The Ultimate Guide to

LONGARM MACHINE QUILTING

- *How to Use ANY Longarm Machine*
- *Techniques, Patterns & Pantographs*
- *Starting a Business*
- *Hiring a Longarm Machine Quilter*

LINDA V. TAYLOR

Editor-in-Chief: Darra Williamson
Editor: Liz Aneloski
Technical Editor: Peggy Kass
Copyeditor: Carol Barrett
Proofreader: Susan Nelsen
Design Director: Aliza Shalit
Book Design and Production: Aliza Shalit
Cover Design: Aliza Shalit
Illustrator: Tim Manibusan
Production Assistant: Jeffery Carrillo
Photography: David Lovelace, unless otherwise noted
Published by C&T Publishing, Inc., P.O. Box 1456, Lafayette, California 94549
Front cover: *Christmas Stars,* pieced by Frances Bagert, Princeton, TX; quilted by Linda V. Taylor, Melissa, TX

Library of Congress Cataloging-in-Publication Data
Taylor, Linda V.
The ultimate guide to longarm machine quilting : how to use any longarm machine : techniques, patterns & pantographs : starting a business : hiring a longarm machine quilter / Linda V. Taylor.
p. cm.
Includes bibliographical references and index.
ISBN 1-57120-184-X (paper trade)
1. Machine quilting—Equipment and supplies.
2. Machine quilting—Patterns. I. Title.
TT835 .T315 2002
746.46—dc21

2002004245

Printed in China
10 9 8

CONTENTS

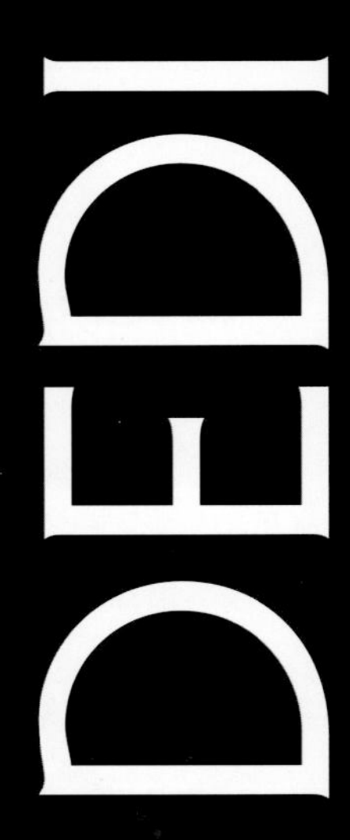

DEDICATION

This book is dedicated to my family and friends who believe in me. I believe in you.

ACKNOWLEDGEMENTS

I found out the hard way that while writing a book you might as well put your life on hold. All your regular activities just go away and sometimes you get cranky. Luckily, my friends did not go away and I am eternally grateful for that.

A Special Thank You

To my family; Rick, Tiffany, and Todd, for their constant support and love, and for stepping around me while I was writing in my studio.

To my sister, Arline, who never hesitated to loan me all the money she had and rejoices in everything I do. You're the best!

To Hari Walner for being my role model, giving me timeless advice, and endless support.

To my accredited teachers; Jana Menning, Beryl Cadman, Merrily Parker, Allison Bayer, and Laurel Barrus for their rally of enthusiastic support, encouragement, and creativity.

To Sharon Blevins, Jane Mitchell, and Laura McGee for believing in me from the beginning.

To Alice Wilhoit and Cheri Meineke-Johnson for trusting me to quilt my dream on their beautiful quilt tops.

To Holice Turnbow who sees so much more in me than I do, Marcia Stevens for her futuristic vision of longarm quilting, and Gwen Meatyard for her truck and willingness to run around for me.

To my little granddaughter, Trinaty Valdean, now ten months old, who made me stop working long enough to "talk things over"—my stress relief.

To all of my students through the years who have told me I made a difference in their lives.

To all the people in this industry who have listened and worked with me to provide for the needs of longarm quilters.

Finally, a big thank you to the patient folks at C&T Publishing for encouraging me to finish this book on longarm quilting. You are all real professionals.

PREFACE

It is always hard making history. We like comfortable. We like acceptable. We like things the way they have always been. It is easier to keep things the way they are today. Change is scary. Change is uncomfortable and sometimes controversial. But I believe the only thing we can count on in this life is change, and change brings growth.

Longarm quilting is a change. It has been called scary. To some quilters, the very subject is uncomfortable and controversial. But I see the use of longarm machines as growth. I believe it is fueling the great upsurge in quilting across the world. Let's be honest, a quilt top is not as exciting as a colorful quilt on your bed or the smiles from your family and friends as you present them with a finished quilt.

Using these machines has enabled some serious longarm quilters to complete more than 250 quilts in a single year! But it is not a contest to see how many quilts can be finished. Longarm machines provide an opportunity for many people to earn an income at home.

The use of longarm machines has also fueled the entire quilting industry. More quilts mean more fabric, batting, and thread, not to mention sewing machines sold, and more demand for quilting teachers and their classes and books. More completed projects mean less guilt and we can all do with less guilt.

There are no drawbacks, except that one little thing called change. Some of the resistence to this type of quilting comes because it is not the way grandma did it. It is not the way it has always been done. But we do not want or need any special rules for this new quilting tool, we want to be allowed the same privileges the rest of the quilting world enjoys. We will abide by the same rules as everyone else, simply good workmanship.

I am dismayed when I hear of people making new rules or banning quilts from shows because they have been quilted with a quilting machine. If these folks had any idea of how much skill, practice, and time it takes to become good enough to enter a show, they would be amazed. And they would be even more amazed if they knew how many "expert" quilters own quilting machines. Not using them is like running in a race barefoot when the best athletic shoes in the world are available.

The group and two-person category entries in quilt shows are growing at an unprecedented rate. I love the two-person team effort since each team member has to do her best on the project to make it complete. We are, indeed, making our own history. May we be remembered as embracing the future and making it brighter for everyone.

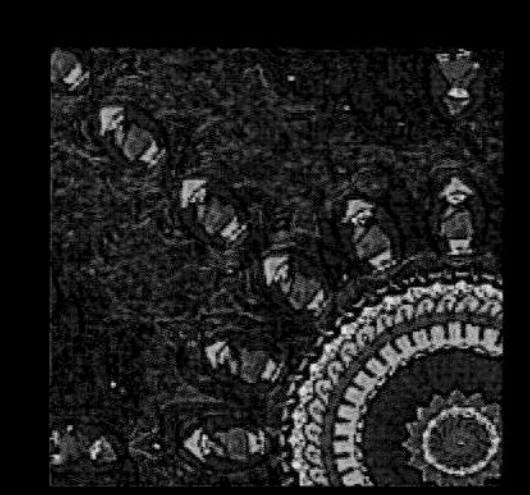

What This Book Is About

This book is about learning to use a sewing tool called a longarm quilting machine. Quilters who use these quilting machines are commonly called longarm quilters.

Chapter One gives an overview of longarm quilting and what tools and accessories are helpful when using a quilting machine.

Chapters Two and Three teach you how to set up a quilt on the machine and quilt an overall continuous pattern from the back of the machine.

Chapter Four gives instruction concerning the specific technical skills needed for custom quilting and using the piecework as your inspiration for how to quilt the top.

Chapter Five offers lessons in free-motion quilting from the front of the quilting machine.

Chapter Six discusses several aspects of setting up and running a professional longarm business or hiring a longarm quilter.

Chapter Seven suggests easy stretching and strengthening exercises for longarm quilters.

There is a gallery for inspiration. Enjoy studying the quilts, all completed by longarm quilters, showing the wide range of patterns and possibilities achieved on the quilting machines.

The last section is a **collection of Continuous-line patterns** for your use on a longarm quilting machine, shortarm quilting machine, domestic machine, or even by hand.

This book is not about the different brands of quilting machines. I work on one brand of quilting machine; however, the techniques and methods are tried and true and can easily be adapted for any differences you may encounter on machines from other manufacturers.

I am right-handed and I have had the opportunity to teach many students who are left-handed. I have observed that left-handed students tend to be more ambidextrous than right-handed people and not only catch on quickly but adapt even quicker. In several ways, I believe being left-handed may be an advantage on a longarm machine because the left hand controls the tools used for custom quilting. The right hand, for the most part, only pushes the buttons. Right-handed people have a harder time allowing their left hand to do the tasks it needs to perform on the quilting machines.

NOTE: You sew from the back of the machine when you are using a pattern under the plastic on the back of the machine. You sew from the front of the machine when you aren't.

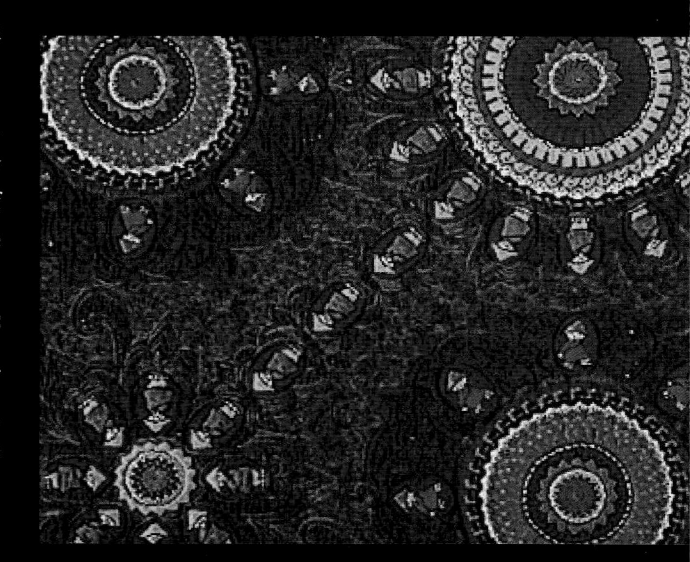

GLOSSARY OF LONGARM TERMS

ACRYLIC GUIDE * a straight piece of ¼" thick acrylic used as a guide to help manipulate the quilting machine to stitch in the ditch, etc. There are other shapes available in acrylic guides such as circles, hearts, stars, etc. Acrylic guides work best when used with an extended base around the throat of the machine to provide a flat surface.

ARCH GUIDE * an acrylic tool developed specifically to help quilt gentle curves like those on Double Wedding Rings.

BASTE OFF * the process of basting the edge of the quilt top to the lining and batting so the quilt top can be unpinned from the top roller.

CANVAS LEADER * the canvas to which the quilt components are pinned on the machine. It is glued and/or taped to the roller bars and allows the user to roll the quilt back and forth with ease.

CHANNEL LOCK * a feature available on most longarm quilting machines that sets the machine in a locked position to sew either horizontally or vertically. This feature can be duplicated manually by holding either the horizontal or vertical wheels on the track.

CUSTOM QUILTING * using the piecework of the quilt top as inspiration for the quilting designs.

DOMESTIC (HOME) MACHINE * a sewing machine made for all kinds of stitching; people use them in their homes to make clothing, piece quilts, and sew for home decoration. Many people also quilt with these machines by making some adaptations.

DOUBLE FOLDED * batting on a roll that is 90" or more in width, but has been folded over and then rolled (usually 20-30 yards per roll) so it is easier to handle, takes up less space for storage, and can be easily shipped.

EXTENDED BASE * a device that provides a flat surface, which can be added around the throat plate of the quilting machine to allow for better manipulation of the flat acrylic tools used for custom quilting. There are several kinds available.

FINGER TRACING * a good way to become familiar with a pattern before you sew it onto the quilt. Use your finger to trace the lines of the pattern to familiarize yourself with the pattern and catch onto the rhythm of quilting it on the machine.

HAND-GUIDED * moving the quilting machine following a pattern or free-motion. The stitch length is determined by how fast or slow the quilter moves the machine, in combination with the motor speed of the quilting machine.

LASER LIGHT * a beam of light used to follow the pattern lines. The light is more versatile and allows for more intricate quilting than the stylus and can be used from the front or back of the machine.

LONGARM QUILTER * a person who uses a longarm quilting machine.

LONGARM QUILTING MACHINE * an industrial machine with an inside throat measurement of 15" or longer, usually on a table 12'–14' long to accommodate a king-size quilt or bedspread. This machine can be used from the front or the back of it.

OFFSETTING PATTERNS * the process of moving a pantograph pattern horizontally, back and forth, every other row, on the back of the quilting machine table. It prevents the stitched motifs in the pattern from lining up directly on top of each other. Some patterns are printed with two or more rows of the quilting pattern already offset.

PANTOGRAPH * a continuous-line pattern that is printed on a long roll of paper. It is made specifically to be placed on the back of the quilting machine table so the user can follow the pattern with a stylus or laser light while the machine is quilting on the top. Pantograph patterns are also referred to as "edge-to-edge" or "overall" patterns. A pantograph pattern is stitched over the quilt regardless of the piecework.

POKIES * tiny bits of thread from one side of the quilt showing through to either the top or back side of the quilt.

QUILT SANDWICH SAMPLE * a small "tester" quilt usually made of an inexpensive material such as muslin. It has batting between two layers of fabric. It is used to run out dirty, oily thread and check the tension on the machine.

ROLL PATTERNS * patterns that generally come on a 10'-long roll of paper, most commonly called pantograph patterns.

SHORTARM QUILTER * a person who uses a shortarm quilting machine.

SHORTARM QUILTING MACHINE * an industrial machine with an inside throat measurement of less than 12". It usually comes with a 12'-long table to accommodate king-size quilts. Generally, the machine is controlled only from the back.

STITCH REGULATOR * a computerized feature that allows you to set the stitch length you desire. This feature is activated by movement. An even stitch is maintained if the machine is moved within a reasonable motion. Not all quilting machines have stitch regulators.

STYLASER * another name for using the laser light to "draw" patterns.

STYLUS * a pointer used on the back of the machine to follow pantographs and other patterns. It is usually made of steel, about the size of a pencil, with a pointed tip.

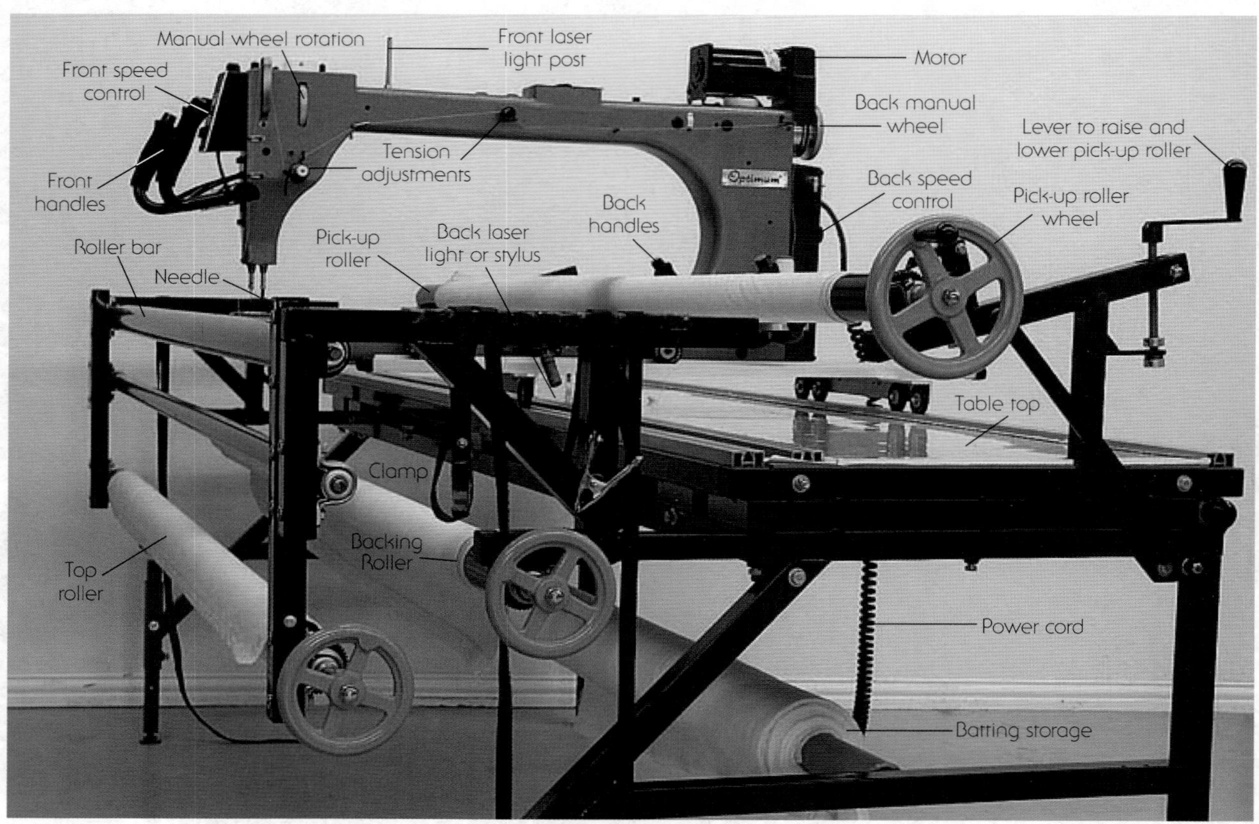

Basic Longarm Quilting Machine

LONGARM QUILTING—HOW DOES IT WORK?

Features

Getting started on the quilting job is always easier and faster if the right equipment and supplies are on hand to do the job effectively. Everything from the batting and thread to the machine itself can affect the outcome of the quilt.

Owning the right quilting machine for the type of quilting you are doing is important. There are many different brands and sizes of quilting machines available today.

Table Size

Nearly all of the quilting machine manufacturers offer at least a 12'-long table, which will accommodate a large king-size quilt. Quilting machine tables that are 14' long or longer will accommodate king-size bedspreads (floor to floor).

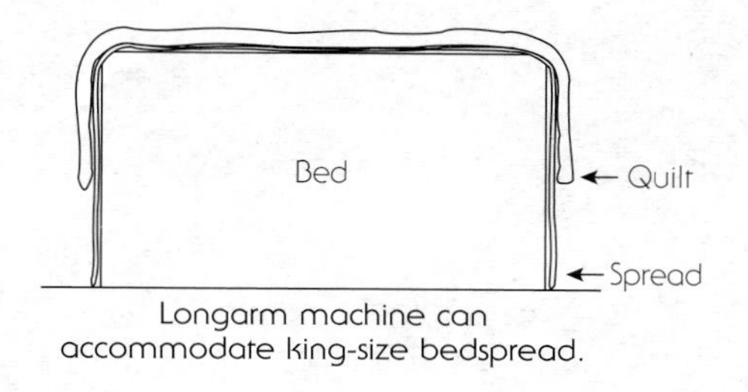

Longarm machine can accommodate king-size bedspread.

Space Requirements

How much space is required? The total width of the quilting machine tables generally measures between 36" and 52". For workable space behind and in front of the table, allow at least 8'–9' total, including the table. On some brands, it is possible to place one end of the quilting machine next to the wall; this way you only need approximately 2½' beyond the length of the actual machine table.

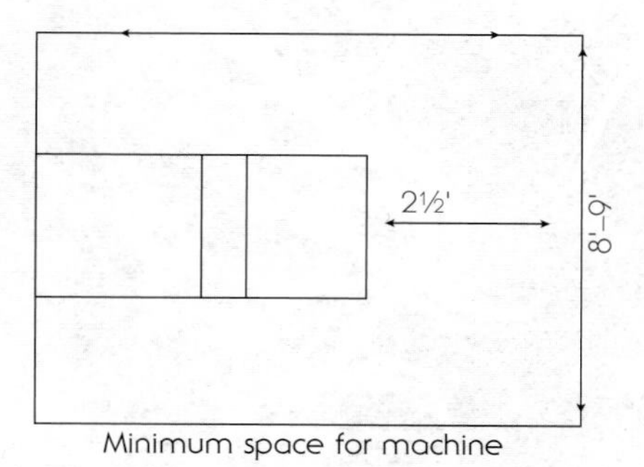

Minimum space for machine

A quilting machine is not just an investment in time and money but also requires a fairly large space. Generally, smaller tables can be special ordered; however, the length of the table determines the size of the quilt that can be quilted.

If you need to move the machine often, wheels or casters can be added to the tables of some brands of machines.

Head and Arm Size

The actual size of the quilting head determines the size of the area you can quilt at one time before you have to advance the quilt to do another area. The size of this area can vary from 6"–36". A larger head on the quilting machine can save you much time and frustration as you are quilting your project because frequent rolling becomes tedious. The longer the inside arm of the machine, the taller the machine itself, allowing for thicker batting and bigger projects.

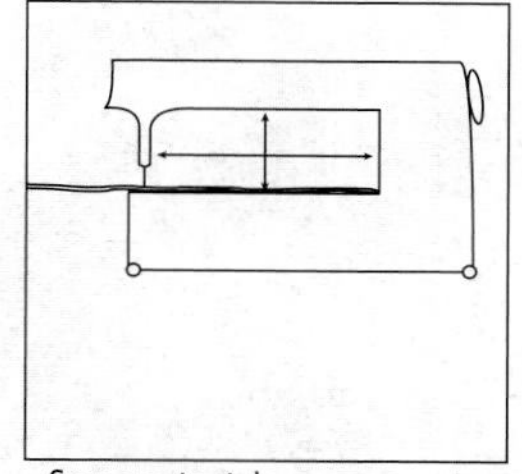
Space inside arm varies.

Since we refer often to the front and back of the machine, imagine the machine as an animal. The front of the machine has "horns" (handles) and the back of the machine has a "tail" (electrical cord).

The quilting machine head moves in every direction, along the track of the table. Ideally, the machine should glide smoothly, with little effort on the part of the user. For the most part, a fingertip touch should be all that is required to move the machine head.

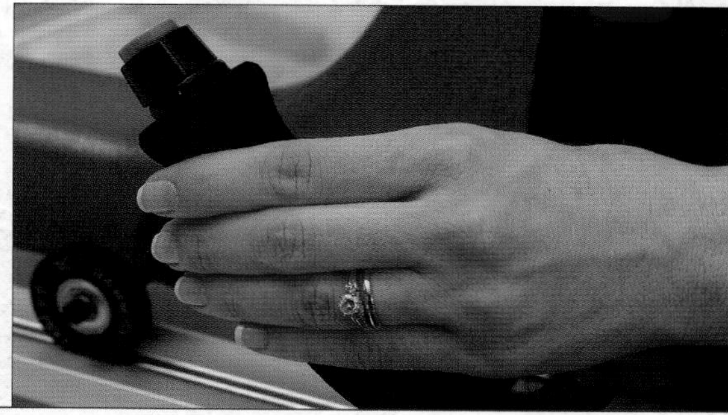
Machine requires a light touch.

Hopping Foot

Quilting machines on the market today do not have "feed dogs." Most are equipped with a "hopping foot." The foot must be adjusted up or down to account for the various thicknesses of fabric and batting in different projects. A few of the machines have an adjustable cam to change the stroke (height) on the hopping foot. The quilter uses this to raise the height of the hop when working on projects with thick batting or fabric such as denim or upholstery fabric. The hop in the foot can also be lowered to glide over the quilt tops with thin cotton batting or flannel. These adjustments allow the user to easily use acrylic rulers and tools for intricate quilting without fear of the hopping foot hitting on top of the tools.

Hopping foot

Rotary Bobbin

The rotary bobbin system, or standard sewing mechanism, is used on industrial quilting machines. This system was designed to use with feed dogs, so the bobbin thread is consistently pulled out in the same direction. When the feed dogs are removed and the machine is moved in every direction, the bobbin thread is also pulled out of the bobbin case in every direction. A basic understanding of the rotary bobbin system helps you understand why quilting on these machines is directional. The best stitch is achieved when the machine is moved in one direction, primarily from right to left when sewing from the back of the machine or from left to right when sewing from the front of the machine. Simply put, this means you start quilting at one end of the machine table and generally move to the opposite end.

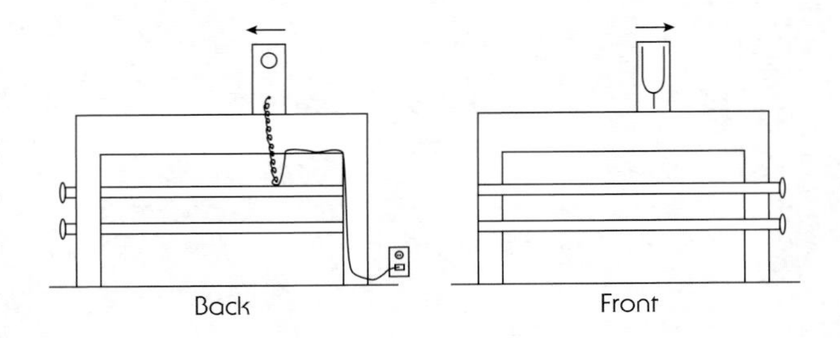

Stitch Regulator

Most of the quilting machines on the market today are hand-guided machines. The user determines the stitch length by moving the machine fast or slow in combination with how fast or slow the machine speed is set.

Manual speed control knob

It takes practice to develop the skill of moving the machine at a steady pace to obtain a nice even stitch length. Even though this is challenging, it can be rewarding and fun to do.

A relatively new feature offered on some brands of quilting machines is called a stitch regulator. This means the machine has built-in sensors that communicate to the machine how fast or slow you are moving it. The objective of the stitch regulator is for the machine to maintain the same number of stitches per inch as the machine is moved by the operator (within a reasonable motion).

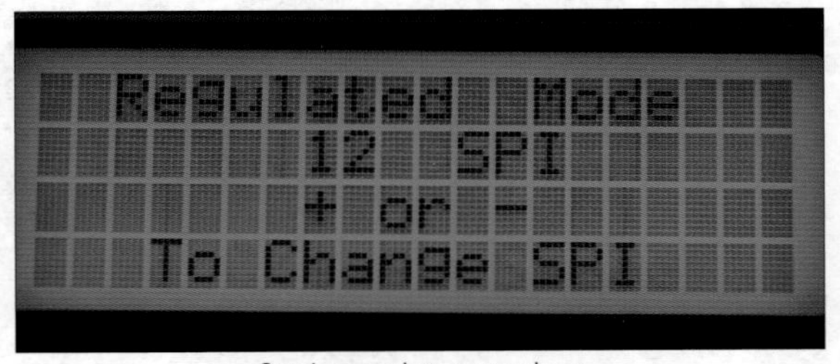

Stitch regulator readout

Having the machine maintain the stitch length is particularly appealing to beginners because they hope it will reduce their learning curve. However, it still takes time and practice to learn how to move the machine as smoothly and evenly as possible. At the present time, some quilt shows do not allow quilts to be entered that have been finished using a stitch regulator.

Quilting on a home sewing machine is similar to moving the paper under a stationary pencil, while quilting on a longarm machine is comparable to using the pencil to draw on the paper.

Additional Features

There are additional special features available on quilting machines that make quilting easier and faster. I highly recommend the needle positioner. This button, generally located on both the front and back of the machine, will raise and lower the needle with one touch. If you start with the needle down in the quilt, it will end in the down position. Oftentimes, as part of the needle positioner function, there will be a button you can push that will do one complete stitch (up and down). If you purchase a quilting machine to use for a business, this feature is a must.

Channel Lock

Another convenient, frequently used feature on the quilting machine, is the channel lock. When the button is pushed the machine will lock in a position horizontal to the roller bars.

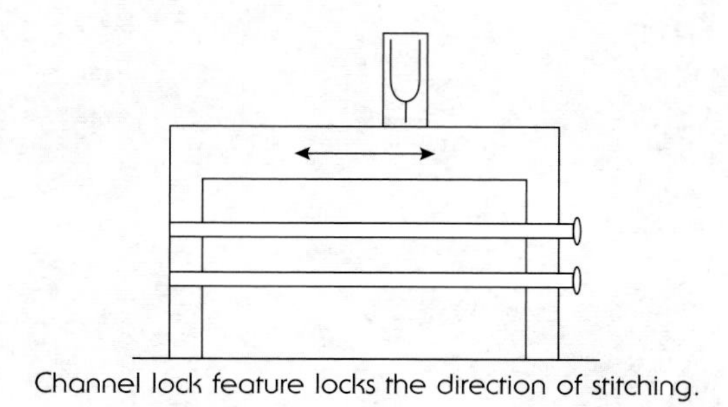

Channel lock feature locks the direction of stitching.

Usually this is achieved with an electronic magnet that attaches to the steel bar to hold the machine in place. I use this feature in the process of mounting the quilt on the frame, in basting quilts for hand quilters, for straight cross-hatching, and as a background stitch for dense quilting. Some of the machines come with a feature for vertical, as well as horizontal, channel lock. The channel lock feature can be duplicated manually by holding the wheels at the back of the machine; it is not convenient, but it works.

Hold the back wheels to simulate the channel lock feature.

Laser Light and Stylus

Quilting machines generally come with a stylus or some kind of pointer built onto the machine to follow a pantograph or border pattern on the back of the table.

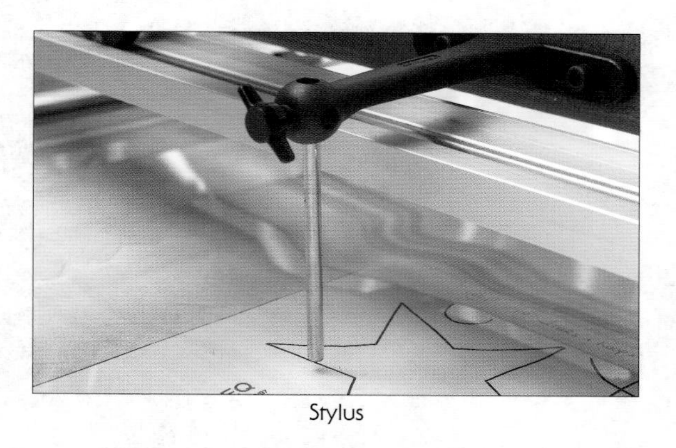

Stylus

Most brands of quilting machines now have a built-in laser light to replace the stylus. This is an extremely useful feature because the laser can be focused at any angle so there is less time spent advancing the quilt. I consider this feature a "must have."

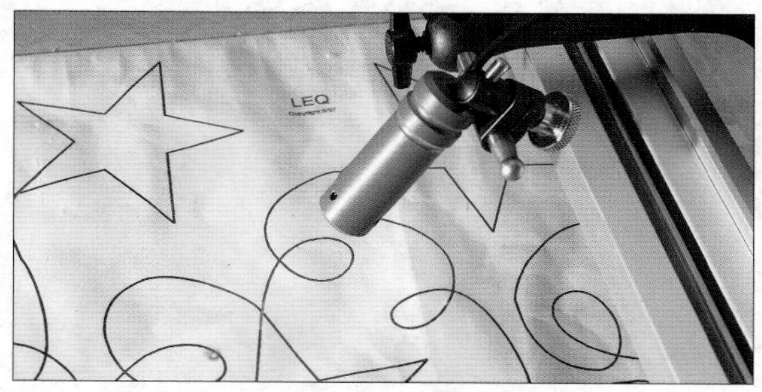

Laser light preferred.

On some brands of quilting machines, the laser can be relocated from the back of the machine and placed toward the front of the quilting machine. This helps accurately stitch intricate patterns from the front of the machine without marking the quilt top.

Machine Maintenance

Your industrial quilting machine should last a lifetime if properly maintained. Quilting machines generally do not need regular "check-ups" by service technicians. The user can efficiently handle minor adjustments, basic cleaning, and oiling. Be aware of the spare parts necessary to keep the machine running smoothly. Be sure to review the owner's manual before working on a machine. The manufacturer or dealer should review machine maintenance with you when your machine is delivered. Ask questions if you are unsure about the maintenance of your machine. It is a big investment and deserves the best care.

Oiling the Bobbin Race

The application of oil is probably the most important aspect of maintenance. Some areas on the machine need oil daily and even hourly. Proper and regular oiling will keep your machine running smoothly for years.

Quilting machines need a drop of oil on the bobbin race approximately every two hours of sewing. It is a good idea to oil and clean this area with every bobbin change. To oil the bobbin race, first turn the machine power off. Make sure the needle is in its highest position, then take out the bobbin case and remove the thread from the needle. Rotate the wheel manually about half way until you see a little shelf of steel. Put a drop of oil on the bottom of this shelf and then rotate the machine wheel to lubricate the entire bobbin race.

Oil the bobbin race.

After brushing and oiling the bobbin case, make sure to sew on a little piece of scrap fabric or your quilt sandwich sample (page 8) until your thread runs clean, otherwise there will be dirty, oily thread on your quilt.

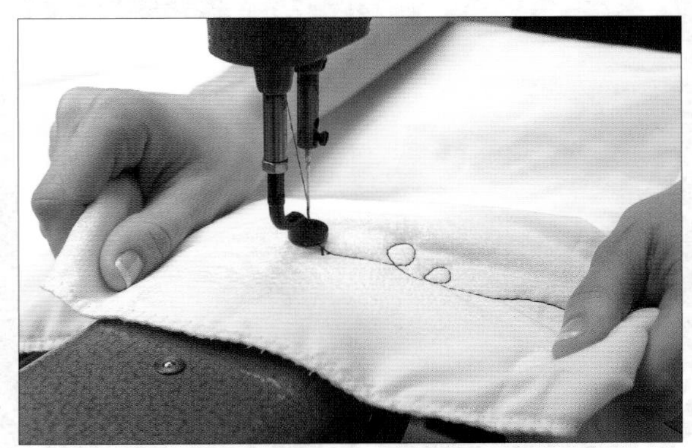

Stitch until the thread is clean.

Cleaning the Tracks and Wheels

Each day the tracks of the table need to be thoroughly cleaned and brushed free of lint and threads. Use a small paintbrush, toothbrush, or vacuum attachment to clean out the tracks. Use a scrap of cotton batting or a soft cloth and rub along the inside of the tracks to clean off any oil and pick up any small threads.

Clean tracks daily.

Using a batting scrap is especially helpful if you have a new machine because a black, oily residue tends to collect on the tracks. Use a pin to clear the tracks of the fine, hard-to-get particles.

The wheels also need daily cleaning. Using a scrap of cotton batting, slide the batting along the edge of each wheel to clean off the lint. This lint is often hard to see.

Clean wheels and check for threads.

Be sure to check the wheels for any threads that may be wrapped around the axles. Even one tiny thread around the axle of the wheel can hinder the machine's movement when you are quilting intricate designs, so make sure the wheels are free of these obstructions.

If possible, once a month lift the machine head off its rolling track and rest it on the table. Now lift the rolling track off the table, turn it upside down and clean the wheels and tracks thoroughly.

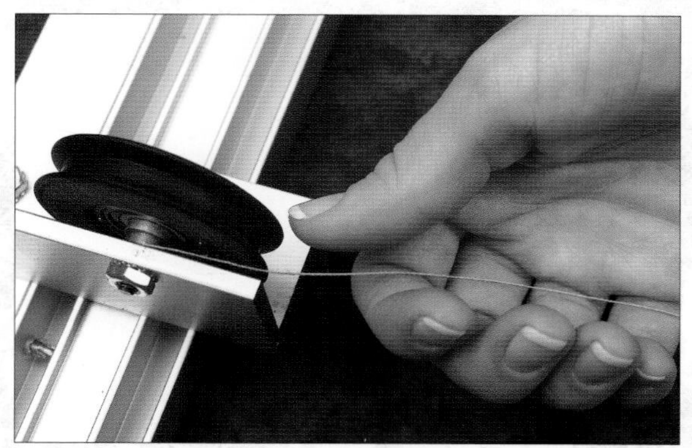

Disassemble and clean wheels and tracks monthly.

Depending on the brand of quilting machine, the track system may not be removable; however, the system still needs to be free of threads, cleaned, and maintained regularly. Check with the manufacturer for details. The wheels and track assemblies never need to be oiled.

Aligned Wheels

If the wheels are properly aligned the machine should glide diagonally across the quilt without stopping or going into a straight line. Check your owner's manual to find out how to make sure the wheels on your machine are properly aligned.

Threading the Machine Properly

It is important that you understand exactly how your quilting machine should be threaded. Most manufacturers give a threading chart for easy reference.

Improper threading of the machine is the cause of many tension problems and thread breakage. If the thread breaks, first check to make sure everything is properly threaded and that the thread has not popped out of the tension disk or flipped up around one of the machine parts.

The bobbin winder may also be the cause of thread breakage. If it is not properly threaded it can wind the thread incorrectly on the bobbin. Make sure the bobbin winder is winding the bobbins evenly. Also, the thread should not be loosely wound on the bobbin. I call that a "squishy" bobbin. Consult your machine or bobbin winder manual to make adjustments.

Poorly and well-wound bobbins

I strongly recommend a bobbin winder independent of your machine for specialty threads and as a time-saving convenience.

Bobbin winder

When it is time to change thread, you do not have to rethread the entire machine. Instead, splice the threads together by clipping the thread on the back of the machine just above the thread spool, then using an overhand knot, tie the end of your new thread onto the snipped piece.

Splice threads (tie on new thread)

From the front of the machine pull the knot in the thread through the threading guides all the way to the needle. Clip it right above the knot and thread it through the needle. This same method can be applied when changing the thread on the bobbin winder.

Caring for the Plastic Cover

Most quilting machine tables have a thin plastic sheet of some kind on the back of the table.

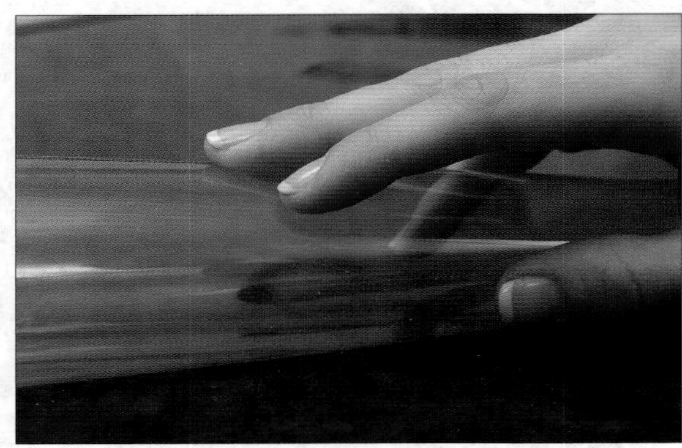
Handle plastic gently.

The plastic is used to keep patterns in place and flat. Take good care of this plastic to ensure it stays in good condition. Be careful when lifting it up to place patterns underneath it so it will not crease or tear. When taping patterns or marking perimeters on top of the plastic, masking tape or painter's tape are the least harmful to the plastic sheets. Do not leave the tape on the plastic for a long period of time because it leaves a hard-to-clean residue. It is a good idea to remove all the tape from the plastic at least once a week.

Safety Alert

Be careful to keep long hair pulled back out of the way of any moving parts on the quilting machines. Also, be alert if the flywheel is at a height near your face.

If you use extension cords for electricity, be careful not to step on or trip over the cord. You can attach the cord to the table with plastic fasteners. Leave the plug hanging down to the floor in the middle of the table to easily reach both sides of the quilting machine table.

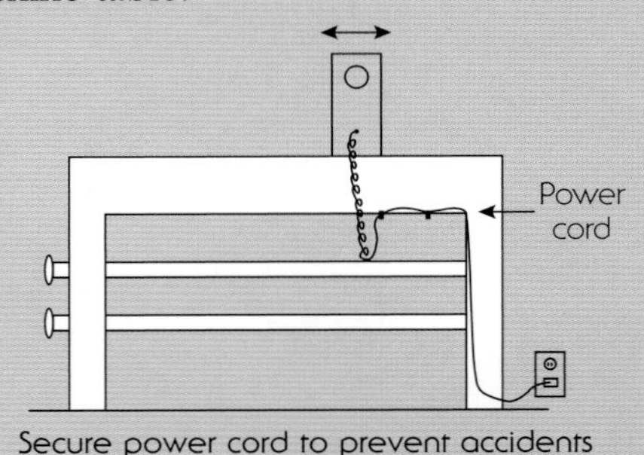

Secure power cord to prevent accidents

And, of course, always watch your fingers when near the needle. As with any power tool, never lose your respect for the power in this industrial machine!

TOOLS AND SUPPLIES

Batting

There are numerous brands of batting available on the market today. Batting can be made from polyester and/or cotton, wool, or silk. Many battings come in different thicknesses or weights.

Most polyester batting is chemically bonded so you can quilt with your lines of stitches further apart without worrying that the batting might shift inside the quilt. Some of the batting manufacturers now make polyester batting that is needle punched. It is soft and lacks the flammable bonding chemicals. Polyester batting shows off the quilting designs because it has loft or puffiness, is lightweight, dries quickly, and is inexpensive.

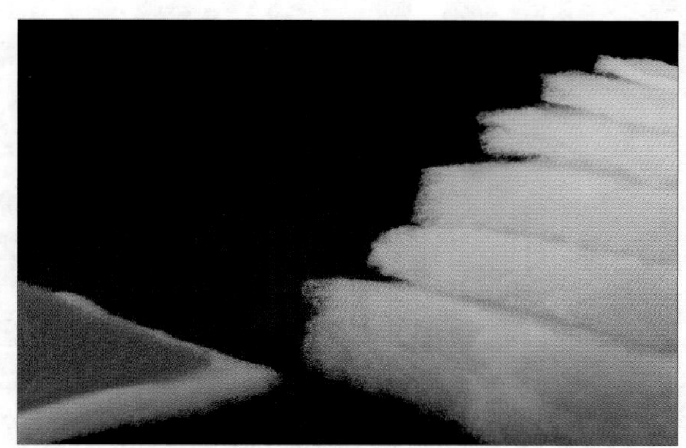
Polyester batting

Another popular batting is a blend of 80% cotton and 20% polyester. It is also relatively inexpensive, lightweight, and needs to be quilted only every 4"–6".

Cotton battings are quickly becoming the preference of quilters in America.

Cotton batting

Cotton lends a flat, traditional look, yet it is soft and pliable. It is slow burning, an important factor in quilts for babies and children. Manufacturers are confident that the new cotton battings will not "ball up" between reasonably-spaced lines of quilting stitches. Some even say the quilting can be 6"–10" apart without worry. This is because cotton batting is generally needle-punched. Some of the cotton batting is needle-punched to a very thin polyester scrim which means it will stretch less and hang very flat.

Needle-punched cotton/with scrim batting

I find the slightly thicker cotton battings are especially good for wallhangings and art quilts that will be used for decorating. There are a few 100% cotton battings on the market that are very thin, almost like paper. This thin batting is good for hand quilting, but use it with caution on the quilting machines because it is easily torn and stretched during the quilting process.

Many cotton battings come in either a natural color (usually with little tiny seeds on one side) or bleached. The bleached battings give a clean, crisp appearance to areas on a quilt with white/light-colored fabric.

Wool batting is readily available in the package or by the roll and is a lovely choice for any quilt. It is generally more expensive than cotton batting and requires a little more care in laundering. Like cotton, wool is a natural fiber that breathes. Quilts with wool batting travel well and creases release better after folding.

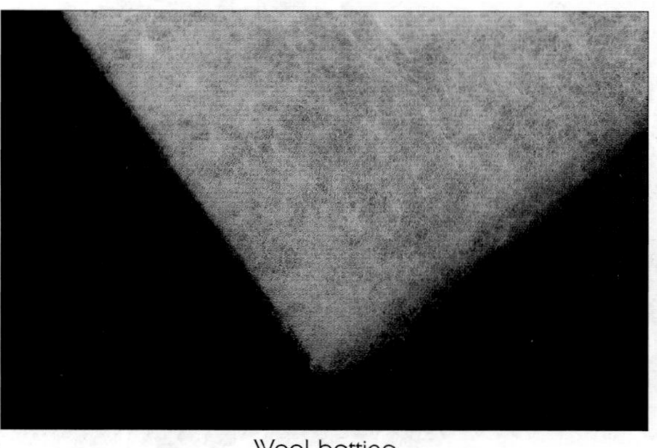
Wool batting

Silk batting is now available in packages, up to queen size. It is very lightweight and easy to work with on the quilting machines. Silk batting is an excellent choice for quilted wearables because of its loft and airy feel.

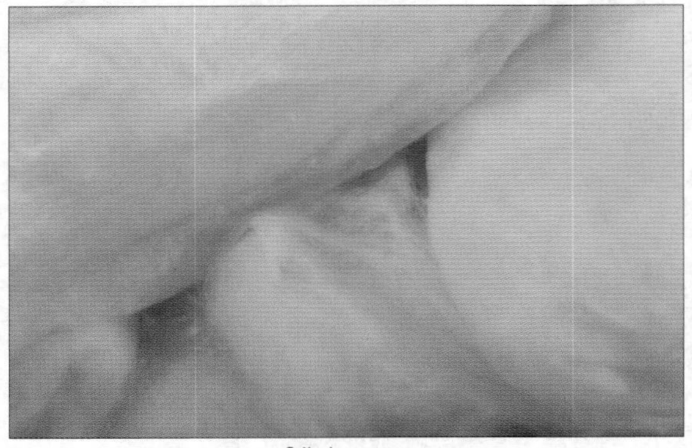

Silk batting

Longarm quilters benefit from purchasing batting on large rolls, usually available in various widths up to 124". Depending on the thickness, the rolls usually include 20-30 yards of batting. The wider battings are shipped double folded. Underneath some quilting machines there is room to accommodate storage for at least two double-folded rolls of batting.

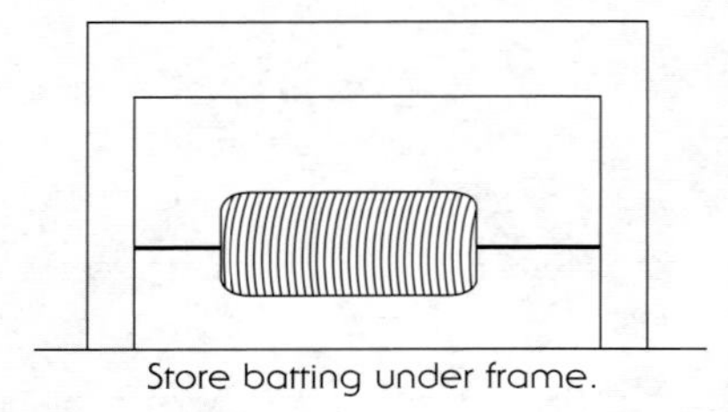

Store batting under frame.

Buying batting on the rolls, rather than packaged, significantly reduces the amount of wrinkles in the batting. However, if you must use the packaged batting there are a couple of things you can do to aid in smoothing out wrinkles. First, take the batting out of the package as soon as possible and allow it to breathe draped over a couch or railing overnight. A warm clothes dryer (on fluff) will help take out some of the folds and wrinkles. If it is extremely wrinkled (and I have seen some really bad wrinkles) you could try steaming the wrinkles out with an iron, but do not apply any pressure on the batting, only steam. Do not use this method for polyester batting.

If you are quilting as a business, you might suggest to your customer that you would prefer using your batting on the roll, and they can use the packaged batting on another quilt. Customers are usually fine with this suggestion, especially when you tell them the benefits of being charged for the amount of batting needed and used rather than having to waste a portion of a packaged batting.

If you want preshrunk batting, I suggest that you put the batting in a pillowcase and safety pin the pillowcase closed before placing it in the washing machine. This method prevents the washing machine from tearing the batting while it is agitating. Use only a gentle cycle on the washing machine. To be safe, always check the manufacturer's directions.

Needles

Because the quilting machines are industrial, the needles are industrial and there are visible differences from domestic (home) sewing machine needles. The industrial needle has a fairly deep groove down the front and an indentation in the back just above the point of the needle. The top of the needle shank is completely round (with no flat side) and must be inserted properly.

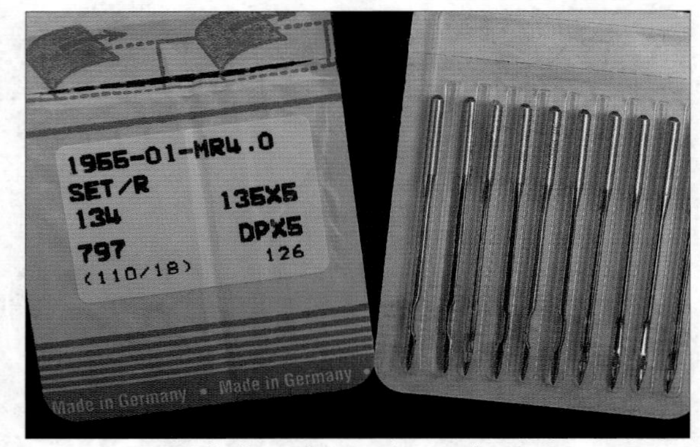

Industrial strength needles

Make sure the needle is pushed all the way up into the needle bar as far as it can go and that it is not twisted or inserted backwards.

The multi-range "MR" industrial needles are beefier, stronger needles. The quilting machines sew multidirectional, and often at high speeds; the MR needles are less likely to break under these conditions. They can be "sharp" or "ballpoint."

The following chart shows the equivalent size of MR needle to its corresponding domestic machine needle and indicates various uses for the five different sizes of needles for the quilting machines:

MR 2.5 (12) - silks, satins, special delicate fabrics, antique quilts

MR 3.0 (14) - antique quilts, cotton quilts with cotton batting

MR 3.5 (16) - most cotton quilts with cotton batting, some specialty threads

MR 4.0 (18) - specialty threads, some metallic thread, heavier threads or fabrics

MR 5.0 (21) - denim, upholstery fabric, comforters (thick batting), specialty threads

Ballpoint needles are also available in most of the common needle sizes. A ballpoint needle should definitely be used on any knit quilt (remember T-shirt quilts are knit). The difference between using a sharp needle and a ballpoint needle is how it enters the fabric. The ballpoint needle moves the fabric threads aside rather than piercing the threads like the sharp needles. The ballpoint needles work well on looser woven fabrics or knits, but not on tightly woven fabric with a high thread count. Ballpoint needles may push the batting or thread through to the backing side in the form of little "pokies" (page 8), depending on the density of the fabric.

Batting may push through to backing.

Because the thread passes by the point of the needle up and down many times before it actually becomes a stitch, sometimes the rounded tip of a ballpoint needle can help curtail thread breakage. This is especially true with some of the cotton, rayon, and specialty threads.

Begin each new project with a new needle. You may need to change the needle part way through a project if you find it is dull. Polyester batting will dull the needle faster than cotton fabric and batting. One indication that a needle is dull is little bits of batting poking through on the wrong side of the quilt. Each time you roll the quilt, make it a habit to check the back of the quilt before quilting a new row.

Sometimes a needle might have a little burr in the eye or on the point of the needle, which causes thread breakage. Again, change the needle.

Thread

Because of the variety of needle sizes, there are many different types and sizes of thread you can use on the quilting machines. Always use a good quality quilting thread, 30-40 TEX (weight). A simplified explanation of "TEX" is the size or thickness of the thread. For example, serger thread is a thinner thread made for serging, 15-20 TEX. It is not the recommended quality for quilting.

Quilting machines are fashioned to hold very large cones of thread, as well as smaller domestic spools. Most convenient, and generally the best value, are the 6000 yard cones. Some of the specialty threads are not put up on such a large cone, but can be purchased in 1000-3000 yard cones. Longarm quilters typically use many cones of thread per year.

Various quilting threads

As much as possible, thread should be stored away from light. I keep mine in a cupboard with doors.

Low humidity also has an adverse effect on thread. Some quilters put their thread in the freezer before using it or lightly spritz it with water.

Polyester-wrapped polyester, or cotton-wrapped polyester thread is usually easier to use because it has more tensile strength and will not break as easily as 100% cotton thread. However, I find cotton thread sews beautifully on the quilting machines if the top tension is backed off slightly.

Occasionally, with cotton thread or specialty threads like metallic and rayon, I find it necessary to sew at slower speeds to avoid thread breakage. Use a slightly larger needle (or a ballpoint needle) and give the top thread more slack when pulling the needle away from one area to another.

Create slack for specialty threads.

It also helps to use a similar weight and kind of thread in the bobbin as on the top of the machine.

If the top thread is breaking often, thread lubricant applied to the thread should help it slide smoothly through the needle eye more easily. I generally apply this lubricant directly on the spool of thread in several places before beginning the quilting process.

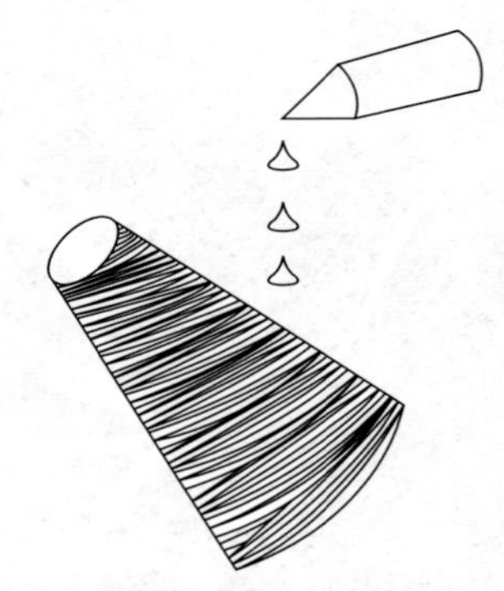

Lubricate thread if needed.

If in doubt, check with your machine manufacturer for their recommendation regarding thread lubricant.

Monofilament thread can also be used on the quilting machines, generally with minimal adjustments to the tension. Today's .004 monofilament thread is thin, like a human hair. It is not fishing line. It is effective for definition when you do not want a thread color to show (like stitch in the ditch on a colorful quilt top). I recommend using it either in the top or in the bobbin, but not both at the same time.

Thread Color

Ask two questions when deciding thread color. First, what color would you use if you were hand quilting? And second, which side is more important, the top or the back of the quilt?

If the backing on a quilt does not match the top fabric or fabrics, my preference is to pick the most pleasing color of thread for the quilt top since that is usually the most important element of the quilt. If the top is colorful, I have no problem in changing the colors in different areas of the quilt, and, at the same time, changing the color in the bobbin to match the top thread. The colorful changes of thread on the back of the quilt create a lovely and interesting effect, oftentimes making the back of the quilt as pleasing to look at as the top.

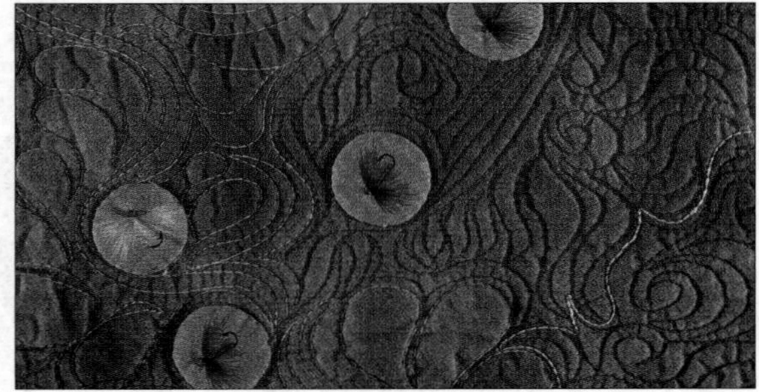

Multicolor threads add interest to backing.

Using contrasting threads on the top and in the bobbin can be a tension nightmare. It is nearly impossible to guarantee perfect tension when you are sewing in a multi-directional fashion with a rotary bobbin system, which is common in all of the quilting machines. Depending on the direction of sewing, it is likely that you will get little "pokies" of color from the back or front at one time or another (especially between sharp black and white contrasting threads).

Low contrast color is preferable.

Less of a contrast in thread colors is generally more tolerable. It also helps to have a busy fabric for the quilt backing.

Pin Types

The quilt top and backing are pinned onto the canvas leaders as the quilt is loaded on the quilting machine table. Use the type of straight pin that works best and is most comfortable for you. I like two kinds of straight pins: the quilt pins with ball heads that are 1¼" long and corsage pins that are sometimes called "hat" pins. Some longarm quilters prefer T-pins (used in drapery workshops). I recommend that you try all types of pins before making a judgment. It really depends on what works best for your fingers. I like the larger ball heads because they are easily inserted into the canvas and can be pulled out quickly.

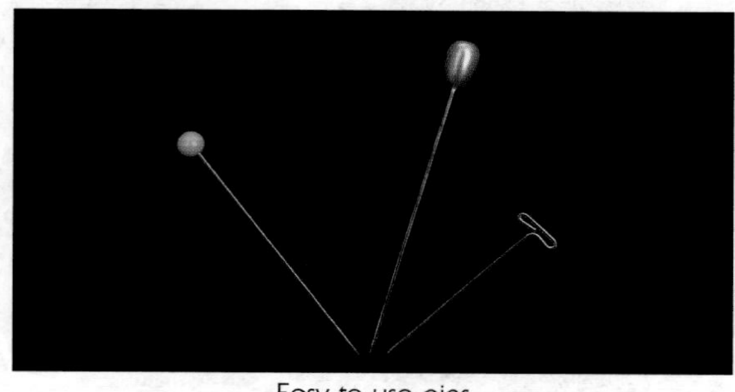

Easy-to-use pins

It is important to use a pincushion wristlet of some kind. These cushions are portable, handy, and easy to use, so you are not chasing pins around on the quilting machine table. I started making my own pincushions out of quilted fabric, stuffed with wool to keep the pins sharp. I designed these pincushions only because I am unable to buy any pincushions big enough to hold the amount of pins I need for a king-size quilt. I have watched students (who, at first, are opposed to wearing a cushion on their wrist) chase their pincushions or magnets all around the table, leaning and reaching over the table to get pins. It looks very uncomfortable. We not only need to save time (as opposed to wasting it), but we also need to be aware of disabling body positions. If our back aches every night after quilting, we are doing something wrong. It should not hurt our bodies to use the quilting machines, aside from being tired because we over-do it. Straps of hook and loop tape on the pincushion seem to fit more people than those with plastic wrist holders. Elastic works well for a while, but over time loses its elasticity.

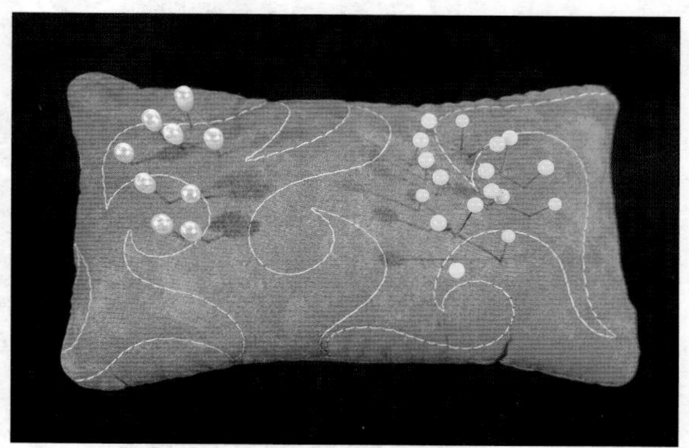

Large wrist pin cushion

Supply Box

Quilting is faster and easier if you have everything you need by your machine. I keep a small plastic container or drawer box at the end of my quilting table filled with necessary items. Like carpenters, some longarm quilters like to wear aprons filled with these necessary tools. For example, scissors—one pair for cutting paper, another pair for fabric, and one small pair for trimming threads—are necessities. The small scissors can be clipped to your shirt, apron, or belt with a retractable holder so they are always with you, or they can be attached to your machine.

Small scissors are essential.

If you are quilting as a business, keep the quilt order sheet near the machine for easy reference. I like to place it right underneath the plastic so I can refer back to the directions as often as needed to help avoid errors.

HELPFUL HINT: I tie a piece of fabric on my fabric scissors. This indicates to other family members which scissors to use for fabric and which to use for paper, wire, and almost anything else they can find to cut.

I always use pins from my pincushion, which is either in the supply box or on my wrist, thereby making pinning and unpinning more efficient. You also need a small container with large, open safety pins; I use a small potato chip can as a container.

Keep a marking pencil or pen and masking tape in your toolbox to help place and mark patterns. A tape measure (I use a steel one) is another good item to have for the placement of patterns and to measure the quilt. Acrylic rulers are also necessary; both the "arch guide" and a straight ruler should be kept in the box.

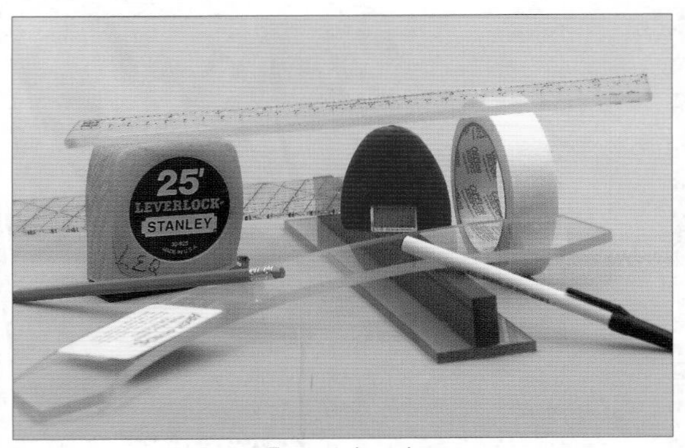

Essential tools

It is a good idea to keep extra needles of different sizes and a small screwdriver or Allen wrench in your supply box.

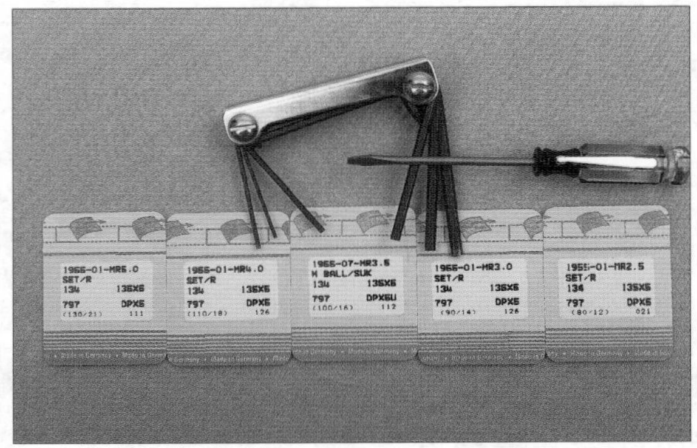
Tools and extra needles

Maintenance items and cleaning supplies such as sewing machine oil and brushes should also be kept in the box for quick and frequent access. You may want to use hook and loop tape to attach the oil bottle to the front of the machine so it is always available. Keep a few cotton swabs handy to clean off the quilting machine's hopping foot and a rag to clean off any excess oil.

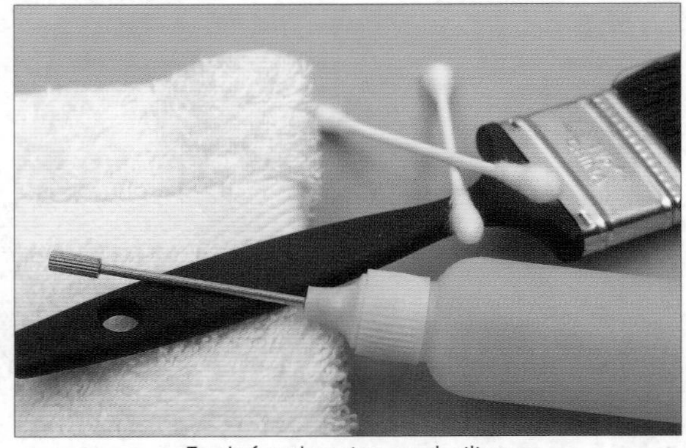
Tools for cleaning and oiling

Be sure to keep a little quilt sandwich of fabric, batting, and backing (I use muslin for both the top and the backing) available when you oil or clean the machine. You can use this quilt sandwich for the first few stitches, running out any oily or dirty thread. It is also handy for checking your tension before you begin to sew and each time you change thread colors or types.

No matter how long you have been sewing or machine quilting, sticking yourself with a pin is always a problem. I always keep first-aid plastic strips and a tissue close at hand, so if I stick myself I will not bleed on the canvas, and especially not on the quilt!

HINT: Your own saliva will help break down the DNA in your own bloodstain, so use that on the quilt or canvas before you use soap and water to prevent staining. Clean off blood as quickly as possible!

Necessary Tools Of The Trade Checklist

- ❑ *Large scissors for fabric*
- ❑ *Scissors for paper*
- ❑ *Small scissors for thread*
- ❑ *Rotary cutter and mat (to square the backing)*
- ❑ *Acrylic rulers: straight and arch guide*
- ❑ *Pincushion: Wear one, do not chase pins around or ruin your back reaching for them.*
- ❑ *Pins: Use what works for you, try different kinds for speed and comfort.*
- ❑ *Masking tape or some kind of marking tape or markers*
- ❑ *Seam ripper*
- ❑ *Tweezers*
- ❑ *Ruler for stitch in the ditch. This is usually an acrylic piece 1/4"–3/8" thick.*
- ❑ *Extra needles: different sizes including ballpoint needles*
- ❑ *Screwdrivers and tools for machine and needle changes*
- ❑ *Brushes to clean the machine; you can also use canned air or a compressor.*
- ❑ *Scraps of cotton batting to clean the tracks of the machine*
- ❑ *Extra bobbins*
- ❑ *Large safety pins*
- ❑ *Tape measure (I use a steel tape measure.)*
- ❑ *First-aid strips just in case (Do not bleed on the quilt or canvas.)*
- ❑ *Machine oil*
- ❑ *Batting on your shoulder to catch threads (sounds weird but saves time cleaning)*

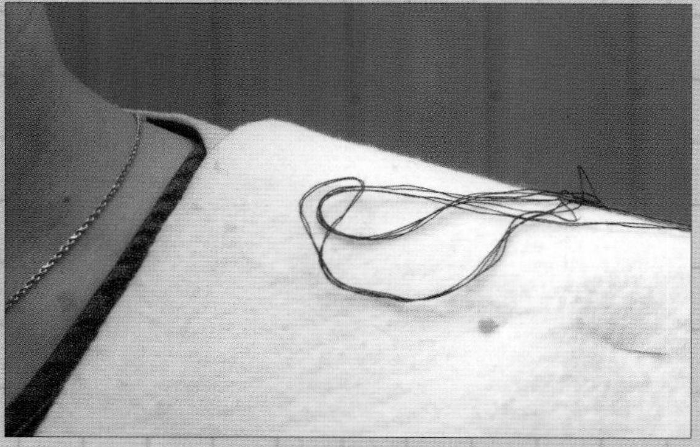

A time saver

Necessary Tools – continued

- ❑ Quilt sandwich sample (to run off oily thread and check the tension)
- ❑ Copy of quilt order for reference
- ❑ Your own design book of ideas (for when you go brain dead)

Optional Tools Of the Trade

- ❑ Apron (to hold tools)
- ❑ Camera (Take pictures for your portfolio and posterity.)
- ❑ Candy, fruit, chewing gum, etc.
- ❑ Music
- ❑ Arm-band (for tennis elbow, really helps when doing a lot of freehand quilting)
- ❑ Drawing pad for doodling
- ❑ Pencils, markers
- ❑ Arch guide for curves
- ❑ Acrylic templates for circles, stars, hearts, etc.
- ❑ Extra bobbin case
- ❑ Miscellaneous machine parts: extra switches, check spring, rubber rings for bobbin winders
- ❑ Toothbrushes and pipe cleaners (to clean table tracks and machine)
- ❑ Silicone lubricant for specialty threads
- ❑ Fingernail file and hand lotion
- ❑ Fray Check
- ❑ Pencil sharpener
- ❑ Basting spray
- ❑ Bodyrite (I highly recommend them for posture counter balance.)
- ❑ Blacklight and glow pencil
- ❑ A container with a handle to keep all this stuff in, to easily carry around the machine
- ❑ Portfolio with pictures of completed quilts

Portfolio

LOADING THE QUILT TOP, BACKING, AND BATTING

Preparing Quilt Components

First things first! It is imperative that you lay out the backing, batting, and quilt top before you start pinning, to make sure that you have enough backing to extend at least 2" beyond each edge. I make mistakes using a tape measure, but my eyes do not easily deceive me.

Lay out backing, batting, and quilt top.

Having taught and trained many people to quilt, I can tell you first hand this is the most often skipped step and a heart-breaking experience to get to the end of the project only to realize your quilt top is longer than your backing or your batting. Oh, if you had only laid out the components of the quilt first! When this happens, you must take the quilt off the machine, correct the problem, then remount the quilt to finish your project.

Square-up the backing, if possible. If necessary, square off the batting on the side that will be pinned to the pick-up roller. The other end of the batting will hang down, so it does not need to be squared.

The quilt top cannot be squared-up unless it is just one piece of fabric, or you will be cutting into the border or the design work on the quilt. Adjustments can be made as the quilt is mounted and quilted on the machine for tops that are not square.

Decide before pinning, which direction the top needs to go on the machine. The quilt top can be mounted in virtually any direction on the table. To determine this, think about it in relationship to the pantograph pattern you are stitching onto the quilt, and whether you will be quilting a border design. It makes a difference if you will be quilting from the front or the back of the machine. Most quilts are rectangular, so two sides of the border are longer. Initially the quilt should be mounted with the long sides parallel to the rollers on the machine to save time rolling the quilt. However, if you are doing an overall pattern, first determine if the quilting pattern is a one-way design, such as ducks, and then which way the quilt should go on the bed, horizontally or vertically. Establish which way you need to pin the top on the rollers in order to apply the quilting pattern in the correct direction.

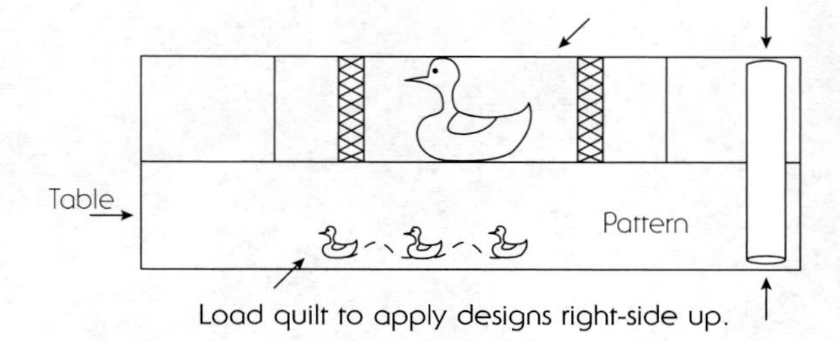

Load quilt to apply designs right-side up.

If the backing has a directional print, consider which way you need to pin it onto the rollers to match the quilt top.

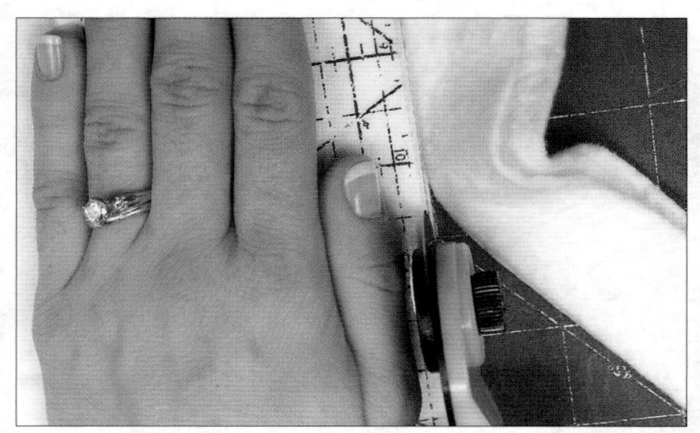

Square-up batting.

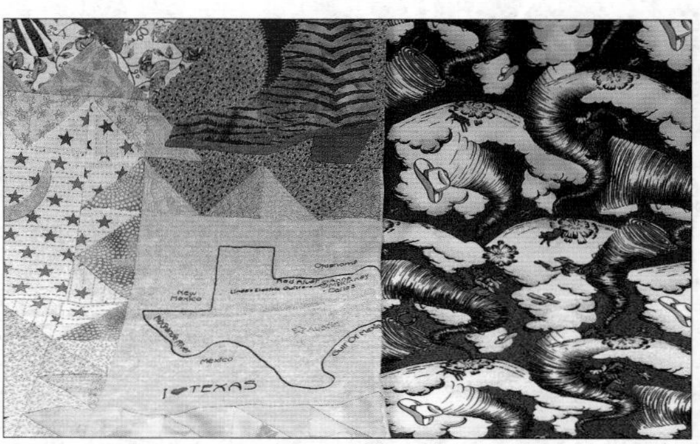

Match top and backing pattern directions.

While working with the quilt top and backing, find the centers of the borders or quilt sides and mark them with a pin.

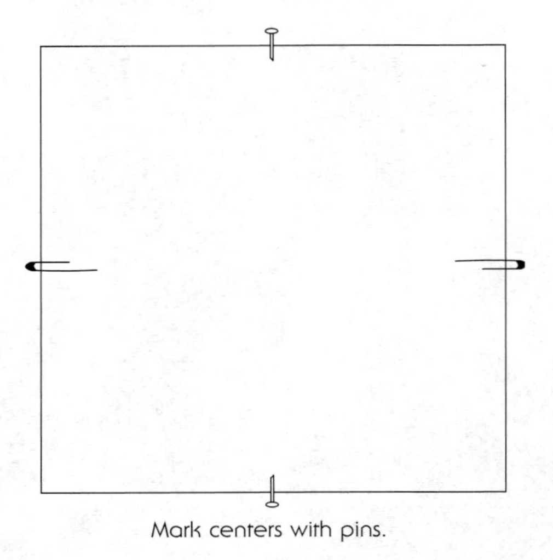

Mark centers with pins.

I work the pin in and out of the fabric with the pin-head outside of the raw edge.

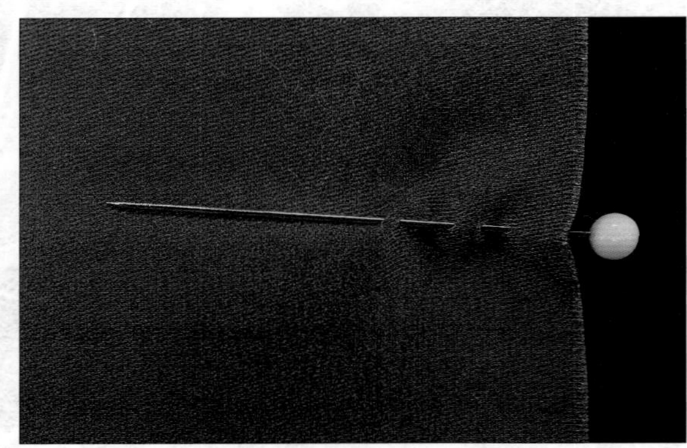

Weave pin to stay.

Notching the top or backing with scissors to indicate the center can be damaging to the quilt top. I do not recommend it.

I use safety pins rather than straight pins in the sides of the quilt top. If you plan on turning the quilt to complete the borders after the center has been quilted, it becomes more tedious to find the exact center on the heavier, bulkier quilt. If you are quilting an overall pattern you need only to find the center on the two ends that will be pinned to the rollers. The exact center is not always where it appears, so fold it in half to find the center, rather than using a fold in the fabric or the pieced work. Be careful not to stretch the edges while you are finding the center. You may need to spread the top on the surface of the table to find the centers on all four sides.

Mounting the Quilt Top

After cleaning the machine and marking the centers of the quilt top and backing, it is time to pin the quilt top onto the appropriate roller. The top goes on first. Although it sounds backwards, if you do it this way, it will save you time. Trust me, I have timed it. Release the top canvas about half way to the floor.

Release canvas only half way to the floor.

HINT: Be careful not to let your canvas leaders out all the way or after a short time they will pull off the rollers.

Now you are ready to lay your quilt top over the roller assembly from the backside of the machine, placing the top right side up.

From back of machine, lay top over rollers.

If the quilt top is very large, most of it will hang neatly over the back of the machine to the floor.

Bring the top canvas up and out, over the roller bar.

Pull top canvas up to meet quilt.

From the front of the machine, bring the quilt top to the canvas edge labeled "Top" (if your canvas is not marked, mark it with a pen) and sandwich the material edge even with the canvas. Pin the center of the top to the center of the canvas placing pins on the canvas side.

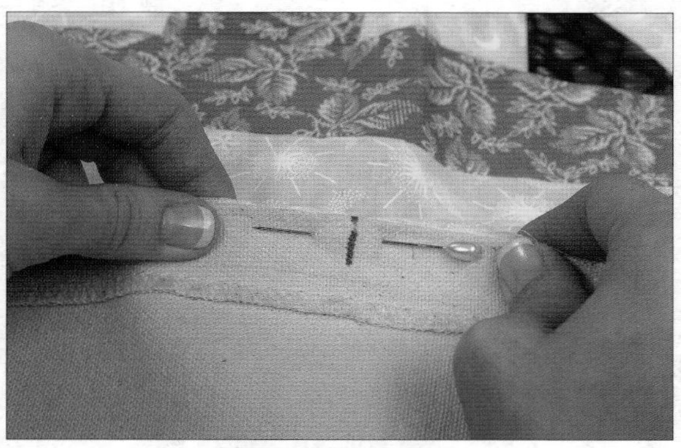
Match center marks.

This method of pinning makes it easier and faster to take the pins out later. Pins should be placed approximately ⅛"–¼" down from the edge of the canvas. Keep pins parallel to the canvas and be consistent across the edge of the canvas leader.

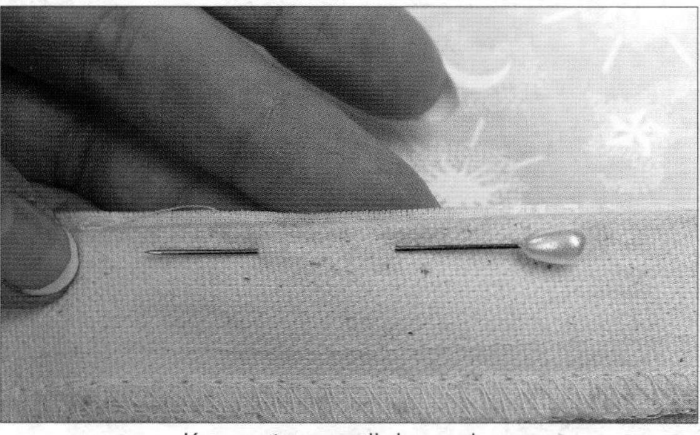
Keep pins parallel to edge.

Next, ease in the border gently, being careful not to stretch it. I pin-baste first, pinning parallel to the canvas every 4"–6", keeping the fabric on a one-to-one ratio with the canvas.

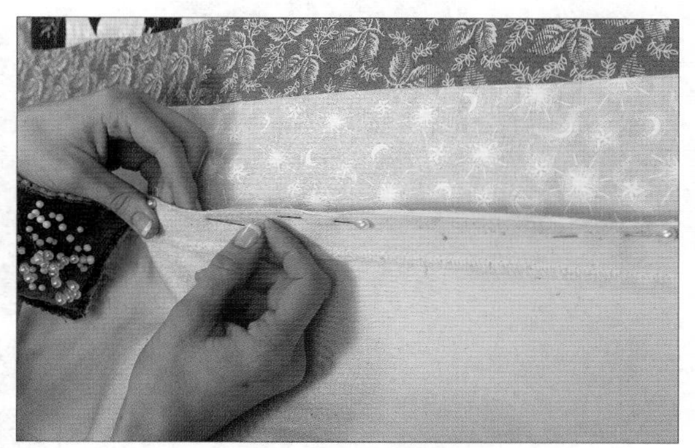
Pin from center to each side.

Pin from the center to each side of the quilt top.

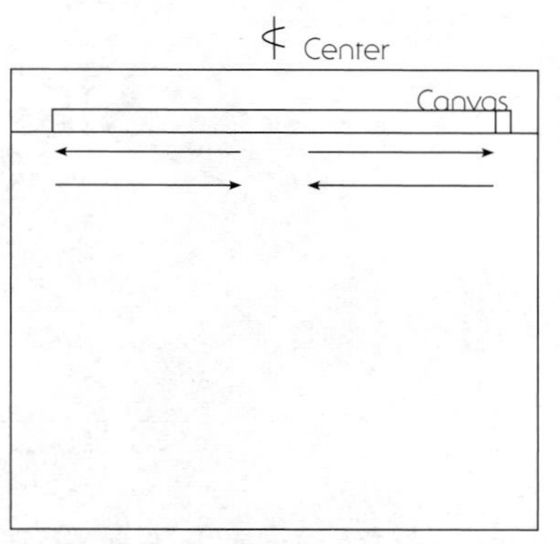

Pin from center to outer edge, then back to center to fill in.

Then, work back to the center by pinning about every 1½" with the pins touching tip to point, without overlapping.

Be careful not to stretch the quilt top while pinning. If you have a quilt top with a flared border, take the following steps: first measure the length of the quilt across the middle (not on the edge) in several places.

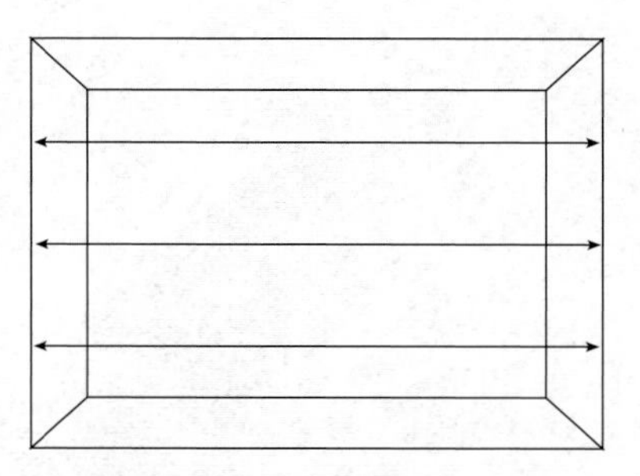
Measure across the middle.

Average that measurement and divide it by half. Now measure from the center of the canvas out on each side using the half measurement and place a pin for a marker.

Mark half way to center on each side, if needed.

Match the center of the quilt top to the center of the canvas and pin them together. Match both edges of the quilt top to the pins you have placed as markers and pin each of them in place. Now half and quarter the remaining quilt top edge and match it to the canvas, easing in any extra fullness in the quilt top. This is a tedious process usually only necessary for quilt tops that are seriously out of square or have very flared borders.

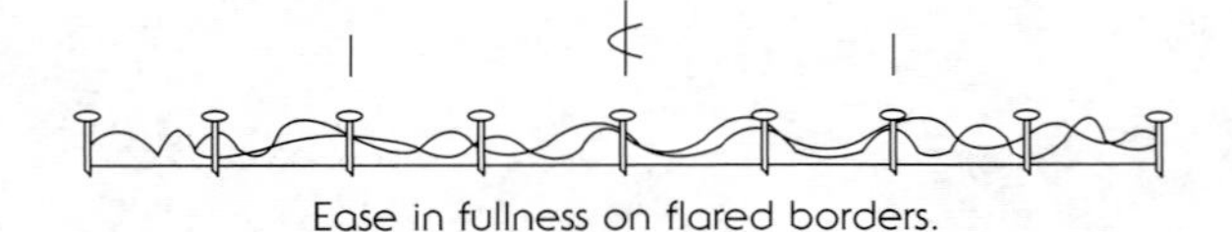

Ease in fullness on flared borders.

Once the top is pinned, it is time to partially roll it up on the top roller bar. Watch the quilt and canvas leaders as you are rolling to make sure they are not twisted. If one side of the canvas leader is twisted and one is not, your quilt will be torqued. The quilt top should roll up smoothly over the back of the table and roller bar.

Quilt should roll smoothly.

Roll until the loose edge of the quilt top rests on the top of the roller bar.

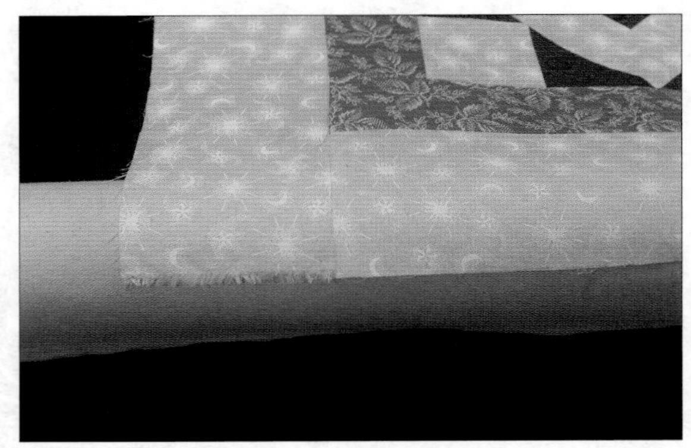

Roll to loose edge.

If you roll any more than this you will have to unroll it later, which will cost you time. When the edge of the quilt top is on top of the roller bar, bring it over toward the front of the machine, letting it fall to the floor underneath the top and backing rollers, or gently lay it on top of the top roller bar; you will pull it up later.

Let quilt top drop while preparing backing and batting.

Mounting the Backing

Lay the backing, wrong side up, over the quilting machine table the same way you did the quilt top.

Lay backing wrong-side up.

Next, find the pins you placed to mark the centers of the edges to be pinned to the canvas. You do not need to worry about the centers on each side because after it has been quilted to the top, the safety pins on the quilt top are enough for center identification.

Let the backing canvas out until it touches the floor but make sure there is still canvas wrapped on the roller. Bring the canvas up between the top roller bar and the top carrier roller bars.

Bring canvas up between bars.

Pin the backing to the backing canvas. (You may need to mark the canvas in the same manner as the quilt top, flush with the edge of the canvas.) Pin-baste first every 6", then fill in pins from tip to point. Your backing should be wider than your quilt top; continue to pin out to the very edge of the backing on both sides so it will roll up evenly.

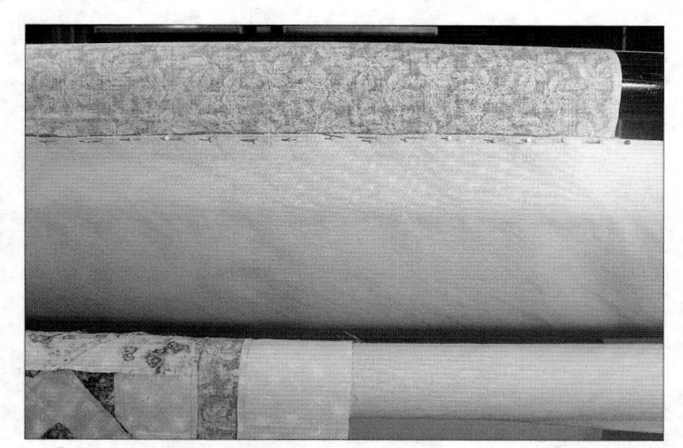
Backing wider than top; completely pinned to edge

Make sure to fill in the pins as much on the backing as you did on the top, because once the quilt has been stabilized, the top canvas will be unpinned. After the backing is pinned to the backing roller, roll it up until the loose end touches the tabletop on the back of the machine. Leave the backing draped over the roller bar assembly and move to the back of the machine table.

Roll up backing until edge touches back of table top.

Now pin the backing to the pick-up roller in the same manner as you pinned the quilt top (pick-up roller is in the arm of the machine). If you are confident that the batting edge is straight, find the center of the edge of the batting and pin it at the same time you pin the backing. Otherwise it can be added later.

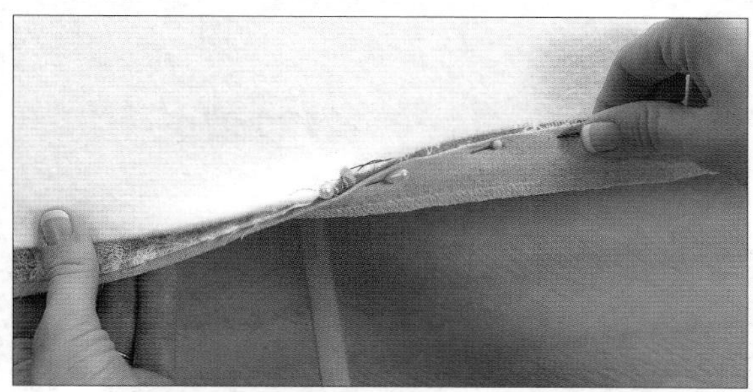
Pin backing and batting to canvas.

Pinning the Batting On

If you did not pin the batting with the backing, find the center of the batting and lay it on top of the backing even with the edge of the canvas. Hold it in place with a few pins. Tuck the other end of the batting between the top roller and the other rollers and let it hang free to the floor.

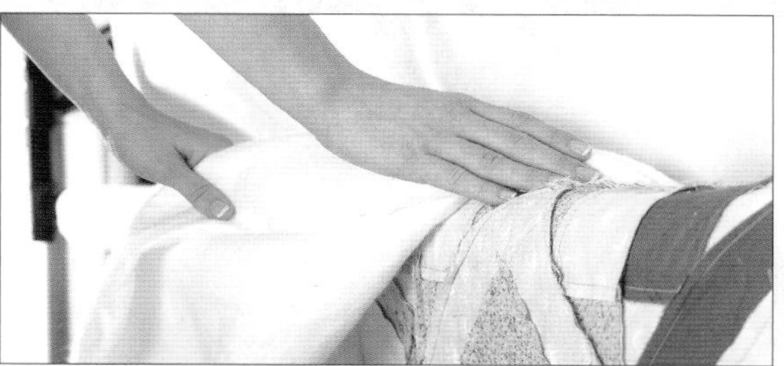
Tuck batting between rollers.

Stitching a Reference Line to "Float the Top"

Let out the canvas on the pick-up roller enough toward the front of the machine for you to easily see and reach the pinned edge of the backing and canvas (no leaning or straining your back). Tighten the backing roller.

Tighten the batting and backing toward front of machine for easy access.

Set the machine on a lower speed for basting (½" stitches) and move the machine into position at the edge of the backing (and batting) about an inch or so down from the pinned edge of the canvas. Note: If you did not pin your batting on with your backing, you will sew the batting to the backing with this line of basting.

Stitch reference line approximately 1" down from pinned canvas edge.

Now turn on the horizontal channel lock and gently sew, moving the machine all the way across the backing and batting to the other edge.

If you do not have a channel lock, set your needle down (from the front) about an inch from the canvas edge, walk around to the back of the machine table, hold the wheels on the vertical track and sew across to the other edge (page 11).

Securing the Quilt Top

Now bring the quilt top up and over the top of the batting and line up the raw edge of the quilt top to the reference line you have sewn. Pin the top along this horizontal reference line to the batting and backing, starting in the center and working out both directions. (The pins should be placed an inch or so below the basting line so they will not be in the way when you sew along the raw edge.)

Place pins well below basting line.

The pinning does not have to be close together, just enough to hold the quilt top in place for you to sew. Now start at the left edge of the top and stitch a basting line across the quilt very close to the edge of the quilt top, approximately ⅛" down from the raw edge.

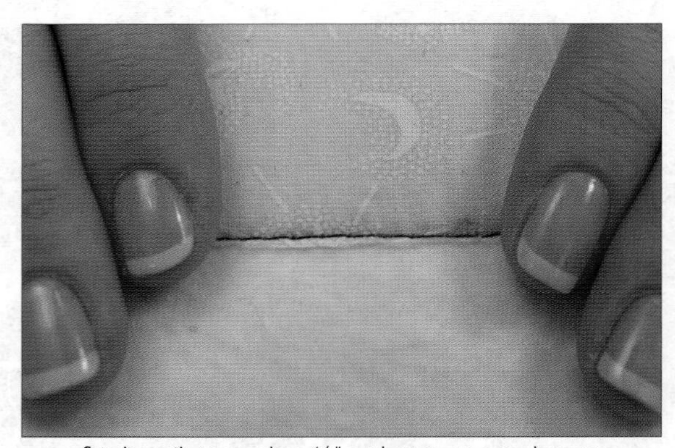

Stitch quilt top edge ⅛" or less to secure layers.

NOTE: Occasionally a quilt top will not be square; appearing "dog-eared" or pointed on the corners. In this case, the quilt top can be adjusted along the reference line. Instead of being placed even with the line, the corners can be extended over the lines so the border will lie flat. This way there will not be any extra fullness created in the side borders.

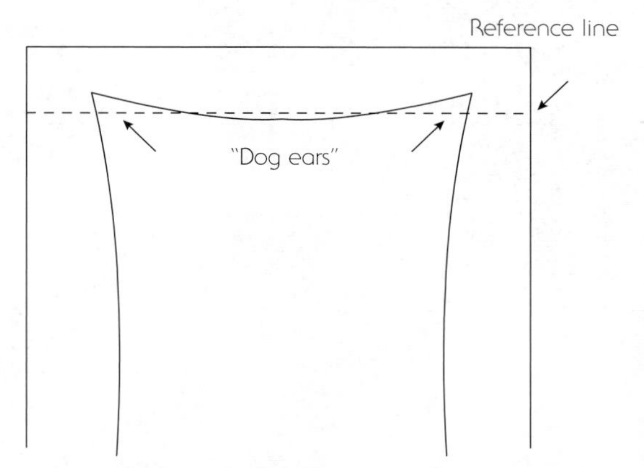

Quilt top corners may extend beyond reference line.

NOTE: If there is not a lot of extra length in the backing it may be necessary to bring the quilt top edge nearly even with the edge of the pick-up roller canvas in order to baste the quilt top to the backing and batting already pinned to the canvas. Occasionally it may be necessary to pin the quilt top onto the pick-up roller with the batting and lining.

Tightening the Quilt

Step over to the gears and wheels on the side of your machine (some machines do not have wheels, just turn the roller bars with your hands). Release, but do not unroll, the top and backing rollers. Advance the quilt (this now includes the backing, batting, and quilt top) back toward the pick-up roller. Tighten the backing roller bar. Move to the front of the machine and smooth the layers..

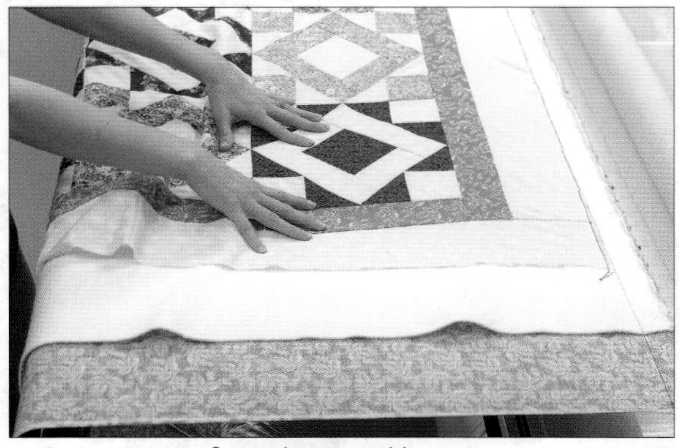

Smooth secured layers.

Visually check your batting; look where the batting hangs down to see if it has a wrinkle. Also, feel along the carrier bar (or "belly" bar) for any wrinkles. Smooth and rake the quilt top with your fingers. From the front of the machine, grasp the top roller and roll it until the top is taut. You may have a little easing in the top and that is okay. If you do not have any easing, you might have stretched it too much, so do not be overly concerned. When you tighten the rollers keep in mind that this is not a rack where the quilts are tortured. Just gently tighten the rollers; there will be some play. You will acquire a feel for how tight the rollers should be. As you tighten the wheels, when you feel resistance you are finished tightening..

Resistance indicates rollers are tight enough.

Each time you roll, make it a habit to look under the quilt at the backing to make sure the pinning is done correctly and that there are no wrinkles, thread, or unforeseen problems to deal with under the quilt.

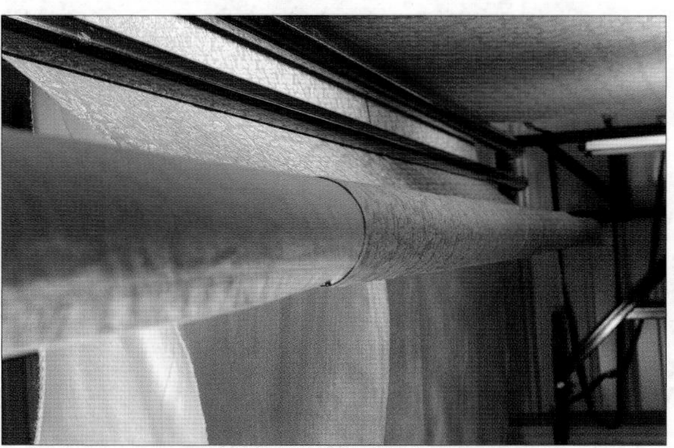

Check underneath for wrinkles.

Check under the quilt to make sure the backing is smooth before you secure the sides of the quilt top to the backing and batting.

Securing the Quilt Top Sides

The edges of the quilt top should be perpendicular to the roller bars. Check this with a square ruler to make sure you will not be stitching any distortion into the quilt.

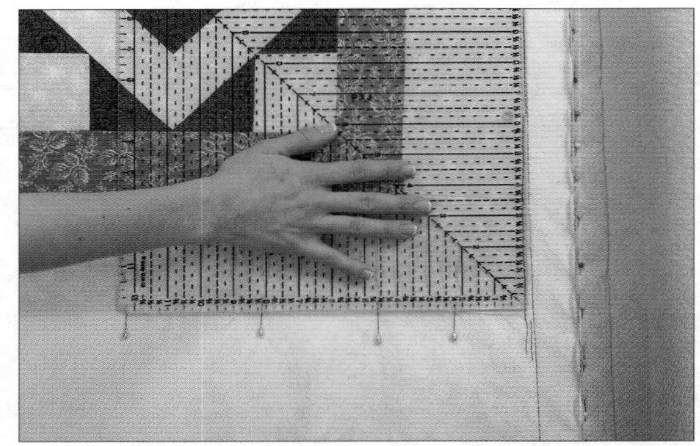

Make sure corners are square and sides are perpendicular to rollers.

Take the pins out from below the basting line and use them to pin the right side of the quilt top to the backing. Place the pins about every 3" in a horizontal position, parallel to the bars, with the pinheads sticking out onto the batting, out of the way of any quilting.

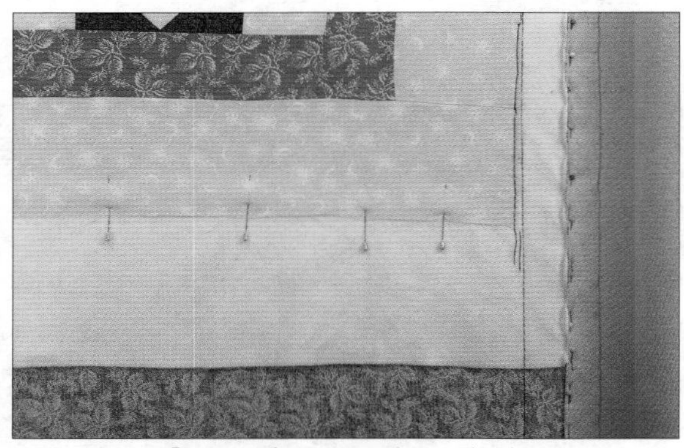

Pin outside area to be quilted.

NOTE: The right side of the quilt top (from the front of the machine) is secured with pins.

On the left side of the quilt top, use the machine to baste down the raw edge of the top, making sure you are ¼" or less from the raw edge. This stitching should be covered with the binding so it will never have to be removed. If you need to ease in extra fullness you may need to pin this edge before stitching.

Sew left edge, easing in fullness and pinning before stitching.

Clamps

Once the top is tightened and you feel the top and backing have an equal amount of tension and the quilt edges are secure, you are ready to put on the clamps. Never apply the clamps until after the quilt edges are secured to the backing, otherwise distortion caused by the clamps can be sewn into the quilt resulting in unwanted wavy seam lines, pleats, or puckers.

There are many different clamps available, some of which are harder to open than others. If you have trouble opening the clamps, find some that work well with your hands. I use the clamps that came with my machine, which work well for my projects. Some of the clamps seem hard to open at first, but your hands will get stronger as you use them.

On the larger machines it is nice to have three clamps on each side of the quilt to keep it taut. The clamps help pull out a little of the easing fullness.

Clamp only to the edge of the backing, not the edge of the quilt top.

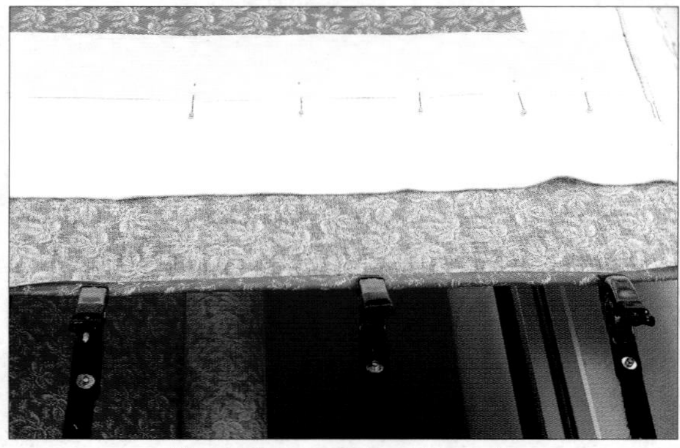

Attach clamps to backing only.

However, if there is no extra backing or batting on the sides of your quilt top you will need to clamp to the edge of the top. Always encourage your customers to give you at least 2"–4" of extra backing all the way around the quilt so you can quilt to the edge of the quilt top.

Important: When you put the clamps on, you should not see any distortion in the quilt top. Check the clamps. If they are pulling and distorting the seams in the quilt top, open them to release the extra tension until the seams in the quilt top are straight.

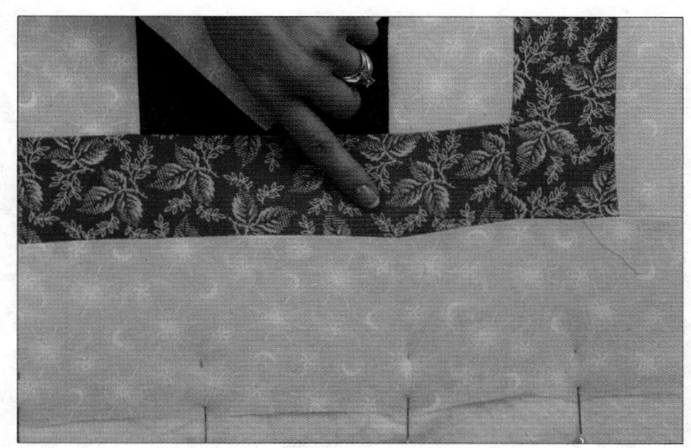

Avoid distortion due to clamps.

It will not make any difference if you have extra batting and backing on the sides of the top. Since the top is basted and pinned to the backing, it is treated as one piece.

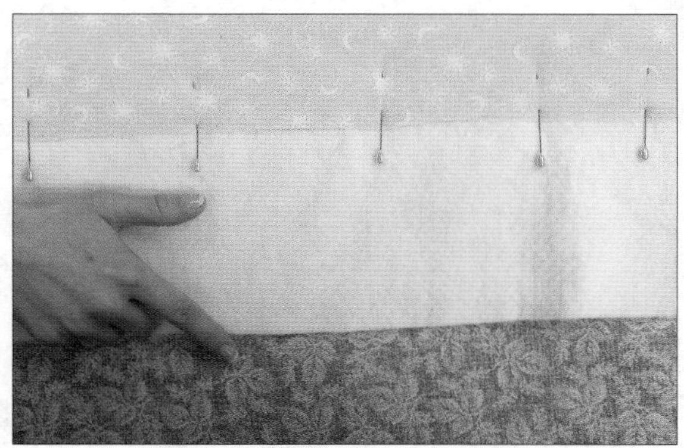

Treat quilt top, batting, and backing as one.

If you are working on your own quilt, you may want to trim the extra backing down to 3"–4". There is no need to trim away extra backing fabric on a customer's quilt; in fact, most prefer to pick up their quilt with extra fabric intact.

DO NOT wrap the hook and loop tape straps around the bar to keep the clamps in place.

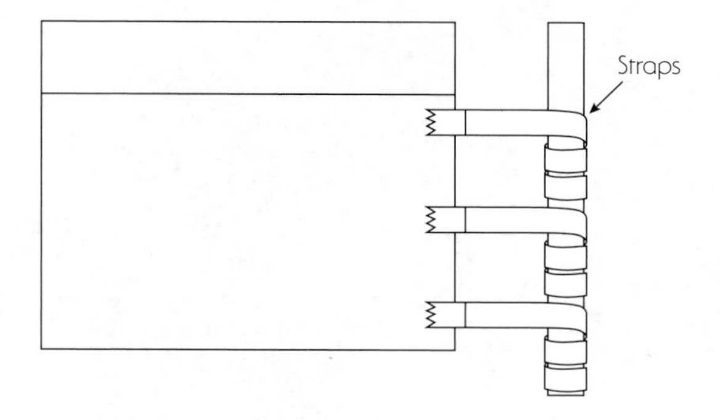

This makes more work when you want to release the clamps. Just position the clamp straps on the hook and loop tape. It will hold firmly. It is a good idea to put wide continuous strips of hook and loop tape all the way across the side bar for convenience.

Keep straps straight

Remember to release the clamps to advance the quilt. If you leave on the clamps, the backing may rip as you roll it.

Check Underneath the Quilt

Once the clamps are attached to the edges of the backing, check the quilt by looking underneath the machine table. It is easy to look under the machine from either side. (I tell my students this is a good time for blood to get to their brain.) Consistently check underneath the quilt, looking first to see how well it is pinned. If the backing or quilt top look loose anywhere, or if there are vertical or horizontal wrinkles, correct them at this point. If there appears to be extra fullness, ease it out by tightening the clamps or the backing roller. Make sure everything looks smooth under the quilt.

Loading a Wallhanging or Odd-Shaped Quilt Top

When you have an odd-shaped or small wallhanging to quilt, it can be loaded and quilted in very much the same manner as a regular quilt top.

For a small wallhanging, load the backing and batting first. Then you can either pin or spray-baste the small piece to the top of the batting/backing and baste around the raw edges. Now it is secure and ready to quilt.

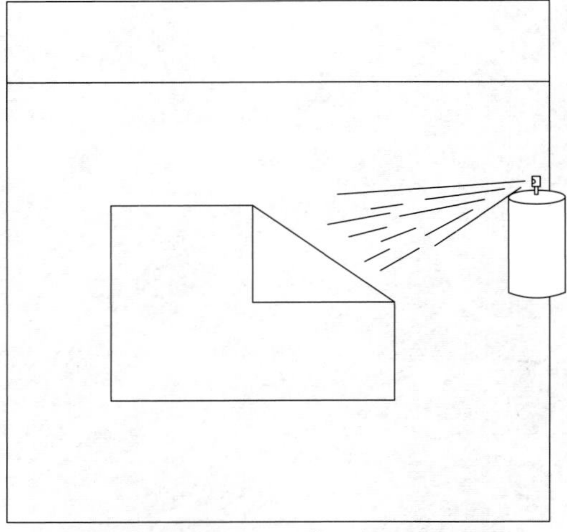

Spray baste small quilt tops to the stretched batting and backing.

Similarly, if you are loading an irregular shaped piece, such as a circle or Double Wedding Ring pattern, fold one edge of the quilted piece up in a straight line so you can pin it on the top roller bar.

Create straight edge on irregular shaped pieces when pinning on "top" canvas.

This edge will be unpinned as you baste off the bottom of the quilt, but you will have even tension on the top as you are quilting it. Next, load the backing and batting and tighten. Stitch a straight line across the top on the batting so you have a reference line. Bring the irregular-shape top edge of the piece to this line and either pin or spray baste it to the batting/backing until you can baste around the top raw edge.

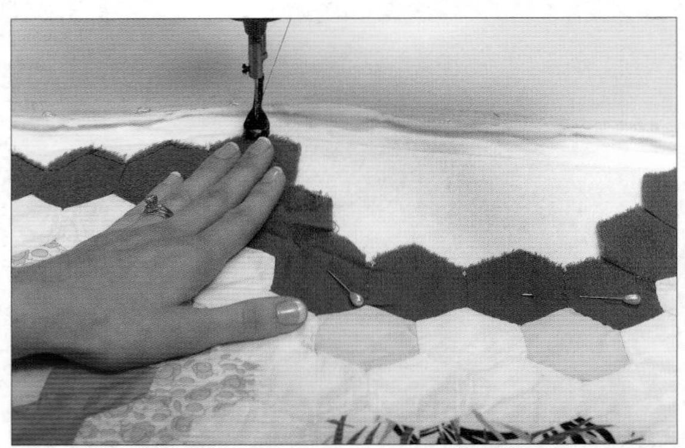

Baste top edge of irregular shape to backing and batting.

Once it is secure, put on your clamps and begin quilting.

QUICK REFERENCE FOR LOADING THE QUILT:

1. Prepare the components, lay out for visual reference, find and pin the centers.
2. Load the quilt top right side up; roll until it touches the pick-up roller bar.
3. Load the backing wrong side up; roll until it touches the back of the quilting machine table.
4. Pin the backing to the pick-up roller (always pin on the canvas side).
5. Load the batting (it may be pinned on pick-up roller same time as backing).
6. Place backing/canvas edges in an easy-to-reach position toward the front of the machine.
7. Tighten the backing roller.
8. Stitch the batting and backing together with a straight reference line approximately 1"–2" down from the canvas edge by using the channel lock or holding the wheels.
9. Secure the quilt top to the backing and batting; first pin, then stitch ⅛" along the edge of the quilt top.
10. Position the backing/canvas edge closer to the pick-up roller bar.
11. Tighten the backing roller, check for wrinkles under quilt.
12. Tighten the top roller.
13. Pin the right edge of the quilt top to the backing and batting.
14. Secure the left edge of the quilt top by basting it to the backing and batting.
15. Clamp the edges of the backing being careful to eliminate distortions.
16. Check underneath the quilt one more time.

PANTOGRAPH, EDGE-TO-EDGE, OR OVERALL QUILTING

Pantograph Patterns

"Edge-to-edge," "pantograph," and "overall" quilting are synonymous terms. "Pantograph quilting" means to apply an overall stitching pattern, from side to side, top to bottom, over the entire quilt, or the designated area of a quilt. The pattern is placed on the back of the machine table, preferably underneath the plastic, and lined up with the lines provided on the quilting machine tabletop. The quilt top is quilted without regard for the piecing design. No matter how the quilt top is pieced, the design of the pantograph pattern is stitched over the entire quilt from the back of the machine. You follow the lines on the table, not the lines of the piecework of the quilt.

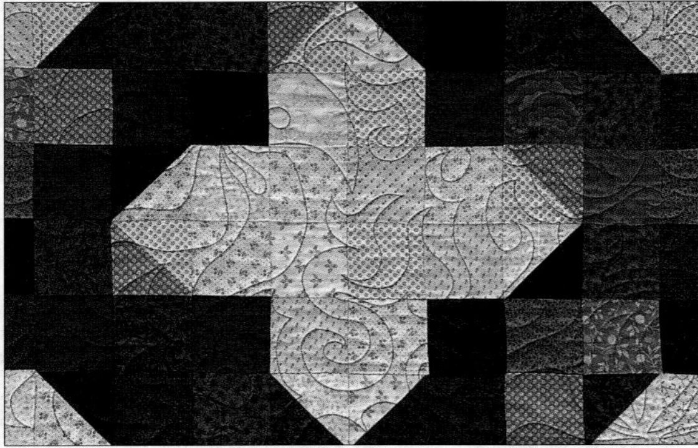
Pantograph pattern on piecework

Practice Piece

Practice is the only way that you will become proficient at stitching a variety of patterns and shapes, and be able to sew neat, uniform stitches. For your first practice quilt, I suggest using an inexpensive solid-colored fabric for the quilt top, perhaps an old sheet. Use an inexpensive batting and backing, and load it on the machine. Begin practicing pantographs at one end of this piece. When you have quilted to the end of the quilt, unpin the top fabric and roll the machine back to the beginning of the quilt. Stitch the practice quilt again using a different pattern. To check your progress, change the thread color each time and focus on the last color quilted. This way you will feel ready and comfortable when quilting on a pieced quilt top.

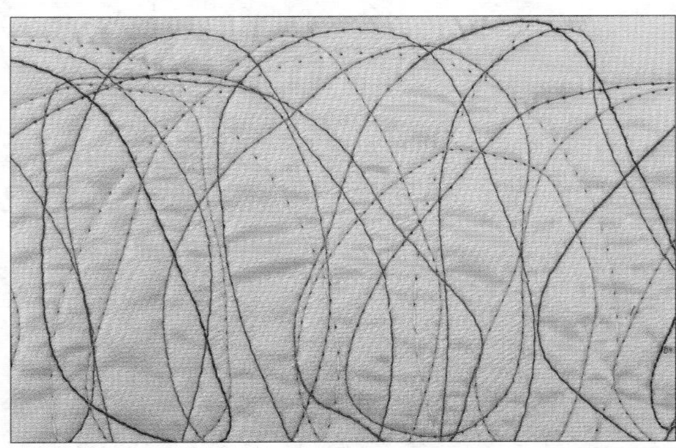
Changing thread colors on practice piece

Pattern Placement

Patterns can be followed from the table at the back of the machine using the laser light or stylus. Place the pattern under the plastic along one of the registration lines on the table. Make sure the pattern is straight and even along the entire length of the table.

Carefully place pattern under plastic along lines.

From the back of the table, position the machine foot at the lower right-hand side of the quilt edge. Set the needle down at this point simply to stabilize your machine while you adjust your laser light or stylus. Be careful not to make any jerky movements with your machine that could rip or tear the quilt.

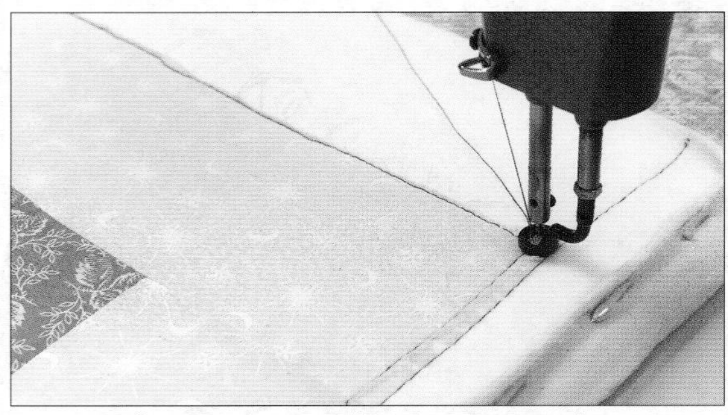
Begin at lower right edge, set needle down to hold machine in place.

With the needle still in the quilt, adjust the laser light so you can see it comfortably when standing behind the machine and make sure it is aimed at the very bottom of the stitching line on the pantograph pattern.

Aim laser at bottom of pattern.

If you have a stylus you will need to adjust the rollers and actually move the quilt to line up with the bottom of the pattern.

Now that the stylus or laser light is set and tightened, bring the needle up out of the quilt. Move the machine along the edge of the quilt top double-checking that all the stitching will be even along the edge of the quilt. Check twice; sew once.

Double-check before sewing.

Position the machine along the raw edge of the quilt top on the right-hand side (from the back of the machine table). Put a long piece of masking tape on top of the plastic on the table along the entire right perimeter of the pantograph pattern by following the end of the stylus or laser light.

This tape is perpendicular to the table and marks the farthest right perimeter of the quilt top.

Mark right perimeter of pattern with tape.

Now move the machine to the left side of the quilt top and place the tape on top of the plastic on the left side of the stylus or laser light to establish the left perimeter.

Mark left perimeter of pattern with tape.

The tape placement on the machine table now indicates the beginning and ending of the quilt top. If you follow the light or stylus and stitch beyond the taped areas, you will be sewing off the quilt top, although you should still be stitching on the batting and backing.

Within the taped perimeter it is easy to see the beginning and ending of the pantograph pattern. You can now easily adjust the pattern from left to right underneath the plastic to find the best place to begin and end the stitching. I call this the "pantograph shuffle." It is best to situate the beginning in a less complicated area of the pattern if possible. Or, a new beginning and/or ending can be drawn on a piece of paper and taped over the end of the pattern so the quilt will be uniform throughout and beautifully balanced.

Pantograph shuffle

Move the machine to the left side of the quilt and check to see where the end of the pantograph pattern will be stitched. Adjust any horizontally placed pins out of the way if necessary. Your smooth quilting lines will suffer if you are worried about sewing over pins at the end of the row.

Move pins away from stitching area.

You have established what I call a "quilt map" or a guide. It is placed on the table; you stand behind the machine and follow the guide while the machine is stitching on top of the quilt. Beginners often have difficulty adjusting to the fact that they are following the lines on the back of the table instead of watching the stitching on the quilt. Also somewhat confusing is the fact that the stitching is offset. For example, if you move your machine needle to the middle of the quilt, you will be about 10"–12" to the left of the middle on the back of the table.

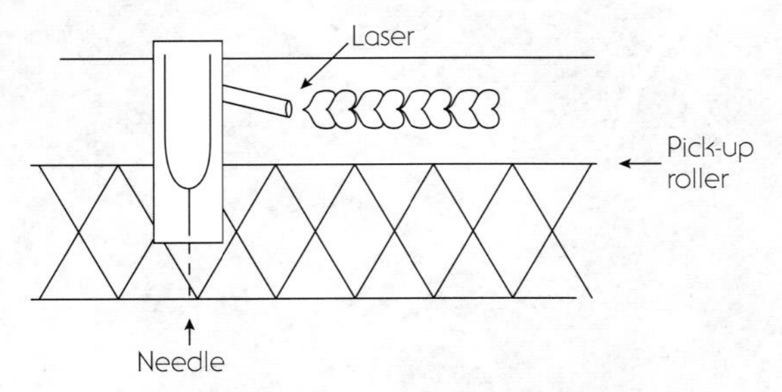

Laser is offset from hopping foot on quilt.

This is due to the location of your stylus or laser light. It will not take long before this seems quite natural.

If the pattern is interlocking, the very top edge of the quilt top (the first part that is pinned to the pick-up roller) will have unquilted gaps in the stitched pattern; the larger the pattern design, the more noticeable the gaps. To fill in these gaps, a portion of the pattern can be stitched at the top of the quilt by marking the edge of the quilt top, and following the laser light on the table. Find the appropriate point on the quilt top by moving the machine foot along the edge and following where the laser or stylus is on the pattern. Do not stitch above the tape mark. Sew straight across to the next point of re-entry into the pattern.

The quilting design to fill in the gaps should be stitched in the quilt at the beginning of the quilting process, but if you forget, the quilt can be rolled back to the top after it is basted off the top roller and the quilting is completed on the bottom end of the quilt. This process works best if the quilt top is floated so quilting can be stitched on and off to the extra backing and batting.

Securing the Stitches

Relax before you begin quilting. Try some stretching exercises, especially for your shoulders and arms. Athletes always warm up their muscles before they begin an activity but longarm quilters often neglect to warm up their arms and fingers. Frequent stretching exercises such as simply bending over to stretch the leg muscles are also important. Be considerate of your body (pages 98-100).

Each time you start stitching you must bring the bobbin thread to the top and secure the stitches so they will not pull out. This also prevents what we call "bird's nests" (clumps of thread) on the back. Beginners usually remember to secure the stitches but forget to bring the bobbin thread up or vice versa; either omission will consequently leave a big bird's nest of thread on the underside of the quilt.

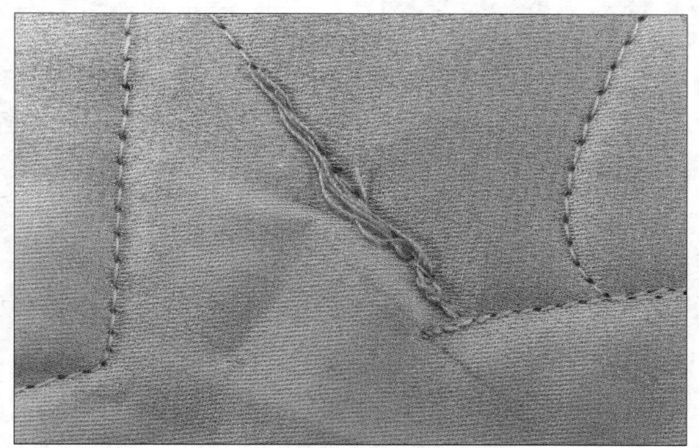

A bird's nest

From the back of the machine, find the place at the beginning of the pantograph pattern where you should begin your stitching. This is at the tape line on the right-hand side where the pattern first enters into view on the quilt map. Move the machine over and place the needle directly over this starting point. For consistency, mark this point on the masking tape. The first stitches are at the very edge of the quilt and will be covered with the binding when finished.

Mark starting point on pattern.

While you are still at the back of the machine, you can bring up the bobbin thread. To bring up the bobbin thread, gently hold onto the top thread, go down with the needle (using the needle positioner button or turning it manually), then bring the needle back to the up position. This means the take-up lever is going to be in the highest position so the bobbin will release automatically. If your machine has a needle positioner, it will automatically stop in this position. As you gently hold the top thread, move the machine over about an inch. By tugging the top thread, the bobbin thread should appear as a little loop. Pull that loop out so you can hold both the top and bobbin threads, both of which need to be brought up underneath the hopping foot.

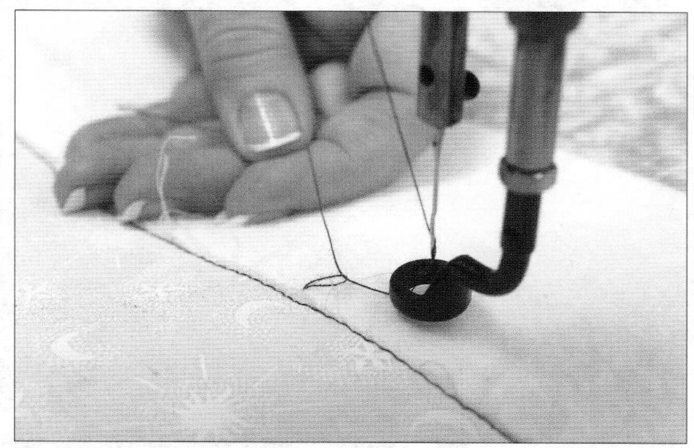

Bring both threads to top under hopping foot.

Gently hold both threads while you continue to take stitches. If you pull them too tight when you make the next stitch, the threads will not catch.

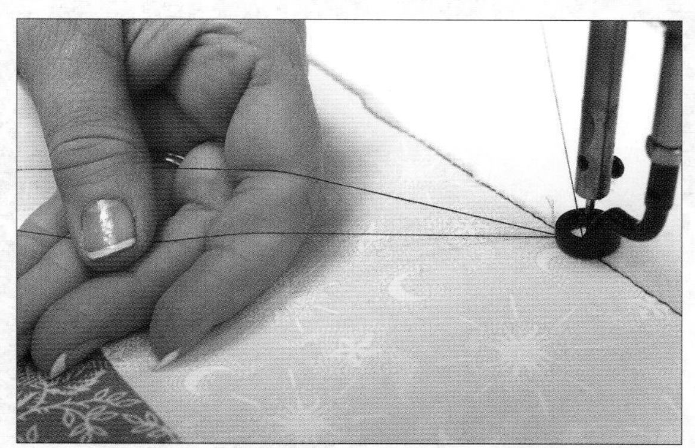

Hold both threads to avoid tangles on back.

Take four or five tiny stitches forward in the direction you will be sewing, looking down at the stylus or laser light point on the pattern. Lightly hold onto both threads as the bobbin rotates; otherwise, the machine will suck one of them down, which creates a loop underneath and ultimately a bird's nest.

The security stitches are at the very edge of the quilt and will be covered with the binding when finished. When you are first learning to secure the stitches, they tend to be exaggerated, but you will get better. With practice the stitches will be much smaller and closer together. Four or five tiny stitches are optimal, they are difficult to pick out and will be sufficient for a secure start and finish.

Start with tiny stitches to lock threads.

If you are going to follow a pantograph pattern, leave the needle down in the quilt. This will hold your place as you position yourself and get ready to start the design. Also, if you are interrupted at any time during the quilting process, the machine needle will stop down and hold the place for you.

If you have to stop sewing for some reason, try to stop at an intersection or on a horizontal line (parallel to the roller bars). This makes it easier and less conspicuous when you start again and creates a transition point. Avoid stopping on vertical lines.

Avoid starting/stopping on vertical lines.

NOTE: Keep interruptions to a minimum! When stopping and starting, the stitches tend to get smaller, especially for beginners. When stitching a pantograph line I do not answer the phone. The world can be on temporary hold until I have finished stitching a pantograph row.

With the stitches secured and the needle in the down position, trim the long remaining threads so they do not get caught in the foot of the machine. Leave the threads about an inch long. If you try to trim closer, you will have to move the machine out of the way, which will cause a loop in the thread.

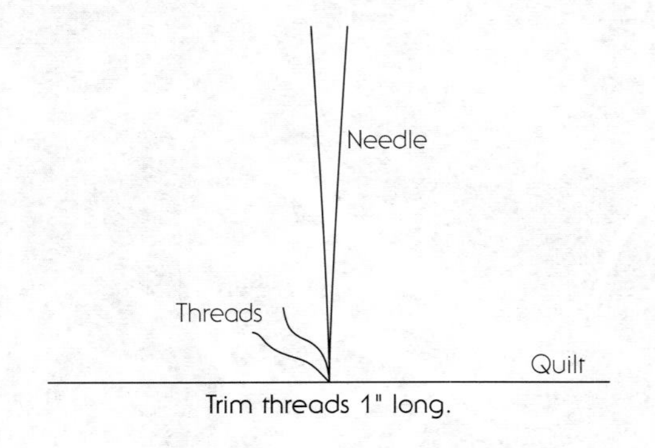

Trim threads 1" long.

Stitching the Design

As you begin, the objective is to get the feel of the machine and the rhythm of the design. In the beginning, do not worry about staying exactly on the lines. If you stray ¼" out of the line, no one is going to know by looking at the quilt, but wavy or shaky lines will certainly be noticeable. This occurs if you stitch too slowly and grip too tightly in an effort to exactly trace the lines.

Wavy lines are caused by gripping too tightly and trying to trace exactly.

Accurate stitching on the line comes with practice. The more you practice, the more easily you are able to stay close to the line. At first, simply focus on the rhythm of the pattern and smooth quilting lines. Start quilting and do not stop until you are at the end of your quilt map.

As a beginner, practice following several different design elements. Practice the round, loopy patterns as well as those with straight lines and points. I suggest starting with an easy loopy design and ending with stars (page 39).

Straight lines and points are usually trickier than loops. To stitch accurate straight lines, I concentrate on locking my arms at my side and using my body. Surprisingly, you may find that the body is much more stable than the arms when stitching many of the intricate pantograph and border designs. And it is fun to do—body-quilting!

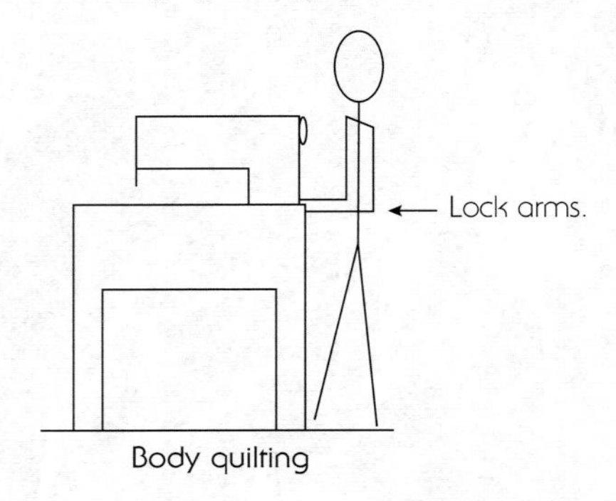

Body quilting

NOTE: When stitching points, be careful not to hesitate too long at the point. Think of the point like hitting a pingpong ball; just in and out. If there is no hesitation the point will be rounded or it will be a loop. There is a fine line between hesitation and lingering. Practice hesitating long enough to make a point, but not lingering to build up a little ball of stitches in the point. The point is not a rest area. It will take some practice to perfect the points and straight lines. Expect it and focus on improving. Allow yourself time to be a beginner.

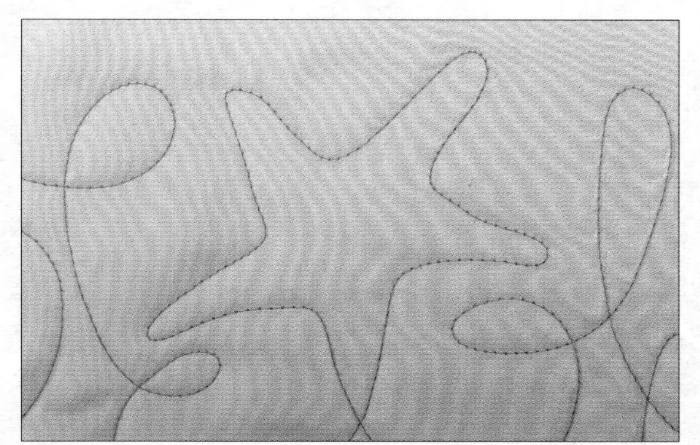

Too fast = Rounded

Too slow = Knots

Consistent speed = Perfect points

Many patterns have intersecting lines. It is important, at these intersections, to cross or connect very closely to the pattern. Pay particular attention to these areas and try to sew accurately at these intersections.

Sew accurately when lines cross.

You may need to redraw some designs so the flow of the continuous quilting seems more natural. Sometimes arrows can be confusing. Highlighting the patterns with yellow or red pens (the pink pens fade over time) may help you more easily follow the difficult patterns. Find a system that works best for you to make your quilting more continuous and smooth. No matter how you mark your patterns, always trace the patterns with your finger ahead of time so your brain and fingers are working together. By doing this, you will not have to worry or stop to think where you will stitch next.

To keep from over-powering or over-controlling the machine, use only fingertip touch when you are beginning. This will help you develop a light touch and realize that you are only guiding the machine. Just guide and slide it over the tracks. Music can help you relax and get into the rhythm of a pattern, smoothing out the lines. Listen to the radio, hum, or do whatever helps you relax. You do not want a neckache from tight muscles. If your body hurts after using the quilting machine, you are doing something wrong.

Stitch Length

Since this is a practice piece, stop after a few inches to check your stitch length. Six to twelve stitches to the inch are acceptable; nine or ten stitches are optimal. A good way to determine the stitch length is to measure a section with a ruler after a few repeats of the design. Stop, measure an inch and count the stitches.

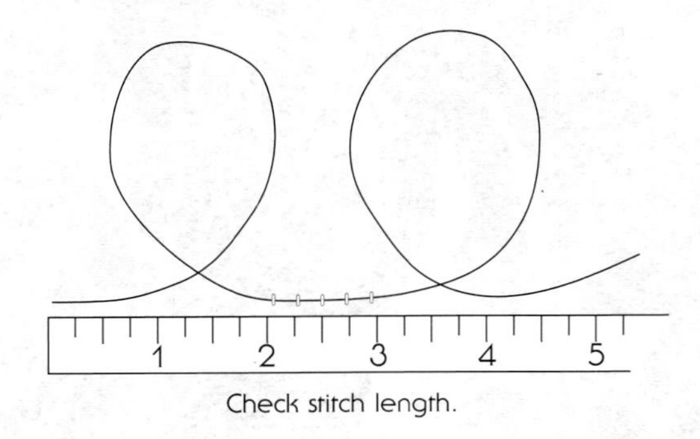

Check stitch length.

Or you can rely on your eyes to gauge it. Quilters are good at eyeballing nearly everything. The more you use your eyes, the better judgment you develop.

Every so often, recheck the stitch length in several places, at points and on curves, so you know if you need to slow down on the curves or go faster in the points. Try to keep the stitches as even as possible—the art of machine quilting. Stitches need to be as even on the long, easy runs as they are on the short little turns and the more intricate areas. The speed control set between 40 and 70 usually yields a good stitch length, depending on the design. Find the speed that is most comfortable for you. Adjust the machine to suit your needs and your speed. You are the operator.

Continue sewing across the quilt following the pattern from right to left from the back of the machine.

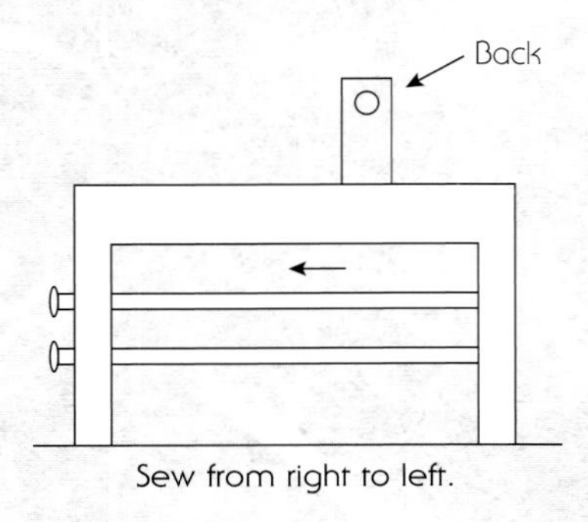

Sew from right to left.

Soon you will discover that you have to take a few sideways baby steps as you are quilting. I cannot give much advice here except to say wear comfortable sturdy shoes and if you are about to fall over, stop the machine! Seriously, everyone learns to walk as they learn to quilt on these machines. Take a step during a time when you are not stitching an intricate part of the pattern. It gets easier with practice. Eventually you won't realize you are walking as you are quilting.

When you approach the tape on the plastic as you sew near the left edge of the quilt, there should be extra batting and backing extending beyond the edge of the quilt top. When you are close to the tape, look up to where you are stitching in order to finish at the edge. While it may be awkward to take a quick glance at the quilt when following the light on the back of the table, you will eventually become more comfortable with your machine. Before you know it, it will become a habit to glance up at the quilt occasionally. After sewing across the quilt to the other edge of the top, you can secure the ending by bobbing back and forth with the machine making wiggly stitches. Make sure you are not more than ¼" from the raw edge of the quilt top while doing this. This ending works well for pantograph quilting because the stitches will be covered with binding. If you prefer, stop and do several small stitches using the needle positioner or hand wheel.

NOTE: The tape is a reference line to show the approximate place to stop sewing. As you roll the quilt, if your reference lines seem to be a little off, simply adjust the laser light or stylus horizontally to make the quilt map reliable for each new row.

The large and more complicated patterns may go off the quilt side edge. However, the pattern still needs to be completed so a bare spot will not be left on the side of the quilt. To ensure that you get a full pattern on the quilt, guide the machine (while sewing) off the edge of the quilt and back on again. Secure the stitches as usual and move the machine to the re-entry point for completing the pattern. Secure the stitches at the beginning, and again as you end the rest of the pattern.

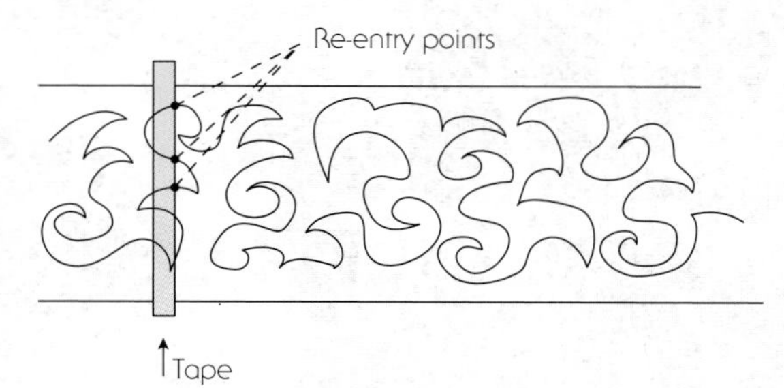

Secure stitches at the re-entry points.

Be careful as you are sewing back onto the quilt top not to get the hopping foot caught under the quilt top. Just remember: tape indicates heads up!

Establishing Reference Points

The first row of quilting is complete. Depending on the size of the pattern and size of the machine, to start the second row you may either roll the quilt or reposition the laser light. In each case, reference points should be established for consistency in the stitched pattern.

If there is not room to stitch another row, roll the quilt (page 42). If there is room to stitch another row without rolling the quilt, off-set the laser light (page 45) and continue.

Reference points can be marked directly on the paper pattern, which saves time for future use, or marked on a small piece of tape on top of the acrylic piece. I call the first reference point "home base" or "top of the pattern." It is marked at the highest point of the pattern line at the top of the paper pattern.

The next reference point indicates where the top of the next quilting row will be. I call this point the "alternate base" or "top of the next row." Most often, the alternate base is vertically straight down from the home base at the bottom of the quilting pattern. However, before deciding exactly where to place this point, first determine how the rows of quilting are going to fit together.

Sometimes the patterns are designed for "rows of quilting." In this case, the alternate base reference point is placed either directly on the bottom line or ¼" below the bottom line of the pattern.

Feathered flowers - rows of quilting

Other times the pattern is designed for each row to interlock into the row ahead of it, making the individual rows less distinct. For these interlocking patterns, the alternate base reference point is placed inside the pattern as far as the next row will comfortably fit without crossing any lines on the already quilted row.

Feathered flowers - interlocking rows

To place the reference point inside the pattern, use a piece of paper and trace one of the repeats. Place it on the pattern to see where the next row can be quilted without overlapping the stitching lines. You want at least ¼"–½" separating the lines of the two patterns in case you happen to stitch outside the pattern lines.

Feathered flowers

Mark the reference point on the pattern or tape; this is the alternate base. Some pattern designers mark these points on the patterns for you.

NOTE: To ensure that the last row ends with a whole repeat of the pattern, the spaces between the rows need to be calculated ahead of time. These unquilted spaces left between rows can be distracting on the quilt. Oftentimes the spaces end up uneven as the quilter tries to adjust the rows toward the end of the quilt. To some extent, these unquilted space calculations are guesswork because of the unknown amount of shrinkage that occurs in the quilting process. The shrinkage of a quilt due to the quilting can vary from 2%–10%. Batting choice, density of quilting, and even the pattern choice are determining factors in quilt shrinkage. It is rare to end the quilt with a perfect space for a final row.

Steps in Rolling the Quilt

There are two common ways of rolling the quilt to begin the next row of pantograph quilting. One way is with the needle down, and the other is with the needle up.

Rolling With the Needle Down

1 Keep in mind that the needle equals the laser light or the stylus. Move the machine so the light or stylus is at home base on the pattern at the back of the machine. The needle should be exactly over the corresponding home base stitched into the quilt. Put the needle down into the quilt at this point (home base).

Home base = Top of pattern

2 Remove the clamps on the sides of the backing. Release the top and backing roller levers (I call them "clickers" because they click).

NOTE: When you release the top and backing roller bars, do not allow them to unroll all the way. It will cost you time to re-roll and it is a pain to make sure they roll back straight, without folds.

3 Slowly and gently roll the pick-up roller bar counter-clockwise. The machine will move with the quilt as it is rolled. Watch the light or stylus as it moves on the back of the tabletop. When the light reaches the alternate base, continue to advance the quilt about ½" past the reference point.

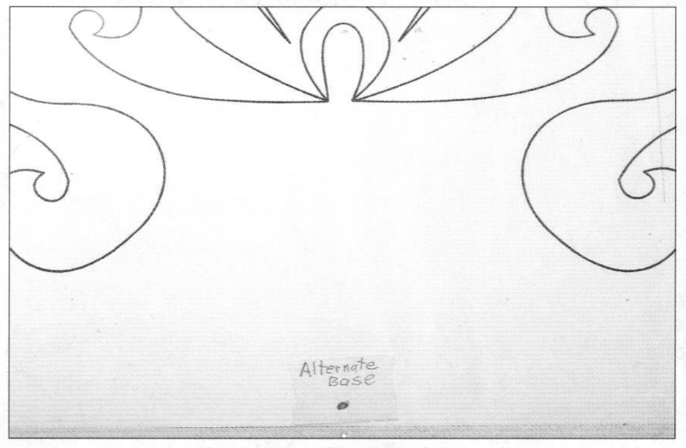

Laser on alternate base

4 With the machine needle still set in the quilt, tighten the backing roller. As you do, the light will move back with the machine to the alternate base reference point on the table. Tighten the top roller bar and attach the clamps to the edge of the backing.

Rolling With The Needle Up

1 Remove the clamps on the sides of the backing. Release the top and backing roller levers.

2 By turning the pick-up roller counter-clockwise, advance the quilt until the quilted area is about 4"–5" from the pick-up roller.

3 Tighten the backing roller and the top roller bar. Attach the clamps to the edge of the backing and batting.

4 Find the home base at the top of the quilted pattern on the quilt top. Position the machine needle over this point and set the needle down to hold the machine in place.

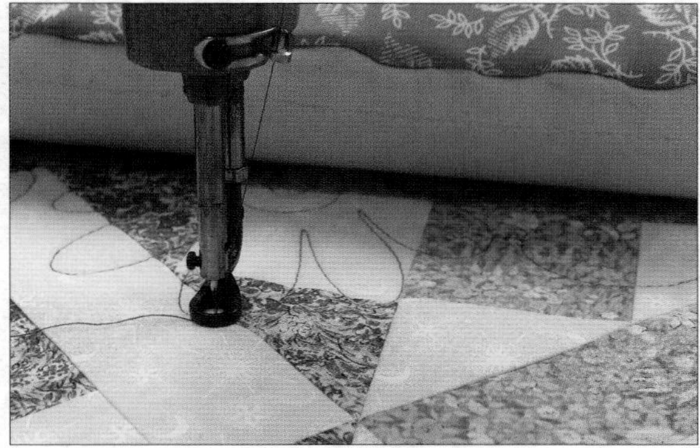

Needle on home base

Loosen the laser light and reposition it on the alternate base point.

Adjust laser to alternate base or bottom of pattern.

Tighten the screw that holds the laser light to make sure it is secure. Bring the needle up out of the quilt and go back to the beginning of the paper pattern on the back of the table.

After Rolling the Quilt

Regardless of how you advanced the quilt, it is now ready for the next row of quilting. Without actually stitching, move the machine to different areas on the pattern and look up at the quilt top to make sure the pattern will be stitched in the right place on the quilt. Check twice, sew once. Consistency in the spacing between pantograph rows is critical.

Double Patterns

Having two copies of the same pattern lined up on the back of the machine table saves time in rolling the quilt. Some patterns conveniently come with two passes already printed. Generally these patterns have the motif offset. For example, you may not want to quilt roses one directly above another, therefore every other row can be offset to the right or left so the roses interlock and do not appear to be in rows.

Interlocking patterns

Large Patterns

Some patterns are too large to lay two rows on the machine table. If offsetting these patterns for every other row is desired, simply slide the paper pattern back and forth under the plastic using the taped perimeters as your guide. Be careful. You may need to redraw the beginning and ending of the offset row.

Losing Your Place

Perhaps you forgot to set your needle on home base before you rolled. How do you find your place? Look at the last stitched pattern on the quilt top and find the home base on the quilt. Set your needle down at this point. Now either roll the quilt (for a stylus) or adjust the laser light to match the home base to the pattern on the table. Once again, the needle equals the laser light or stylus. Be sure to double check where you will be stitching to make sure you are in the correct position. Consistency in the spacing between pantograph rows is critical.

The End of the Quilt

Before you stitch the last row of quilting, but after you have quilted and rolled to the bottom of the quilt, you are ready to "baste off" the bottom edge. Release the top roller so it is easier to remove the pins; however, leave the backing roller tight.

Remove some pins from the top canvas and the quilt top leaving one pin every 3"–4". Tighten the top roller again. Place a clamp on the left side of the quilt even with the bottom edge of the quilt to hold the quilt taut. Turn the speed on the machine down to 15 or 20 for a basting stitch.

NOTE: If you remove all the pins at once, the quilt top will no longer have the proper tension.

Beginning at the left side of the quilt, baste to the right across the quilt bottom, staying about ⅛" from the raw edge. Stop and remove each remaining pin as you are basting in order to sew close to the quilt edge.

Remove pins as you baste bottom edge.

NOTE: If you sew in too far on the quilt, the raw edge can get flipped back and sewn down to the right side of the quilt top as you are stitching the last row of the pattern.

You have basted the quilt top to the backing and batting. The top canvas can now be rolled back on the top roller bar out of the way, since you no longer have the top pinned to it. Hopefully, there are several inches of batting and backing extending beyond the quilt top pinned to the edge of the backing roller canvas.

The Last Row

If you basted off the quilt top, remember to turn up the speed on the machine now to complete the last row of stitching.

Generally, only part of a pattern will fit in the last row. Of course, this is always true if the pattern is interlocking.

So how do we end the quilting with a pantograph pattern? With the quilt top basted to the batting/backing, the pattern can be completed without worrying about the bottom raw edge of the quilt. The pantograph can be stitched on and off the edge of the quilt top and batting/backing; this works well if the pattern is not large.

Pattern can be stitched on and off quilt top.

A portion of a large pattern can be stitched at the bottom of the quilt by simply marking the edge of the quilt bottom, following the laser light, on the table with masking tape. Find the quilt bottom by moving the machine foot along the edge and following where the laser or stylus is on the pattern. Do not stitch above the tape mark. Stitch straight across to the next point of re-entry into the pattern.

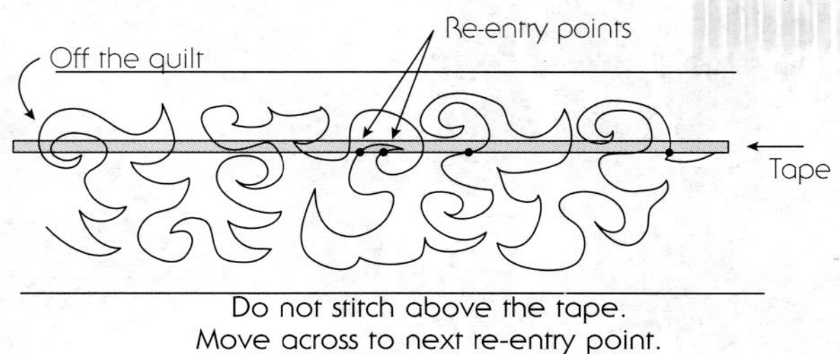

Removing the Quilt

When the last row is completed, you are ready to remove the quilt. Loosen the backing roller and remove the pins. Without loosening the rollers, it will be more difficult to remove the pins and some pinheads may even be pulled off in the effort. Always remove the pins approaching them from the head side so there is less chance of the sharp end sticking your fingers.

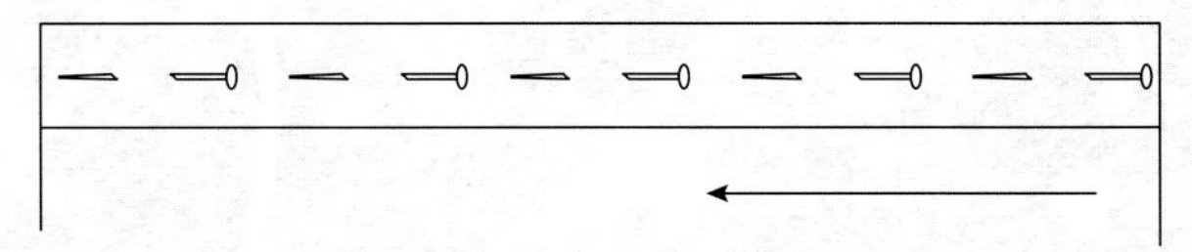
Approach pins from head side to remove.

Now, from the back of the machine table, slowly unroll the quilt, carefully checking the back of the quilt and clipping loose threads one roll at a time.

Remove the remaining pins from the pick-up roller canvas and the quilt is off.

MULTIPLYING PATTERNS

If there is enough room to complete another row of the pattern without rolling, the laser light can be offset instead of actually rolling the quilt. This will save a lot of time by rolling every two or three rows instead of each row.

To offset the laser light, find and mark the reference points in exactly the same manner explained on page 41 Move the machine needle to the home base on the quilt (the row you just finished) and lower it into the quilt to hold the machine in place while you adjust the laser light. With the needle in the quilt, adjust the laser light from the home base to focus on the alternate base on the pattern on the table.

Laser on alternate base

Make sure the laser light is tightened and will not move while you are quilting. Bring the machine needle up and double check where the machine will be stitching on the quilt while you are following the pattern on the table with the laser light. When you are sure you will be quilting in the right place, proceed to stitch the second row.

After stitching the second row in this manner, if there is room enough to stitch another row, follow the same procedure to move the laser light. Always double check exactly where on the quilt you will be stitching before you actually begin to stitch.

After completing as many rows of the quilting pattern as possible, follow Steps 1-4 in Rolling the Quilt with the Needle Up (page 43).

Note: The laser light should remain a light dot. If the angle makes it look like a line, the casing can be removed and the light can be refocused. If this seems like too much work or you are in a hurry, simply put a piece of masking tape over the end of the light and poke a small hole in the tape with a pin to make the light a dot again. Always make sure the laser light is screwed on tight and do not bump it or you will be unpicking stitches!

BASTING WITH THE LONGARM MACHINE

When we talk about basting, we tend to think of basting the quilt to prepare for hand quilting; however, there are other reasons for basting a quilt. Occasionally, we might need to baste a whole cloth quilt to stabilize it for intricate quilting. Sometimes we need to baste large areas on a quilt to stabilize it and complete the border designs. And, as we are setting the quilt up on the machine we generally lightly baste the quilt top to the backing and batting. Likewise, at the end of the quilt we most often baste off the end of the quilt top.

So how do we baste on the quilting machine? Of course, the stitches need to be much longer than usual. In order to achieve this, the speed of the machine must be lower and the machine must be moved faster over the quilt. The ideal basting stitch length is two or three stitches to the inch.

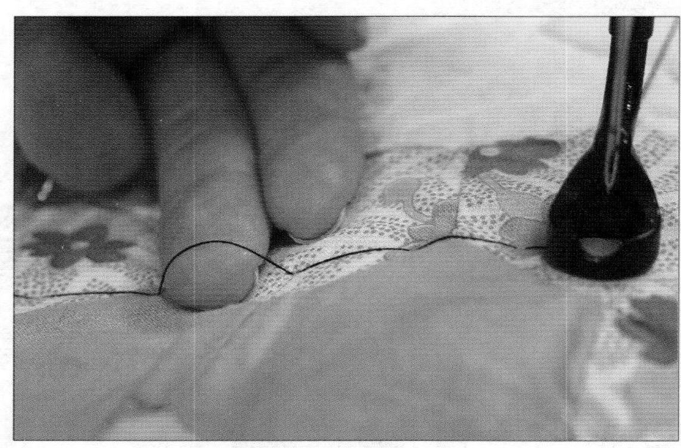

Ideal basting

Try to sew the stitches evenly. You do not want little stitches anywhere in the basted quilt since they will be more difficult to remove.

Basting one direction every 4" is plenty of stabilization for most hand quilters. Basting both directions just creates extra work in taking out stitches. Remember longarm basting stitches are much more secure than hand basting stitches.

On most longarm machines, turn the speed down between 15 and 20 or about 20%. Use only cotton thread for basting and use a small needle size. Moving the machine too fast at this speed may cause the needle to deflect and break, so be careful. Gently push the fabric down behind the needle as you stitch across the quilt to relieve some of the pressure on the needle.

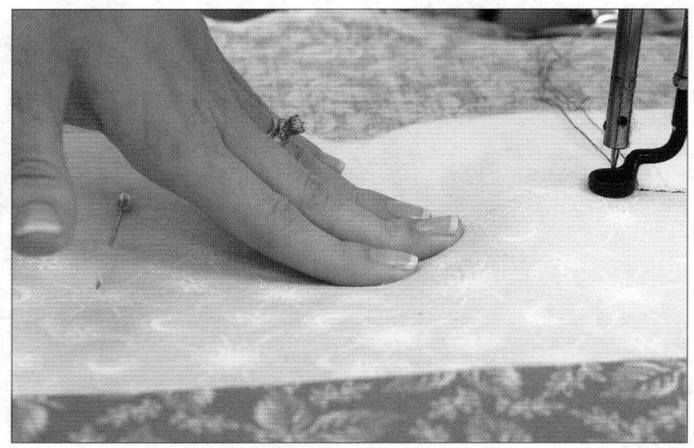

Ease in fullness.

This is also a good way of easing in any extra fullness in the quilt top.

Avoid basting over delicate appliqué areas or over photos on quilts. Use good judgment; some quilts have special fabrics where the holes from the basting will not disappear, like batiks. It is easy to skip over these areas without breaking the threads. Simply stop the machine, move over to the next area, and resume basting. The long threads dragged across the unbasted areas can be easily clipped later.

Using the channel lock from the front of the machine is an easy and accurate way to go across the quilt. When using the channel lock to sew even, straight lines, always measure and set the channel lock in the *middle* of the quilt. Then move the machine over to the left edge and sew to the right edge. The sides of the quilt can be volatile. The middle is stable and will give you more accurate, even lines of stitching.

OVERALL FREEHAND MEANDERING

Overall freehand "meandering" seems to be a popular way to finish quilts. Meandering lines are more than ¼" apart, as opposed to "stippling" where the lines are less than ¼" apart. Meandering and stippling are also sometimes referred to as "vermicelli." This technique is easy and fast. If you are paying someone to quilt your quilt top, the large meandering is also the least expensive method to consider.

Overall meandering is generally accomplished from the front of the machine. This is an excellent way to work in extra fullness throughout the quilt or in borders that are flared. While working the quilt from the front, the user can gently push down around the throat plate behind the needle with the left hand. This eases in the extra fullness without creating tucks in the fabric. This method works best without an extended base around the throat plate.

A traditional meandering technique is easy and fun to learn. Practice it on paper before trying it on a quilt. There are three basic rules to follow: first, all the lines are rounded, no points; second, do not cross lines; and third, try not to establish a pattern in the freehand stitching, make it a true meandering.

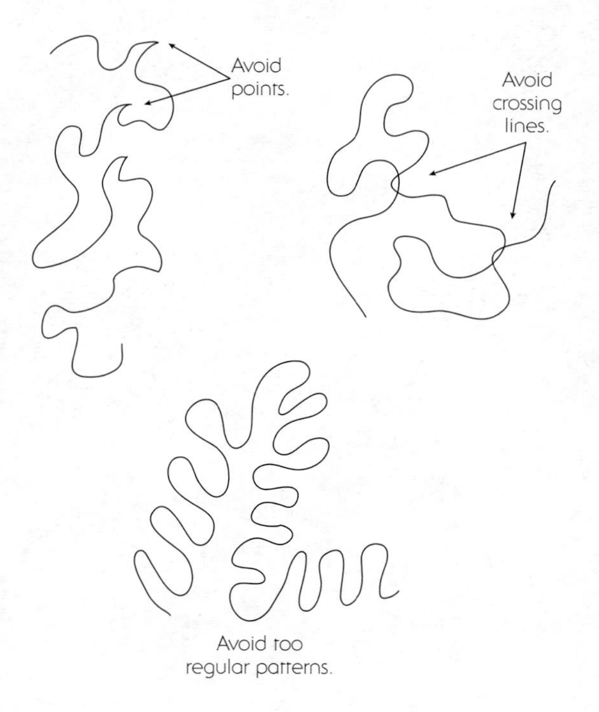

Avoid too regular patterns.

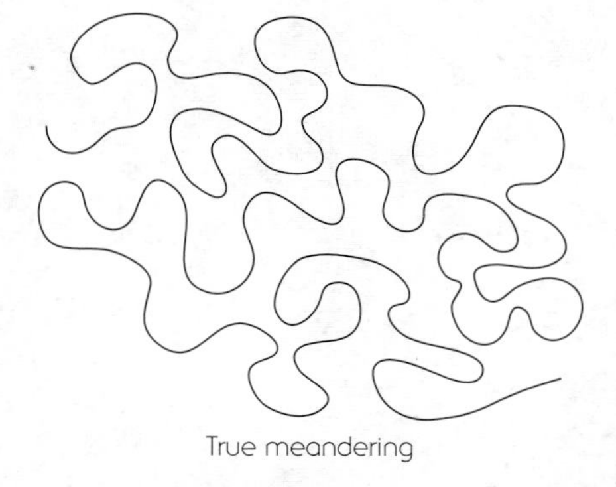

True meandering

There are a variety of meandering patterns, many of which do not follow these rules. You will find your own signature meandering pattern. It is similar to handwriting, each person's style is different.

TIP: Keep the distance between the lines as even as possible so the meandering is consistent. I like to keep what I call a "stippling or meandering strip" right by the machine as I am meandering. I can compare the size on this strip to the work I am doing on the quilt as I am working. This way, the size of the meandering or stippling will be consistent throughout the quilt.

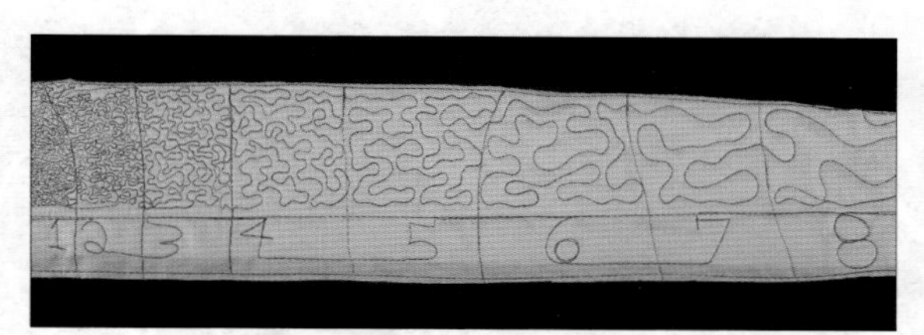

Stippling or meandering strip

To make a stippling strip, load an approximately 5" x 36" piece of muslin or solid-colored fabric, batting, and backing on the machine. Divide the strip into seven segments and fill each segment with a different size of stippling, from very tiny to very large. Making a stippling strip is also a very good practice piece for beginners.

A stippling or meandering strip is especially important if you are quilting as a business. It allows your customers to choose which size of meandering they want on their quilts. Pricing will be different for each size of meandering or stippling.

OVERVIEW OF SET-UP AND PROGRESSION ON CUSTOM QUILTS

Custom quilting (as opposed to overall or pantograph quilting) is choosing quilting designs that enhance the piecework of the quilt. Most often, this will include stitching in the ditch, outlining the appliqué (if included), and setting designs in specific open areas of the quilt. This generally involves using rulers and tools developed for the longarm machines to aid in precise execution of the technical skills. You sew from the back of the machine whenever you are using a pattern that is placed on the back of the machine. You sew from the front of the machine whenever you are using freehand techniques.

IMPORTANT NOTE: This section is an overview of the set-up and progression and technical skills used for all custom quilting on the longarm machines. Whether you are setting in border or sashing designs, block patterns, or stitching around appliqué, the process of stabilizing the quilt on the quilting machines is the same. A clear understanding of this process can alleviate subsequent problems encountered by many longarm quilters.

Stabilizing the Quilt, Setting in the Border Design

There is a natural progression when custom quilting on the quilting machines. It is different from hand quilting but similar to methods used by other machine quilters. The quilt must be stabilized before much of the design work and heavy quilting is applied. If this does not occur, the borders and outsides edges of the quilt will be ruffled. This is because as the quilt is stitched it shrinks.

Since most quilts are rectangular, load the quilt sideways, pinning the longest sides to the roller bars first (page 23), unless the pattern requires upright loading (page 23).

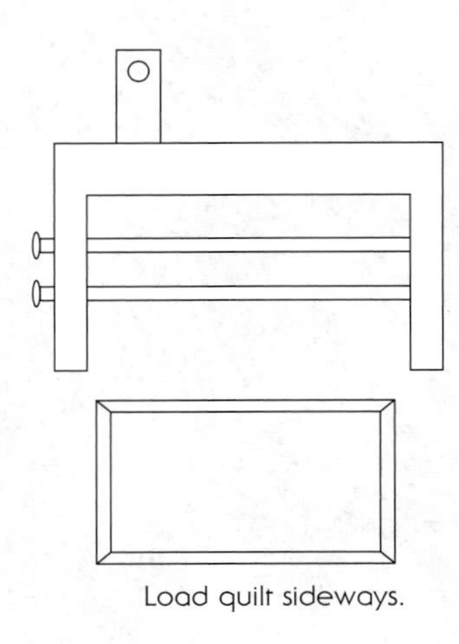

Load quilt sideways.

To stabilize the custom quilt, begin with stitching in the first border design including the corners. Then proceed to outline the areas on the quilt that you will later enhance with motifs or dense free-hand quilting. To outline areas; stitch in the ditch (page 59), stitch ¼" from the seamlines (page 61), use simple cross-hatching (page 64), or stitch around the appliqué motifs (page 61).

Continue to advance the quilt and outline the necessary areas. Do not leave an area larger than 14" without some stitching inside it. Sometimes, basting across a large square is necessary to stabilize it. The entire quilt must be stabilized as you advance to the opposite end of the quilt.

When you reach the other border, reposition the corner patterns, turn the border pattern upside down and repeat exactly what you did when you placed the first border design. Stitch the border and corner design in this second long-side border of the quilt.

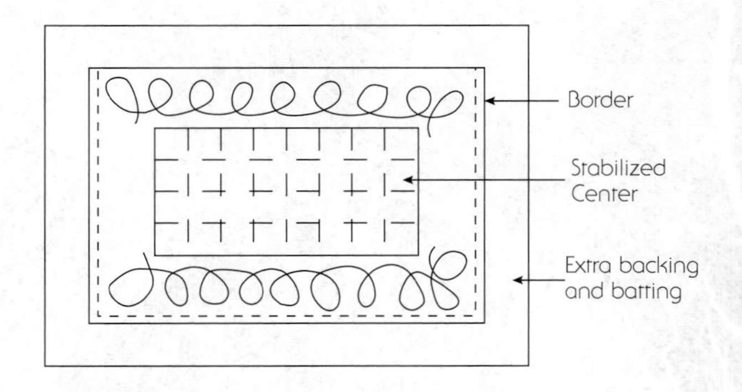

Unpin the entire quilt and rotate it one-quarter turn.

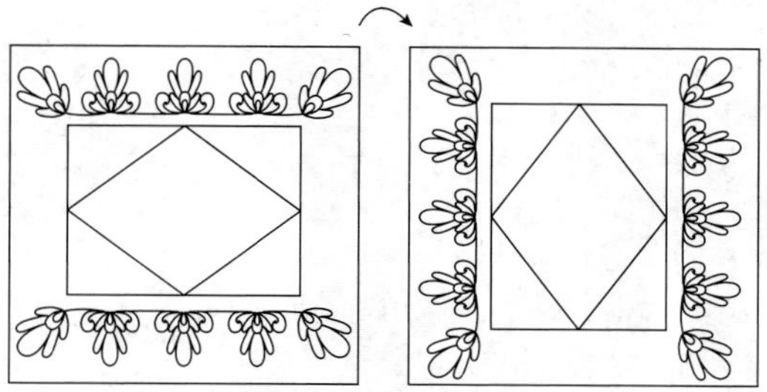

Turn quilt 90° and pin.

Repin using the edge of the quilt top, which is more likely to be square than the edge of the backing. On my machine, I generally re-pin to the pick-up roller bar and the backing roller because it is easier to reach both bars at the same time without leaning or bending over. Remember your back is important.

NOTE: Before remounting the quilt, many longarm quilters trim the excess backing and batting to approximately 2". I find the backing and batting do not interfere in any way with the quilting process, so I leave it on the quilt to save my time and allow my customers the opportunity to deal with it as they choose.

Once the quilt is re-pinned, the border that is pinned onto the backing roller needs to be positioned so it is closer to the pick-up roller. This places it in a position that is easier for you to reach from behind the machine table. The border pattern is already facing the correct direction to be stitched. If you have a stylus, you can move the quilt into position with the pattern using the rollers. If you have a laser light, simply find the center of the border design ¼" up from the seamline and put the needle down on this point; refocus the light to the corresponding point on the border pattern. In either case, be sure to double check the distance from the seamline all along the border to make sure you will not be sewing out of the border area. Take the corner patterns off the table so you do not sew them again.

Stitch this border and roll the quilt to the opposite border pinned onto the pick-up roller bar. Match the reference points and stitch this border in a similar manner. (You need to turn the pattern one last time for this border.)

Now the motifs can be stitched in the design areas (page 62).

Only after the quilt is stabilized and the designs are set can you begin the heavier quilting such as stippling or meandering (pages 70-73). Heavy quilting should be consistent throughout the quilt for balance.

This method of stabilizing the quilt means less chance of flared borders on the quilt due to shrinkage in the middle of the quilt. It is also practical. The quilter is forced to focus on one technique at a time and can execute that technique with accuracy and consistency.

Freehand Borders

If you are quilting a freehand border design, the stabilizing process is the same except you will complete the freehand border design as you advance the quilt.

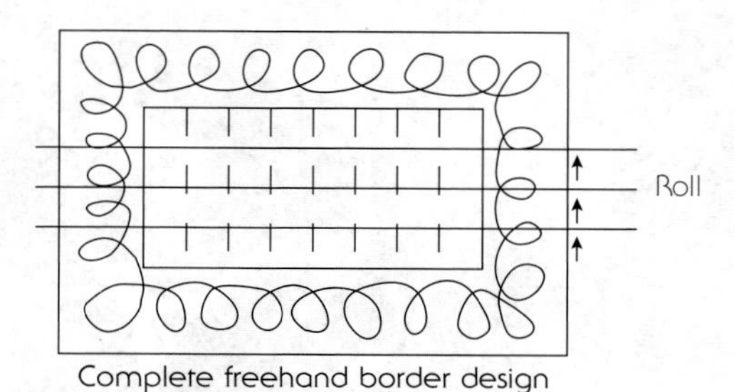

Complete freehand border design as you advance the quilt.

Each time you stabilize and advance the quilt, complete the freehand border designs on both sides of the quilt as you roll. When you have stabilized the entire quilt to the other border, complete the last freehand border design and baste off the edge of the quilt (page 44). Now you can begin to set the motifs in specific areas of the quilt, working from the bottom up. There is no need to roll back to the top of the quilt because you have already stabilized the quilt.

BORDERS AND CORNERS

Border Designs

Many continuous-line border and block patterns can be purchased. Some printed patterns are long enough to fit the border, while others are only a portion of the pattern. There are several ways to duplicate the pattern to make it long enough for the quilt border. It can be traced on paper, such as long butcher paper. It can be scanned and resized on a computer and printed on a printer or plotter, or it can be duplicated on a copy machine and taped together. In any case, make sure the pattern is recreated or duplicated with reference lines to help with placement on the quilt. These lines mark the bottom of a border or indicate miter lines on corner patterns and block patterns.

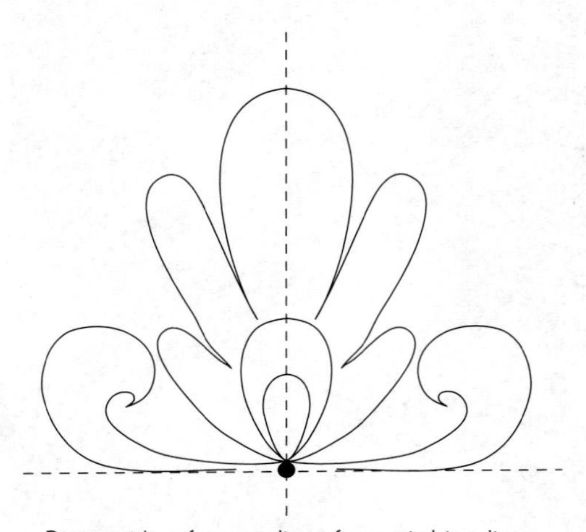

Distinguish reference lines from stitching lines.

The reference lines can be dotted lines or marked in color to distinguish them from the stitching lines.

NOTE: Never resent the time it takes to manually trace a pattern.

While tracing, practice using your whole arm, moving it as evenly as possible around the motif. Your brain does not distinguish between tracing on paper and quilting on a machine; therefore, you can practice the design before you ever start stitching it on the quilt.

Measure the width of the area where the border motif is to be stitched. Make the pattern for this area 1"–1½" narrower overall. This will give you ample space to allow for uneven piecing or slightly inaccurate stitching. If the border measures 6", you will make a paper pattern 4½"–5" tall.

NOTE: Occasionally I already have a border design traced, but find it is 2" or 2½" smaller than the area measured. To save time, rather than trace a slightly larger pattern, I will use the pattern I already have and simply echo or stipple around the outside edge of the pattern to fill in the extra space. This is a successful, lovely effect.

Echo stitch to fill in small spaces.

Placing the Border Designs

Traditionally, area motifs, corners, and borders can be traced on the quilt with a variety of tools, then stitched over; later the marks are removed. Sometimes quilters actually stitch the pattern right through the paper onto the quilt and later remove the bits of paper left under the stitches. These traditional methods are readily available for study in many quilt books today.

There are several ways to conveniently stitch corner and border designs using the features on the quilting machine engineered to save time and effort. These methods are unique to the longarm machines.

Method One: The Border Shuffle

This method is successful at least 90% of the time. I always try it first because it is so easy and will save time on the project.

Every quilt border has a natural miter line; no matter how the border is pieced. The miter line starts at the inside corner of the border and follows out to the outside corner of the border.

Setup

1 Place a piece of masking tape along the miter line on the quilt top from the inside corner of the border to the outside corner of the border.

Tape edge of miter line.

The two corner patterns are traced separately from the long border design. Miter lines should be marked on each corner pattern as well as a reference point.

2 Place one of the corner patterns on top of the actual quilt border and line it up with the taped miter line on the machine table.

Place corner pattern to preview palcement.

3 Insert a pin through the reference dot on the pattern and down through the quilt top. Lift up the corner pattern slightly and mark a dot right on the tape edge where the pin enters the quilt.

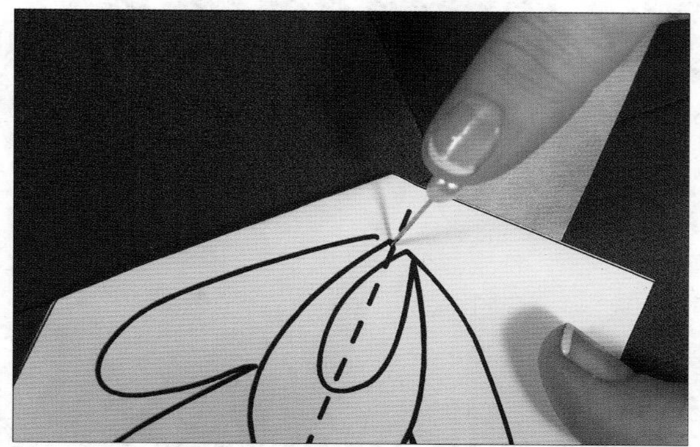

Place pin through bottom of corner pattern to mark dot on tape.

Also mark a line on the edge of the tape indicating where the actual seamline of the corner starts.

Mark corner seam line.

4 Measure the distance from the inside corner line to the reference dot on the edge of the tape.

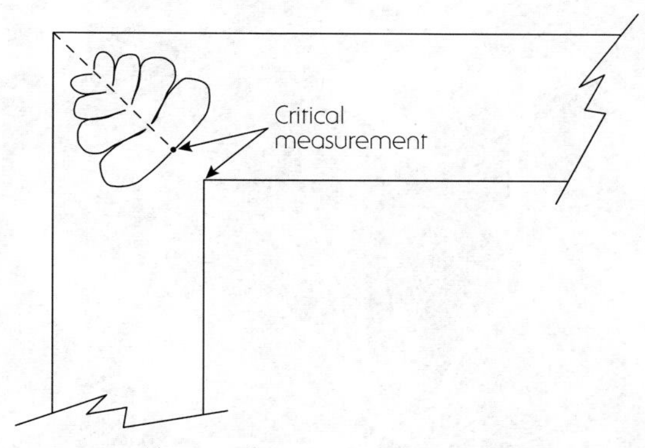

Measure from corner to start dot.

Measure and mark the tape on the opposite border exactly the same.

5 Put the needle down through the reference dot at the edge of the masking tape.

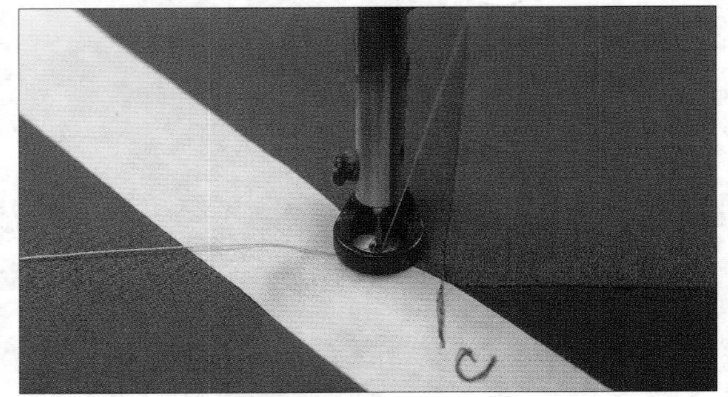
Set the needle down to position pattern.

6 Place the corner pattern on top of the plastic on the back of the machine table and use the stylus or laser light to match up with the reference dot on the quilt top. (This is the reference dot, NOT the corner line.)

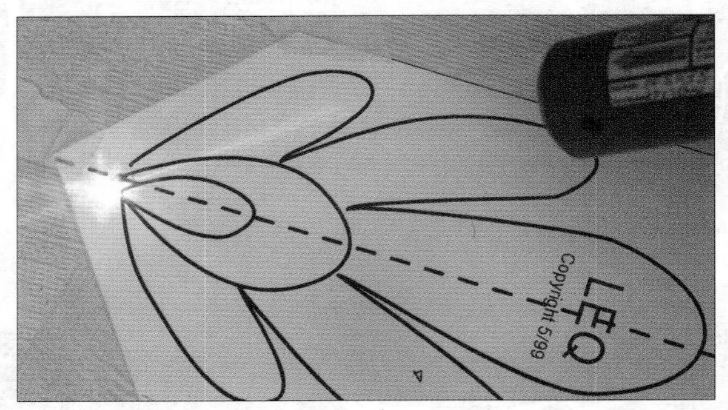

Focus laser or stylus on reference dot on pattern.

7 Moving the machine, follow the miter line along the edge of the tape on the quilt partway up toward the corner of the quilt.

8 Following the laser light or stylus, position the miter line on the corner pattern on the table to match up with the miter line on the quilt and securely tape the pattern to the tabletop plastic.

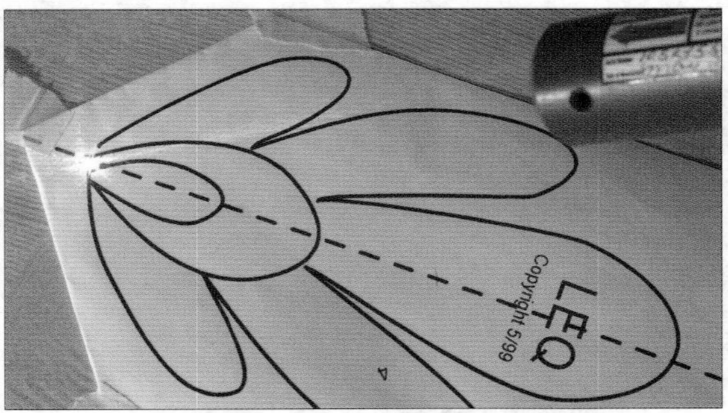

Match miter line on pattern and quilt top.
Secure pattern to table.

9 Repeat for the opposite corner. Tighten the laser light to make sure it will not move out of place. If the light moves, repeat steps 2–8.

Both corner patterns are in position on top of the plastic.

10 Place the border pattern under the plastic. Move the border back and forth, checking the beginning and ending of the border design in relation to the corner patterns. This is what I call the border shuffle. Sometimes it is helpful to position a motif in the center of the border and work out to the corners.

Position at bottom of border center
and work out to corners.

Once you are satisfied with the way the border corner looks, check the distance between the border and body of the quilt.

11 Move the edge of the hopping foot along the seamline and match the bottom of the border pattern to the laser light.

Adjust pattern, not laser light.
Seamline even with edge of foot.

Do not adjust the laser light (or stylus) or it will not be set correctly with the corners. If needed, slightly move the border pattern under the plastic to line up with the laser light.

12 Now, a transition line must be established between the border and the corners. For the quilting line, place a short piece of masking tape on top of the plastic from the corners to the border and redraw a line that will flow smoothly.

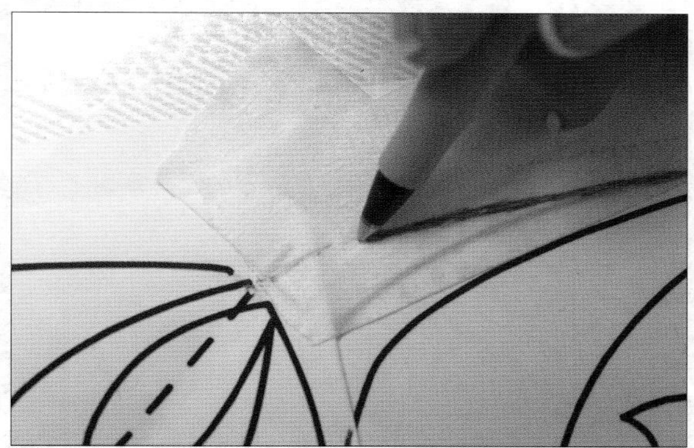

Draw transition line between border and corner.

You will be amazed how easy this is to do.

Move the machine over the quilt and double-check the pattern placement with the laser light. Check twice; sew once.

Quilting

Before you start quilting, remove the masking tape strips from the quilt top. Place these strips out of the way on the tabletop plastic. Put the right tape on the left side and the left tape on the right side and the markings will coincide exactly when you get to the opposite border of the quilt.

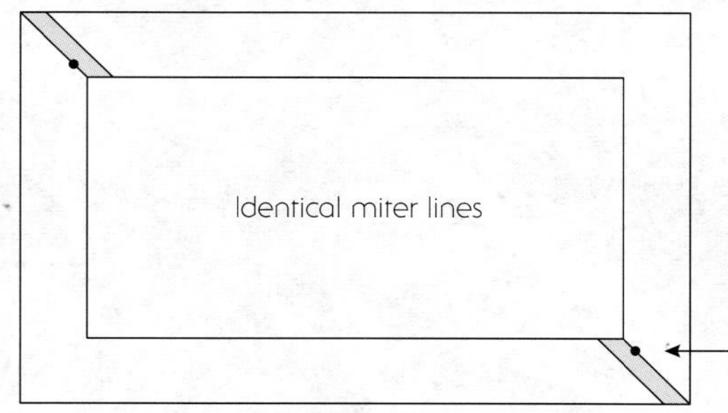

Markings should coincide on all corners.

This saves time in measuring and marking since it is hard to remember what you did when you finally get to the other end of the quilt. It is helpful to make a notation on one of the pieces of tape for exactly what motif is in the center of the border.

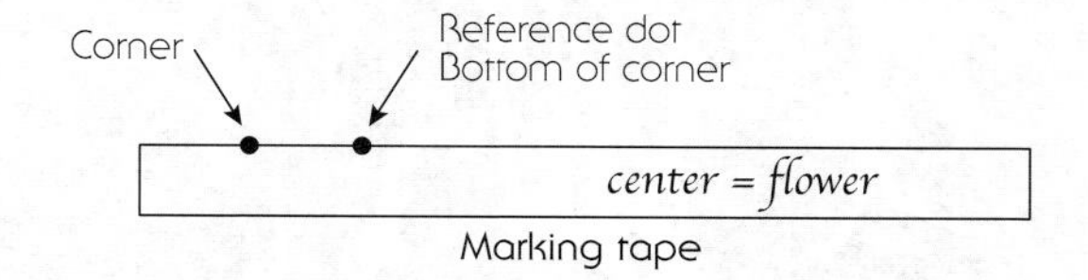

This will also come in handy at the other end of the quilt and on the other borders.

Now you are ready to begin stitching from the right-side corner (from the back of the machine), across the border design, and flow directly into the left corner. It is important that starts, stops, and reconnecting stitches be undetectable.

The Process

1 To secure the threads, put the needle down on the starting line and walk around to the front of the machine. Bring the needle up in the front of the machine and bring up the bobbin thread. Pull both bobbin and top threads under the hopping foot and out in a direction away from the imminent stitching. Stick a pin through the quilt top and over the threads, then down into the quilt again. Now wrap the ends of the threads around the top of the pinhead several times. Push the pin all the way into the quilt.

Secure threads.

This will secure the stitches as you begin stitching so there will not be a bird's nest of thread under the quilt. Since you will quilt to this line when connecting the other border, you can secure the stitches of both lines right on top of these beginning stitches with four or five tiny stitches. This makes the start and stop virtually undetectable.

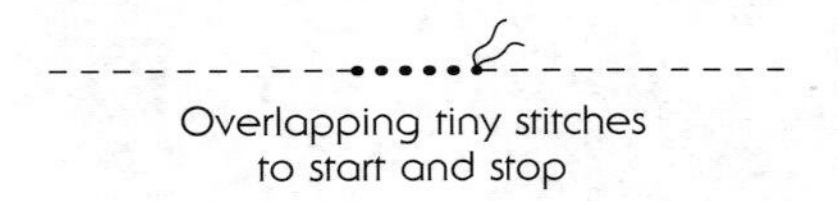

Overlapping tiny stitches to start and stop

During the custom quilting process there are frequent stops and starts throughout the quilt. Here is how to end a line of stitching:

Secure the end of the stitching line with 4–5 tiny stitches. With the thread still intact, move the machine about 6" away from the area. Use your finger to lift up the thread that was dragged from the stopping point to the machine needle. Move the machine back to the same point (or very close). You now have a loop of thread around your finger. Move your needle down and back up. Now move the machine away again for the last time. You should see three threads. You have not let go of the loop of thread with your finger. Do not bother to try to separate these threads, simply take your scissors and clip all three threads close to the quilt. Clip close because you don't want "whiskers" on your quilt. That's all there is to it. No tails to trim underneath the quilt when you are finished! This process may at first seem tedious but it becomes second nature after one quilt.

2 To achieve the smoothest quilting lines, if possible, stitch the corners and border without stopping the machine.

3 Once this side of the border has been stitched, including corners, you can begin the process of stabilizing the quilt body to the opposite border. Stabilize the quilt by quilting in the ditch (page 59) or ¼" (page 61) around all squares, triangles, or other piecework. Sometimes it is necessary to stitch around any appliqué for stabilization (page 61).

4 When the quilt is stabilized and advanced to the opposite border, make sure the border is rolled to a position close to the pick-up roller so the border is easy to reach from behind the machine.

5 Place the miter tapes (previously marked and reserved on the tabletop) on top of the quilt corners and match up the corner miter lines with the corner patterns using the laser light or stylus. Do this exactly as you did previously except that the patterns need to be turned upside down. Remove the border pattern from under the plastic, turn it upside down, and replace it under the table plastic. Center the motif you noted on the masking tape and work out to the corners.

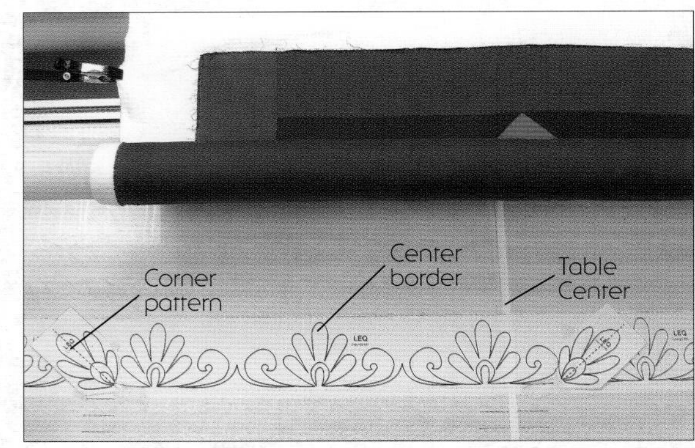

Pattern turned upside down.
Border rolled close to pick-up roller.

6 Line up the edge of the hopping foot with the seamline while matching the border pattern with the laser light. Redraw connecting lines if necessary.

7 Remove the tape from the quilt and sew this side of the border with corners exactly as you did the first side.

8 Baste off the end of the quilt (page 44).

9 Release the rollers and unpin the quilt.

10 Turn the quilt one-quarter turn and pin back onto the backing and the pick-up roller bars.

11 Pin back onto, or close to, the edge of the quilt top, not the backing sides. The quilt top is more likely to be square than the sides of the backing.

12 Roll the border that is pinned to the backing roller close to the pick-up roller to be near you as you work from the back of the machine. The pattern under the plastic is still facing the correct direction to sew this border.

13 Move the machine foot to the center of the border keeping the edge of the hopping foot even with the seam of the quilt top (page 52). Adjust the laser light to the middle of the border pattern already in place. Check the distance the pattern will be stitched from the seamline (back of hopping foot edge against the seamline of the quilt top) and adjust the pattern if necessary.

14 Take no chances. Remove the corner patterns from the plastic so you do not sew them again. You have already stitched them in the border of the quilt.

15 Move the machine to the left side of the border (standing behind the machine) to see where the border flows into the corner. Put a "stop" sign on the plastic (a piece of tape will do) about 1"–2" before the point where you will be quilting onto the beginning corner stitching.

Place "stop" sign.

16 Step around to the front of the machine. On the left side of the border, put the needle down about ¼" into the existing pattern stitching. Bring the bobbin thread up, and holding onto both threads, gently take four or five tiny stitches on top of the existing stitches. This will secure both the previous stitching line and the new stitches you are starting.

17 Return to the back of the machine. Look where your laser light is focused on the pattern. It should be very close to flowing into the border pattern. You can place a piece of tape on the plastic and draw the line where you will stitch to flow into the border; or, when you become more experienced, just smoothly start stitching into the pattern. Continue quilting. Stop when you reach your stop sign.

18 Once again, go around to the front of the machine. Turn the speed down in the front and freehand the small connecting stitches. It will only be 1" or 2". You can do it. Using tiny security stitches, overlap the line of stitching where you started. Bring the bobbin thread to the top and trim your threads. Good for you, you did it and it looks great!

19 Roll the quilt to position the unquilted border closest to the pick-up roller. Turn the border pattern upside down for the last time and repeat the process of stitching the border design from behind the machine.

When the border design is complete all the way around, you are ready to begin setting designs in the other areas on the quilt and completing the more complicated stitching throughout the body of the quilt.

But before we move on, I want to point out how easily border patterns can be changed to suit your needs, particularly directional border patterns (those with a one-way design).

On a traditional border, the motifs face toward the center.

However, for a wallhanging, or a quilt that hangs over the side of a bed, you may not want the one-way motif on the bottom border to be upside down.

The border and corner patterns can be placed facing upright. Then simply redraw the connecting lines to the side borders so the design flows smoothly.

If you are quilting as a business, it is important to point this out to your customers. Let them make the decision of how they want the border pattern applied to their quilt.

Method Two: Fold or Split

On some border patterns it is easy to see that with just 1"–2" leeway, the border design could flow freely into the corner designs. You can either take a fold between each of the motifs on the border design, shrinking the length of the border pattern to fit, or you might split the pattern and redraw it leaving extra space between the motifs so it will flow freely into the corner designs.

Take a fold between each of the motifs.

Method Three: Use an Alternate Corner Design

If drawing a connecting line from the border to the corner patterns does not work on a particular pattern, choose a completely different corner design. For example, you could use a simple leaf design for nearly any floral border pattern. I suggest you keep some generic-type corners on hand that make an easy transition from one design to the next.

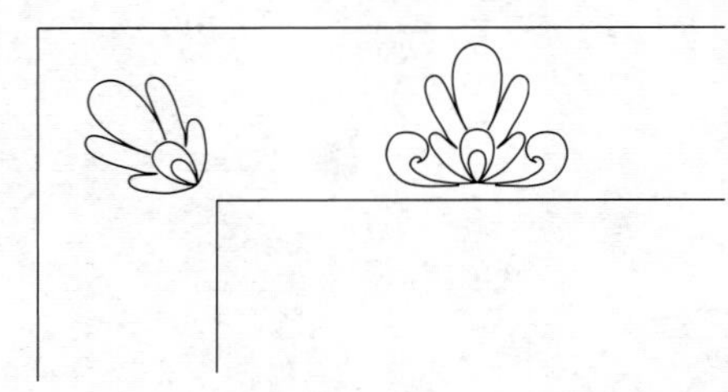

Generic corner patterns are useful.

Another alternative is to redesign the corner pattern, which can be a really fun thing to do. Make sure you keep these alternative corner patterns; you may want to use them again.

Method Four: Adjust the Middle of the Border

Sometimes you may want to leave the transitions from the borders into the corner designs exactly as the designer intended and either adjust the pattern in the center of the border or fill in with an additional center design.

To accomplish this, tape the corner patterns onto the border pattern. Be sure the miter lines are marked on the corners. Using the masking tape to mark the miter lines on the quilt, match the miter lines on the quilt body with the miter lines on the corner patterns. Check the distance from both the vertical and horizontal seamlines.

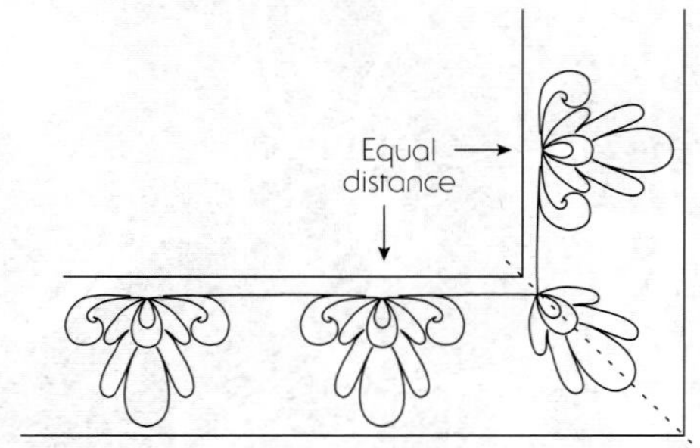

Check horizontal and vertical distances.

Now find the middle where the two sides of the border patterns meet. Place the middle pattern there and redraw connecting lines.

Redraw connecting lines for new middle motif.

Proceed to quilt the other borders as you did the border shuffle.

Method Five: Sew As You Roll

Some patterns are busy enough that you can sew them all the way across the border like a pantograph pattern. Then, using a portion of the pattern placed in a vertical position on the back of the table, you can easily find an inconspicuous place to start the next section of border design and sew as far as you can reach with the machine. This way the border design is quilted as you are stabilizing the quilt, and the quilt will not need to be turned and remounted.

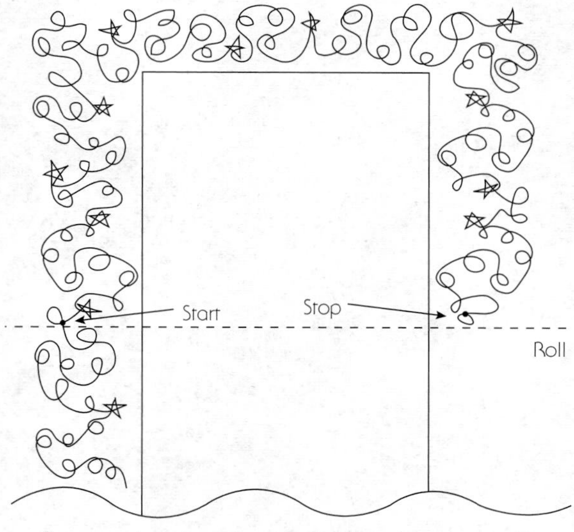

Reconnect and continue vertical border as you roll.

Method Six: Freehand Borders

When stitching freehand borders from the front of the machine start at the left side as close to you as the machine will reach. Proceed with your quilting to the top of the quilt and across from left to right.

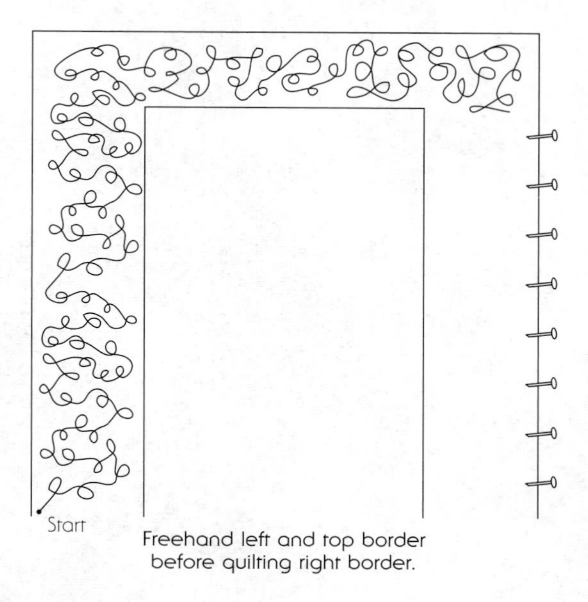

Freehand left and top border before quilting right border.

Stop and stabilize as much of the quilt as possible at this point, before freehanding the right border design.

Proceed with this method as the quilt is rolled. Stitch the left border, stabilize, then stitch the right border.

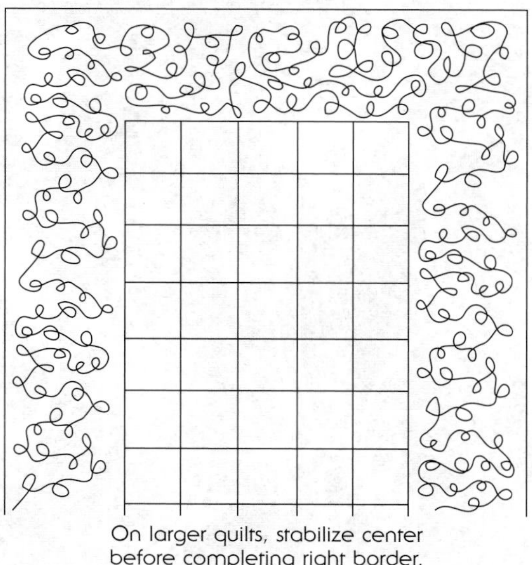
On larger quilts, stabilize center before completing right border.

Method Seven: Integrated Border Design

Sometimes the border is pieced so it intermittently flows up into the quilt. This kind of border is easily accommodated by cutting the border motifs apart, using the laser light or stylus to line them up on the back of the table in order to place them exactly where they need to be in the border. Then redraw connecting lines between them. This method is successful and attractive.

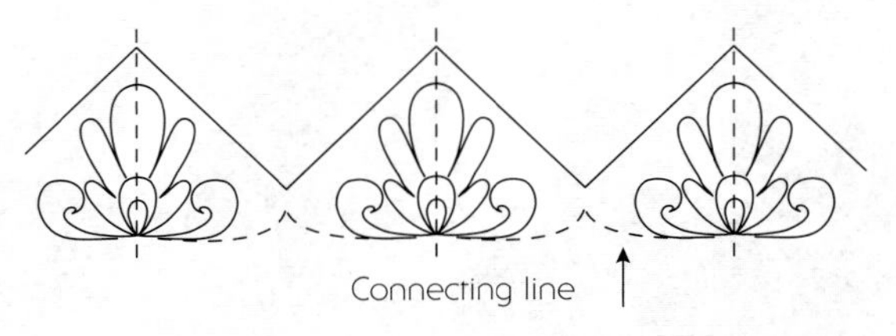

Redraw connecting lines.

Freehand quilting can be beautifully adapted to this type of border as well.

Method Eight: Dead End Border

If the quilt top is pieced with squares in the corners of the border, also called "cornerstones" or "corner sets," a dead-end border is executed between the cornerstones.

Many different patterns can be adapted into dead-end border patterns. Start and stop the quilting design inside the two inside border seamlines. I usually make sure I am at least ½" inside each seam.

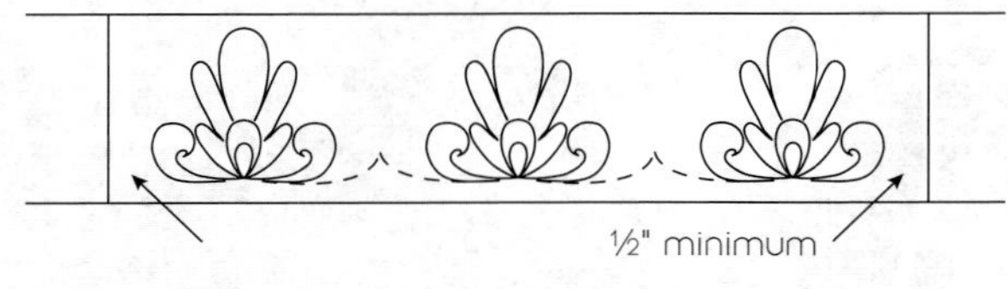

Dead end border

The cornerstone area is lovely quilted with a separate block or circle design.

NOTE: A custom quilt is worked from left to right as the quilt is stabilized (from the front of the machine). Therefore, each time the quilt is advanced, stitch the top to the backing and batting on the left side. Then, place the pins horizontally every 3"–4" along the edge of the quilt top in the right border. This will keep the top from creeping over to the left as it is stitched. When you have finally stitched in the ditch between the quilt and the right border, you can remove the pins one at a time as you baste the top on this side to the backing and batting before you roll.

I have found that if I baste the right side of the quilt before it is stabilized, there tends to be a little bubble of extra fullness next to the basting that must be released before quilting.

After completely stabilizing the quilt, having the edges of the quilt top basted to the backing and batting all the way around the quilt makes it easier to rotate the quilt and complete the border designs.

Starting and Stopping Stitching Lines

When starting and stopping on the same line of stitching (for example, stitching around a square or circle), try not to create extra bulk in the line of security stitches. Start by holding onto both threads under the foot with your left hand or secure them with a straight pin. Then as you complete the stitching and come to the same place you started, carefully place security stitches right on top of the beginning stitches, thereby securing both the beginning and ending stitches. This way you can confidently trim all four threads close to the fabric without fear of the stitches coming loose and with very little extra bulk.

When stabilizing areas on the quilt or stitching designs try not to start or stop in a corner. Start stitching approximately ¼" on top of an existing stitched line with tiny stitches, pivot when you reach the corner and continue with regularly spaced stitches. If there isn't an existing stitched line, start in the middle of a line, not in a corner.

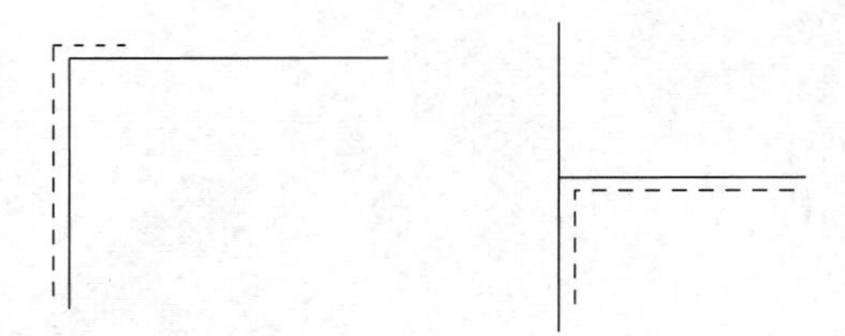

Start and stop stitching before corner.

If you have matching thread and fabric, where you started and stopped will be well hidden. If you have contrasting thread and fabric there is only a slight increase in thread color for about ¼", very minimal.

STITCHING IN THE DITCH

Stitching "in the ditch" is one of the more difficult techniques to master on the quilting machines. It is executed from the front of the machine where you can easily see where you are stitching. Using a simple straight-edge tool can greatly aid in this task. I also find an extended base of some kind attached around the machine throat provides a larger flat area to work with the tools.

Extended base

Accurately stitching in the ditch takes consistent practice to judge the ¼" distance to stay in the ditch. The trick is to securely hold the ruler on the quilt ¼" from the seam using the left hand while the right hand slides the machine down the side of the ruler.

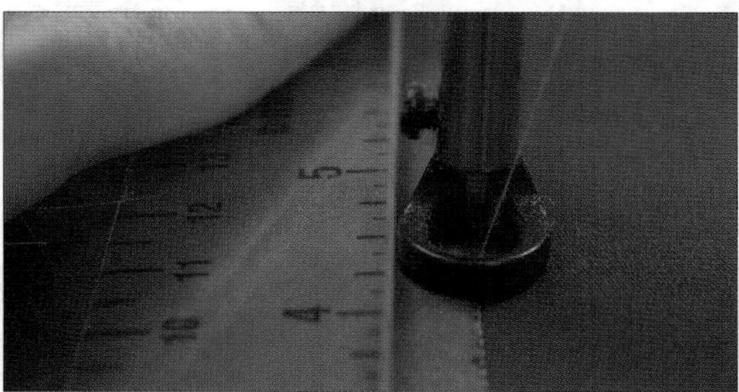

Using a ruler increases accuracy.

NOTE: I use an acrylic ruler that is at least ¼" thick. Since the diameter of the hopping foot on most of the quilting machines measures ½" and the needle goes down through the middle of the foot, the measurement from the needle to the outside of the foot is ¼".

Reduce the speed on the machine (between 15-40). Try not to control the machine with your right hand. The left hand determines where the needle stitches. The right hand simply propels the machine. Finding a balance between pushing down too hard to secure the ruler in place and not holding firmly enough to slide the machine along the ruler's side takes practice. In order to achieve a beautifully completed quilt, the importance of stitching in the ditch between borders, around blocks, and pieced work and outlining appliqué cannot be overstressed.

Practice until you can stitch from front to back, side to side, and back to front equally well. When stitching the perimeter of a square, you must stitch in all directions with a continuous line for smooth quilting. When the machine is stitching away from you, it is difficult to see the ditch. With practice, you will learn to judge the right distance from the seam to place the ruler to accommodate the width of the foot and stay in the ditch.

Diagonals can also be stitched accurately by using a tool. Remember to keep the ruler on the left side of the hopping foot.

DANGER: Do not cross your hand with the ruler on the right side in front of the needle.

When using any of the acrylic guides, try to keep your hand in a position that is comfortable for you. I like to keep my left hand as flat as possible. Sometimes I am stitching in the ditch for hours so I need to make sure my hand is not in a cramped or awkward gripping position.

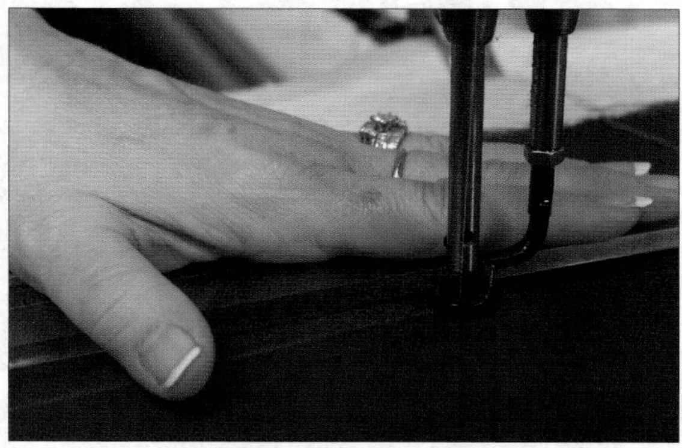

Keep hand flat on ruler.

Some of the machines have a hopping foot with a cut-down area in the front of the foot. Be careful not to use the ruler directly in front of this kind of hopping foot because it could jump on top of the ruler, or the needle may strike the ruler causing an accident (e.g., bent, broken needle; chip out of ruler). But on all the other sides of the hopping foot you can use the ruler in every direction.

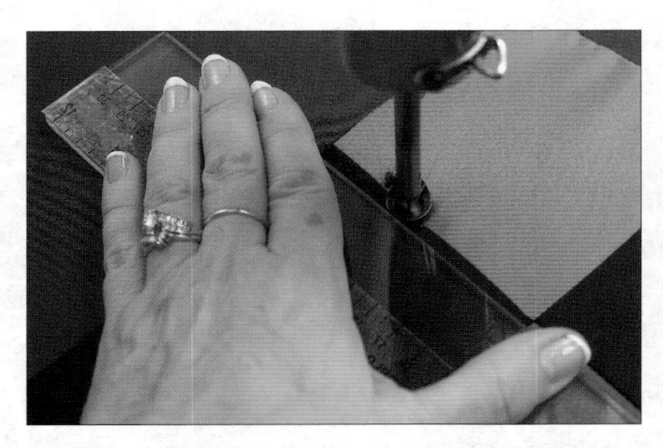

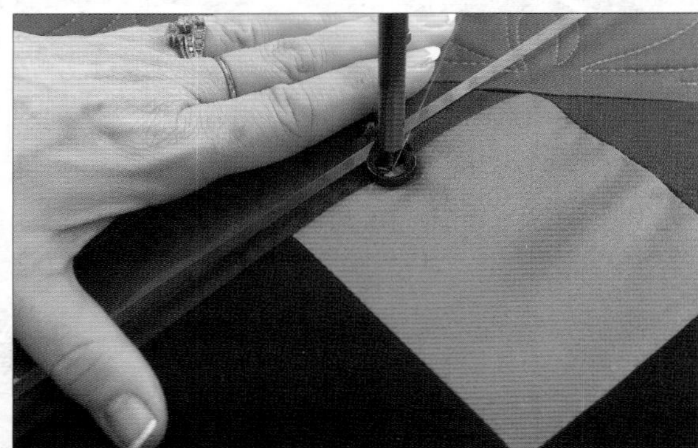

Use the ruler on any side of the hopping foot.

Some machines have a hopping foot with sides that are thick enough all the way around to protect the needle. Simply check the foot on the machine to determine how you can effectively and safely use the ruler on your machine.

Pressing also affects the ease with which you can quilt in the ditch. I have quilted on some quilts so well pressed I could not fall out of the ditch. But not all quilts are well pressed, or the seams twist or flip-flop back and forth and seem to throw the machine needle out of the ditch. Take your time. Slow the machine speed down to 10-15 until you can control it.

The ruler is useful for short, diagonal lines and for vertical lines. When I stitch the horizontal lines (parallel to the roller bars) I find that freehanding works well if I can concentrate on just guiding the machine, not controlling it. I use a light, two-finger control. Try everything and do whatever works best for you.

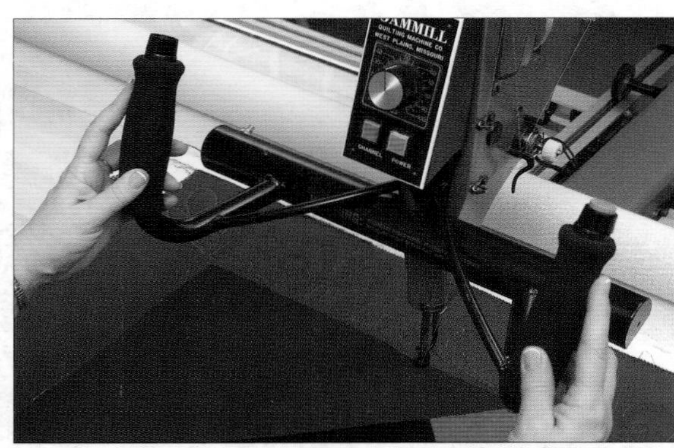

Use a light touch to guide the machine.

Some quilters use a serpentine line instead of stitching in the ditch, and there are times where that is appropriate. If a quilt is badly pieced, the seams are damaged, the quilt is unraveling and very old, or the seams are pressed open (since you would be stitching on just thread), you may choose not to stitch in the ditch. With old quilts, the extra stress and thread you put into the old seams might cause damage, so a serpentine line works well. I have also seen serpentine lines work well on the inside of a Dresden Plate. But for the most part, stitch in the ditch or quarter-inch stitching is the traditional way of stabilizing the quilt.

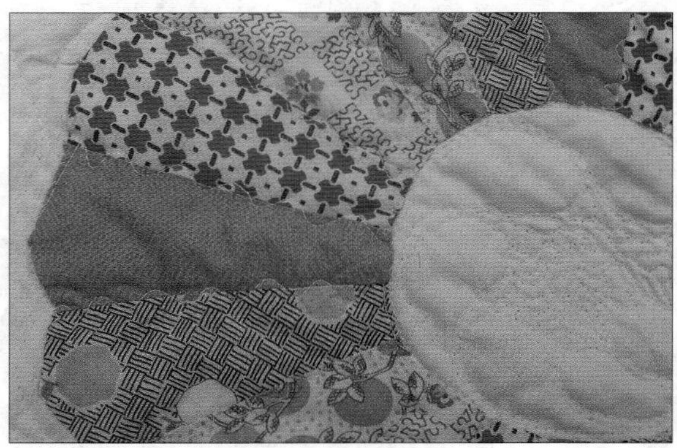

Serpentine line

QUARTER-INCH STITCHING

Quarter-inch stitching is similar to stitching in the ditch. Since the hopping foot is ½" thick and the needle goes in the middle, if the edge of the foot is on the seamline, the needle will be stitching ¼" from the seam. Hold the ruler even with the seam and slide the machine along the edge of the ruler; voila, quarter-inch stitching. This is a good option for seams that are pressed open.

Accurate ¼" for open seams

STITCHING AROUND APPLIQUÉ MOTIFS

To stitch around appliqué, slow the speed of the machine until you can easily control where you are stitching. It is important not to stitch on top of the appliqué as you are outlining, but stay very close to the edge. Outlining the appliqué will set it apart from the quilt.

It is helpful to use some kind of stitching guide for the left hand to help control where the needle is stitching. Acrylic guides can be purchased for this purpose, or you can gently hold onto the back of the hopping foot.

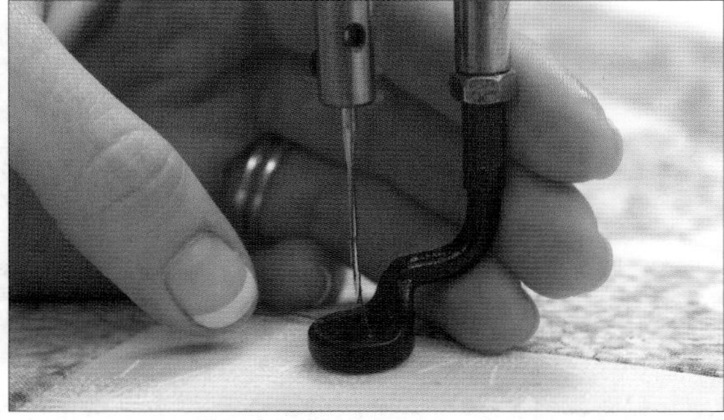

Gently guide hopping foot.

Stitching On Appliqué Motifs

Machine stitching on top of appliqué can greatly enhance the quilt. Do not be afraid to use the stitching to separate sections of the appliqué. This makes the appliqué appear more realistic. For example, sewing between the petals on a flower will make the flower appear more real.

Stitching on appliqué

Large areas of appliqué without simple outline stitching on the appliqué motifs will appear to poof out from the quilt and look unfinished.

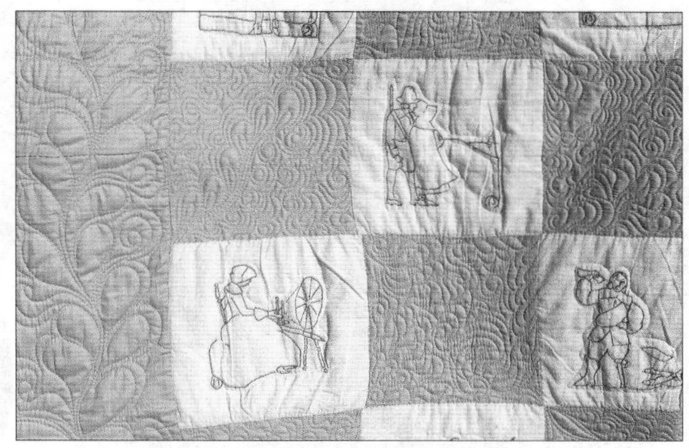

Unquilted appliqué or embroidery

When stitching on appliqué, I like to use decorative embroidery threads. Variegated threads blend in well with most appliqué.

Details can be added on some appliqué designs that clearly enhance the quilt. For instance, veins on appliquéd leaves, shingles on a roof, and faces on angels can all be added with the stitching. These touches are definitely an artist's touch. If the quilt is being quilted for a customer, always ask permission to sew on the appliqué prior to quilting.

Enhance appliqué with quilting

SETTING DESIGNS IN THE QUILT

After the quilt is stabilized, you are ready to place the design elements within the stabilized areas. There are a couple of options to accomplish this task.

Setting Designs in the Quilt from the Back of the Machine

The preferred option is to place the paper pattern exactly where you want the pattern to be stitched on the quilt and mark several reference points. I use pins to mark these points so I never have to worry about removing marks from the quilt. Simply insert the pins directly down through the paper pattern and into the quilt. Then gently lift the pattern up partially and with another pin mark the spot where the first pin enters the quilt top.

Mark location.

To save time, while you are at the front of the machine, move the pattern to each of the exposed areas where you want to stitch the design and leave pins on the quilt top for the reference points.

Take your pattern to the back of the machine table. Using the stylus or laser light, line up the reference lines on the pattern with the reference pins on the quilt top.

Line up reference points with laser light.

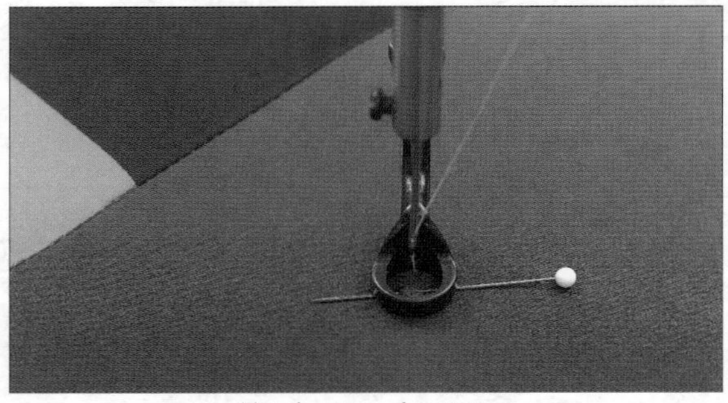

Match pinned points.

The pattern can be placed one of several ways: under the plastic on the table; taped to the top of the table; or taped to the underside of an acrylic or Mylar piece and positioned on the table.

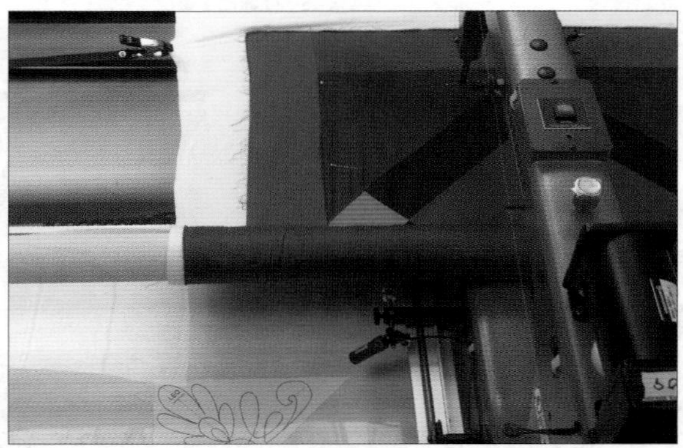

Place pattern under plastic.

Placing the pattern under the non-glare Mylar is the fastest way to position the pattern behind the machine.

It is most convenient to have two copies of the paper pattern; position one on the front of the quilt and one on the back of the machine table for stitching.

Once the pattern is lined up with the pin markers on the quilt, and you are ready to quilt, remove the pins or marks you used on the quilt top.

Be sure to finger trace the motif before sewing the design on the quilt. Be aware of the direction to stitch through intersections and the areas on the pattern that may be more intricate and difficult to execute.

Do not start stitching in the middle of the motif; start somewhere on the outside of the pattern so the start and stop is easy to connect and undetectable.

Perhaps the piecing of the quilt top will aid you in finding the best place to start and stop. Mark your starting point in one of the busy fabrics on the quilt top. Starting in an inconspicuous spot saves time and worry in connecting your stitches.

Using this method of placing the design, you do not have to remove marks on the quilt or paper bits under the stitches. It also utilizes the unique features on the quilting machines. You can become extremely proficient with this method.

Setting Designs in the Quilt from the Front of the Machine Using the Laser Light

Another wonderful option for placing a motif in a stabilized area of the quilt is moving the laser light to the top of the front of the machine so it can be focused on the quilt top. This option is particularly suited to smaller patterns, 10" or less in diameter.

1 Use a flat surface on which to place the pattern for stabilizing it during the stitching process. This eliminates the vibration but also provides a fast way to place the pattern without tape, pins, or marking of any kind. I use a clear piece of acrylic for this flat surface, which I call an acrylic table. Additionally, I use a smaller scored piece of acrylic on top of the paper pattern.

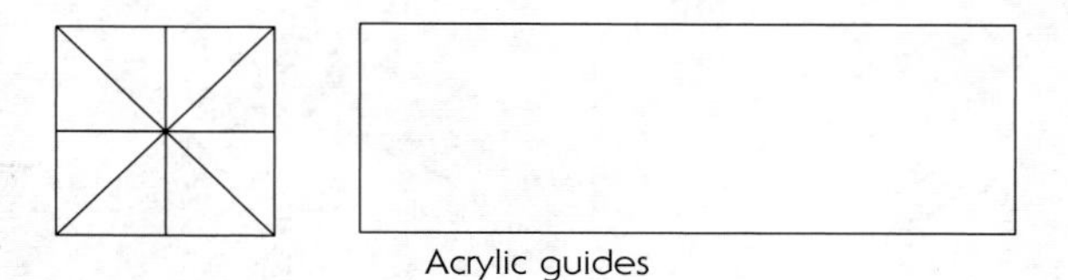
Acrylic guides

The smaller piece is scored to aid in accurate pattern placement. A ruler and a razor blade can be used to score the acrylic. The pattern is taped to the back of the smaller piece of clear acrylic and is easily adjusted on the larger acrylic piece as it is placed for stitching.

The large acrylic table can be placed on either the left or right side of the machine, on top of the quilt.

As you are doing rows of motifs, the acrylic table will need to be changed from side to side at the end of the rows to remain on top of the quilt.

2 Practice stitching the designs from both the right and left so you will be equally proficient in either direction. The laser light will, of course, need to be adjusted to the right or left, according to which side the acrylic table is placed on the quilt.

3 Position the quilt so the areas you want to stitch are close to you at the front of the machine. Place the paper pattern (under the small acrylic piece) back toward the pick-up roller. This way the laser light will be focused directly down on the pat-

tern and not aimed at so much of an angle. If there is too much of an angle, the laser light can be distorted.

Aim laser light as straight as possible, less of an angle.

4 Eyeball the center of the area to be stitched, or chalk in a cross-section and position the machine needle over this point. Focus the laser light in the middle of the pattern. Now move the machine following the score lines on the acrylic piece out to the edge of the quilt square and adjust the pattern, if needed, to line up with the score lines. In this manner, you are able to position the pattern squarely where it should be stitched without taping or pinning.

5 Using a very light touch, stitch the design on the quilt. Before stitching the design, I sometimes remove the top thread from the needle and stitch around the design without thread to get the feel of the design. This also shows you how accurately the design is placed. This is not necessary for each design, but it will help build confidence as you begin stitching the designs on the quilt. If you see little needle holes from the dry run after you have stitched the design, lightly spritz the area with water and gently rub the holes with a soft, clean cloth and they will disappear.

OTHER OPTIONS

Other options for sewing the designs in areas on the quilt top include traditional methods for marking the quilt. The methods are common to hand and machine quilting in general and can be studied in books written on these subjects. Some of these methods include marking the top with water-soluble markers, transferring the pattern to tracing paper and sewing directly on top of the paper, drawing the pattern on the quilt using chalk pencils, or using pouncing powder through a plastic stencil. All of these options not only involve more time for marking, but also for removing marks. If you are in business, always obtain permission from the customer to mark on their quilt.

Of course, if a customer has already marked the quilt top before bringing it to you, these marks can easily be followed using the quilting machine and the customer is responsible for mark removal.

DIAGONAL LINES

Using a Long Guide

Using a long ruler makes it easier to quilt long diagonal lines with the quilting machines. There are a variety of tools available for this purpose, usually available from the machine manufacturer.

Some of the long guides are to be used specifically with a certain hopping foot on the machine. Be sure to check with your manufacturer to see if there is a special attachment or recommendation for your machine.

When using a long guide, gently place the right hand on the machine handle and slide the foot of the machine down along the side of the ruler, while the left hand firmly holds the ruler in place. If the ruler is firmly held in place with my left hand, I have no trouble stitching where I intend to quilt.

Hold long guide firmly in place.

Marking a side edge and the top edge as you are beginning will help establish a guide for the distance you want between the diagonal lines. Measuring and marking on masking tape will work well, or you can buy easy-to-use tape, pre-marked in different increments.

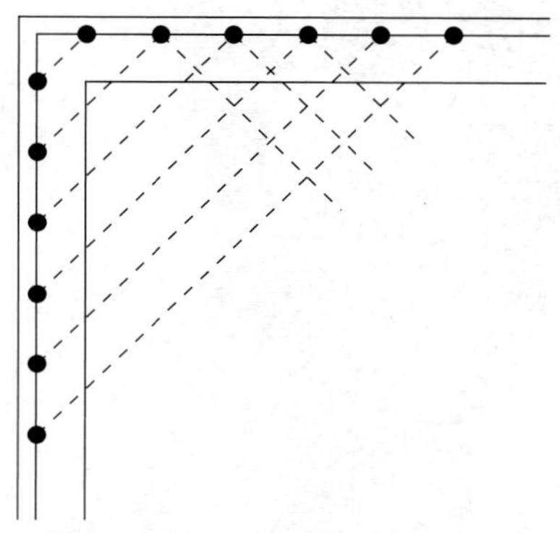
Use masking tape on sides of quilt for cross-hatching guide.

Using the Gam Guide

Almost all of the quilting machine manufacturers have developed methods and tools to be used with their machines to quilt diagonal lines. Ask your manufacturer how this is accomplished on your quilting machine. Since I am most familiar with the Gammill machines, here are the guidelines I find most helpful for using the Gam Guide tool for quilting diagonals.

1 The pick-up roller needs to be a little higher than you would usually keep it so you can hold the Gam Guide in place and keep it snug against the pick-up roller.

2 Your fingers need to be between the carrier roller and the Gam Guide because the machine body that is underneath the quilt is actually higher than the carrier roller. Because of this, if you are pushing the Gam Guide down on the carrier roller, as you bring the machine forward you will actually be pushing down on the machine and it will be hard to move. So, do not push the ruler down on the carrier roller.

3 Also, make sure nothing, including the Gam Guide, is between you and the machine so that at all times you can pull the machine toward your body. In other words, the guide always goes behind the needle, never in front. The back of the hopping foot on your machine is made to glide along the Gam Guide.

When using the Gam Guide you will need to turn the speed up a little. You will be amazed at how fast you move the machine when you are using the guide, so watch your stitch length.

It helps to use a piece of batting between the "wings" on the Gam Guide and the quilt. Some students actually fit batting or fabric over the wings to help the Gam Guide stay in place.

USING ACRYLIC TEMPLATE TOOLS

There are many acrylic template tools available for the quilting machines. All of the tools work best with a large flat surface around the throat plate on the machine; therefore, an extended base is needed. This base creates a stable surface for the acrylic template tools.

The tools must be held firmly in place with the left hand while the right hand guides the machine around the template. Be sure to keep the machine foot tightly next to the template. If you push too hard to keep the template in place, you are pushing down on the machine.

Press template snugly against hopping foot.

Like all techniques on the quilting machines, this skill takes practice.

Small dots of sandpaper applied to the underside of the templates help hold them in place for the stitching. The acrylic pieces are generally easy to see through, and many of them are scored to make accurate placement easy.

Besides the acrylic templates, most of the machine manufacturers have some kind of "circle-maker" to help you stitch perfect circles on your quilt. Be sure to see this demonstrated so you will know how to use it on your machine.

WHOLE-CLOTH WALLHANGING

Sampler quilt

Use this project to practice freehand techniques sewing from the front of the machine. I suggest that you do not preshrink the fabric or batting. The slight puckering that occurs after it is washed and dried gives the quilt a fabulous heirloom look.

Materials

Muslin 40" x 40"

Backing (can also be muslin) 45" x 45"

Binding: ⅓ yard

Batting 45" x 45"

Matching or contrasting thread

Prepare the Quilt

1 Mark the guidelines for your practice quilt top lightly with pencil, chalk, or water marker.

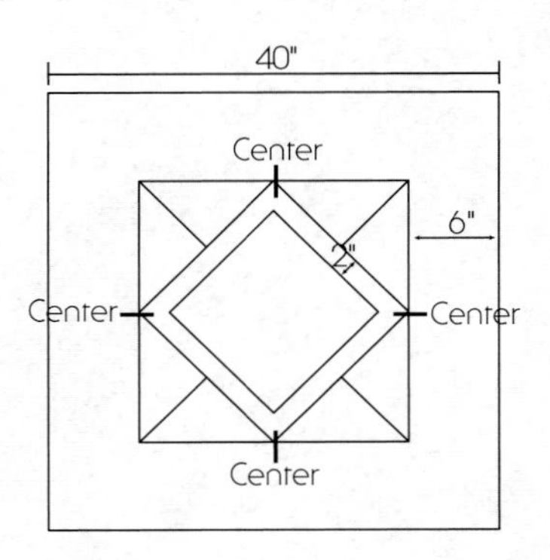

2 Load the quilt according to directions given in Chapter Two (page 23).

Freehand Feather Border

As you stabilize the quilt (Chapter Three), you can stitch the freehand feather design in the outside border. Before you actually start stitching, read through this section and visualize the procedure of quilting the feather border design.

It is easier to stitch the stem of the feather first so you have a guide for where to sew the feathers. If you are unsure of where to place the stem, try marking the stem on the quilt first. I usually sew the stem and then stitch the feathers down one side of it.

When creating the feathers on the stem, think of half hearts. The top is rounded, then it flows back and follows the stem for a little ways. This will set you up for the next feather.

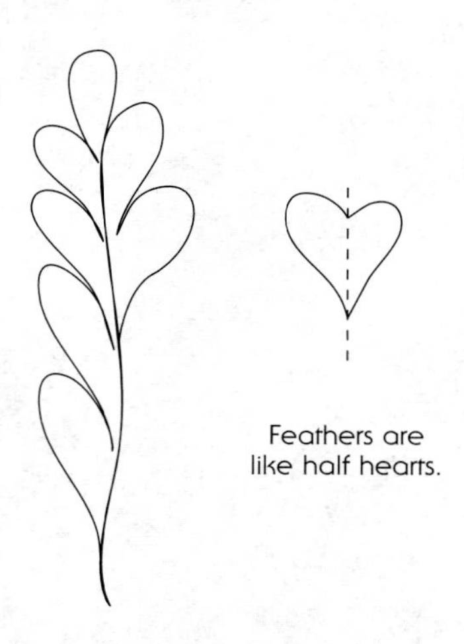

Feathers are like half hearts.

Feathers have a direction. For the most part, they lie down on the stem.

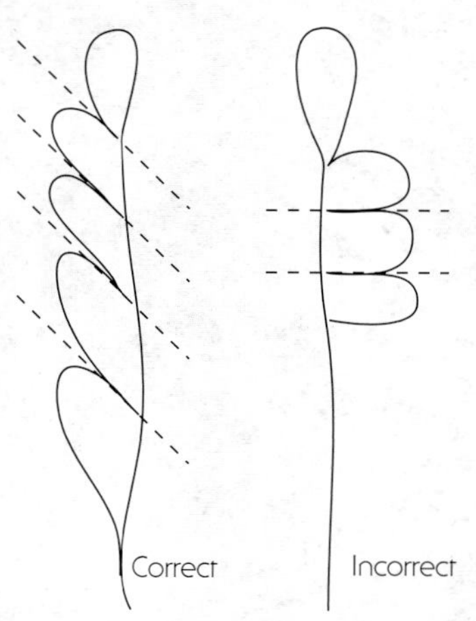

Slant the feathers

Do not be too critical of your first feathers. Give yourself time to be a beginner and have a positive attitude. You will develop your own style as you practice.

Stitching the Feather Border

1 Stitch the stem in a flowing, curvy shape starting on the left side of the quilt, across the top, and down the right side.

2 Add the feathers on one side of the stem.

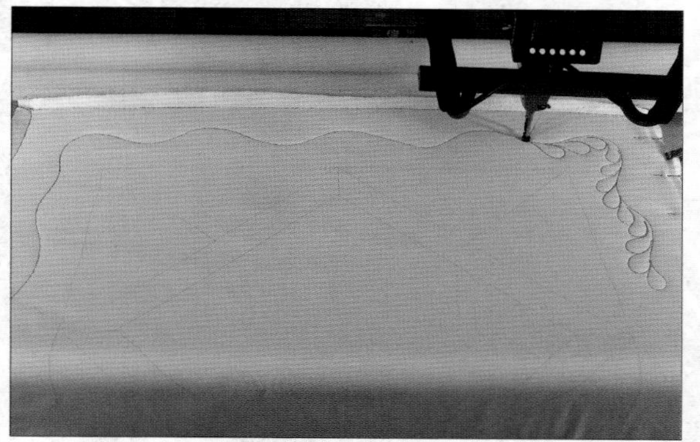

Add the feathers on one side of stem.

3 Double the stem and stitch the feathers coming down the other side.

Double stem and stitch other side.

Double stems look more real, flowing and growing. The lines in the stem do not have to be exactly ¼" apart; in fact, they can touch in some places to look more realistic.

Remember that freehand is not exact. It is not a stencil look. You have the artistic license to create your own interpretation.

Beginning freehand quilters frequently observe that one side of their feathers turn out much better than the other side. I believe it is a right brain, left brain phenomenon. Keep practicing and soon both sides will look equally wonderful.

4 Continue to stabilize the quilt by stitching on the lines you have "drawn". When you have advanced to the bottom of the quilt, complete the feather design in the remaining bottom border.

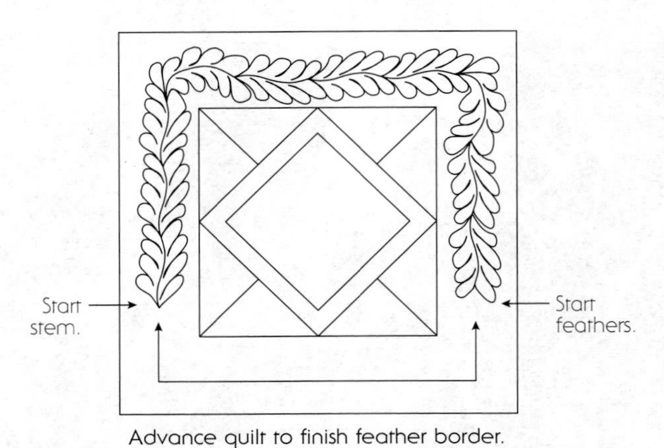

Advance quilt to finish feather border.

5 Unpin the top fabric from the top roller canvas.

6 Now the quilt is stabilized. The quilt is still pinned on the backing roller and the pick-up roller, so the quilt can be rolled back and forth to complete the rest of the quilting.

Freehand Feather Medallion

Once the quilt is stabilized and the border design is stitched on the quilt, you may set design elements anywhere on the quilt.

1 Stitch a circle in the middle square of the quilt, using an acrylic template or the circle-maker for your machine.

2 Mark the center medallion cross lines up to 1" from the outer edge of the circle. Then mark reference dots 3" out on the diagonals from the middle intersection.

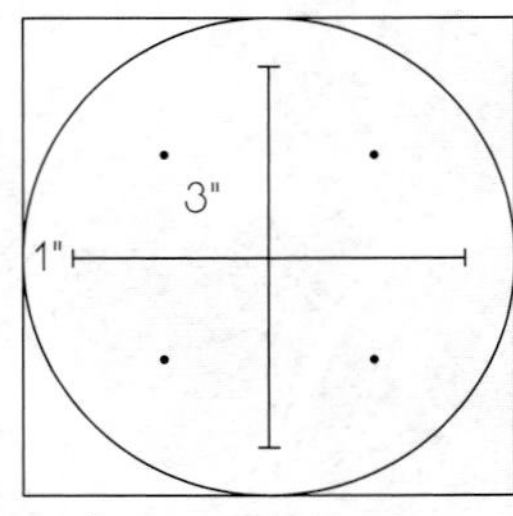

Reference dots for making circles.

3 Put the needle down and secure the stitches in the middle of the square or circle.

4 Sew a double figure-eight and then sew up the middle line and form a teardrop feather at the end of the line. Continue making feathers moving down to the center. Remember, think of half hearts as you are making the feather shapes.

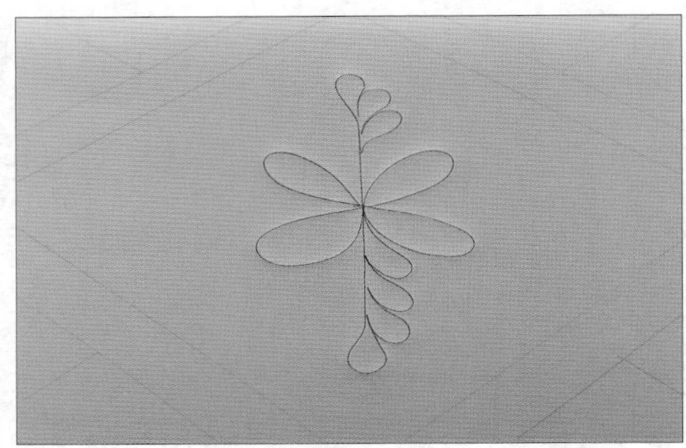
Double figure-eight with feathers

5 Double the stem and make feathers moving down the other side.

6 Complete each stem in the same way. These feather motifs can be placed within squares, triangles, circles, and all other shapes. Practice them and you can save a lot of time on quilts.

7 Stitch out from between the feathers to begin stippling or whatever meandering technique you like (pages 70-73).

Stipple strip sampler

To maintain an even stipple pattern, keep a stipple strip sample (page 47) close by while you are working.

SIMPLE SASHING IDEAS

The following ideas can be used in borders as well as sashing areas. They are simple because each one uses a half-circle design. With a little practice and focus, you can complete these sashing designs nearly perfectly with freehand machine stitching.

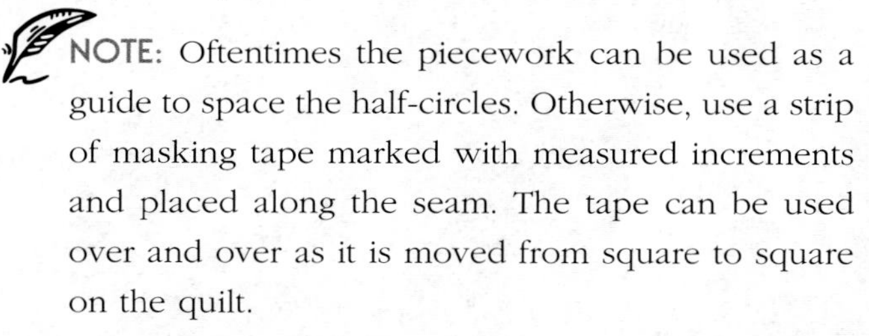

NOTE: Oftentimes the piecework can be used as a guide to space the half-circles. Otherwise, use a strip of masking tape marked with measured increments and placed along the seam. The tape can be used over and over as it is moved from square to square on the quilt.

Variations of Stained Glass Design

Stitch the following sashing designs on your practice piece. Using the piecework or the marks on the masking tape, begin in one corner and stitch half-circles across the sashing area. Secure the stitches when you get to the other side.

Begin in the corner on the opposite side of the sashing area and complete half-circles stitching in the opposite direction from the previous line.

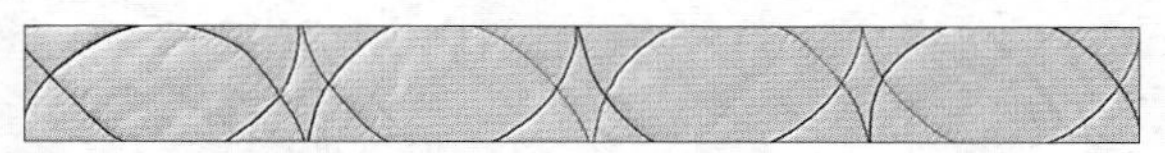

Stitch half circles across one direction. Then, stitch half-circles in the opposite direction.

The secret of stitching an even stained glass design is to cross lines in the middle of the sashing or border.

Stained glass design

By placing masking tape across the square just inside the seamline as a guide for the top of the half-circle, you can create a stitching guide to make the stained glass design take on a different look.

Tape for stitching line

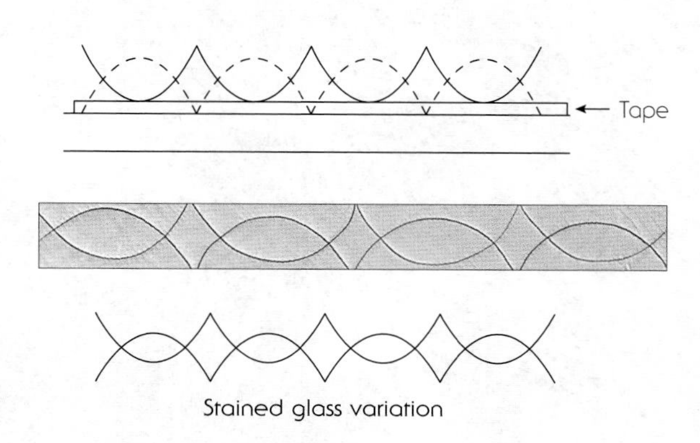

Stained glass variation

Pumpkin Seed Design

This design is commonly called pumpkin seed. It is easy to do freehand if you focus on nice round half-circles. You stitch in one direction for the first row of half-circles, leave the needle in the same corner where you ended, then stitch half-circles back in the other direction for the second stitching row.

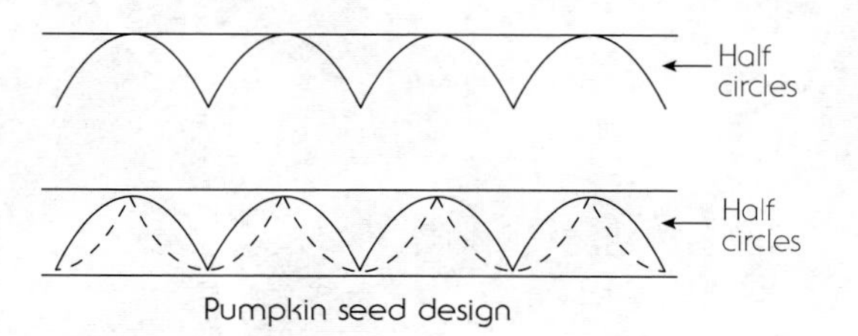

Pumpkin seed design

Circle Sashing Design

Place the edge of the masking tape along the center of the sashing as a guide to complete the first row of half-circles and stitch the pumpkin seed design.

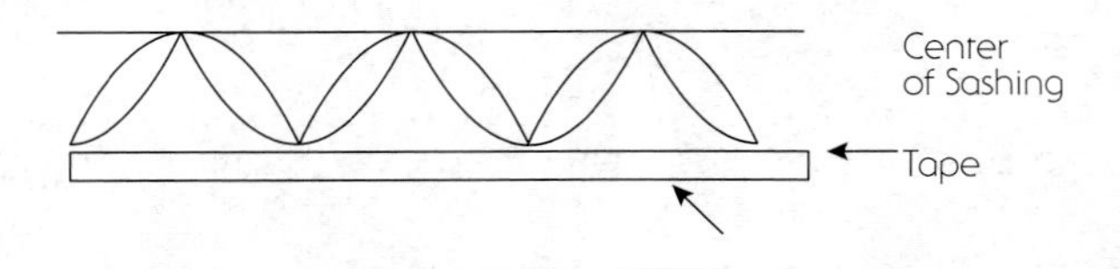

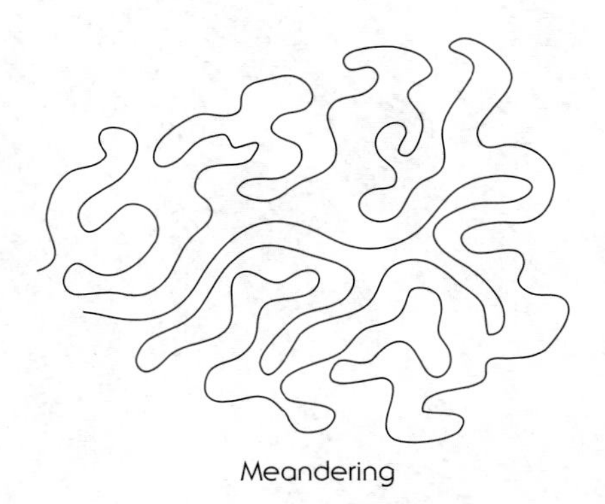
Meandering

Now remove the tape and use the top of the existing half-circle as a guide to complete the second line of pumpkin seed designs.

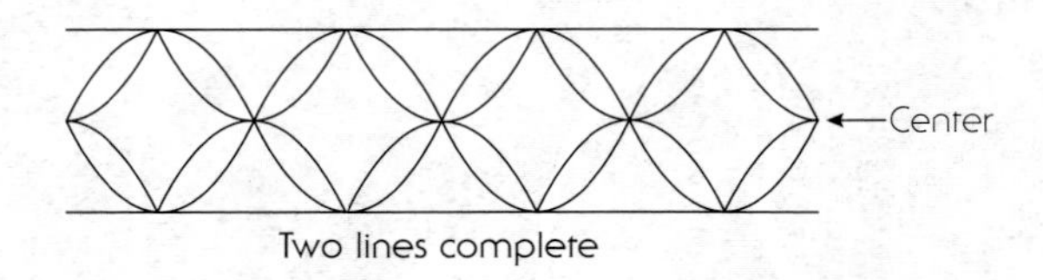

Two lines complete

Make sure the top of the half-circles meet in the middle and touch each other to complete the design.

BACKGROUND QUILTING TECHNIQUES

Traditional Meandering or Stippling

Traditional stippling and meandering designs are common in the quilt world. Stippling lines are generally less than ¼" apart, while meandering is much further apart. Either way, there are three rules to follow:

- All lines are curved, no points.
- No crossed lines.
- Try not to get into a pattern, but truly meander. If you start getting in a pattern, take off in a little worm-like line, then fill in around it. With a little practice you will do great!

Everyone's stippling or meandering is different. It is like a signature. Practice with a pencil and paper. When you are talking on the phone, practice meandering doodles on paper and soon you will be able to do it with ease.

Be sure to:

- Create meandering spaces that are close enough together so the design you are meandering around doesn't blend in too much.

Motif can be lost in too large meandering.

- Follow the central design close enough to set it apart from the background. It is necessary to outline the design rather closely with the stipple or meandering design. To accomplish this, simply stipple or meander in and out around the design first, then continue with the freehand technique to complete the area or block.

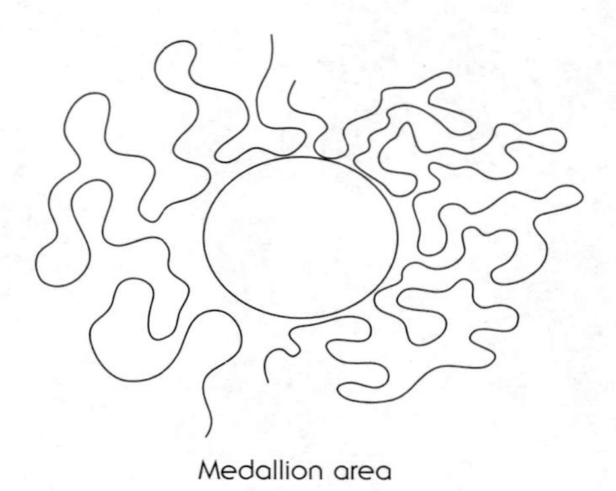

Medallion area

Use the small stipple design to fill in the space around the feather medallion in the middle of your sampler.

Echo Stippling

Another type of stippling or meandering that is even more fun to stitch is what I call "echo stippling." It is also less stressful on your arms and hands because it is performed with somewhat smoother lines.

Start with a long worm and echo it. As you continue to echo this worm shape, come out with other worm-like shapes.

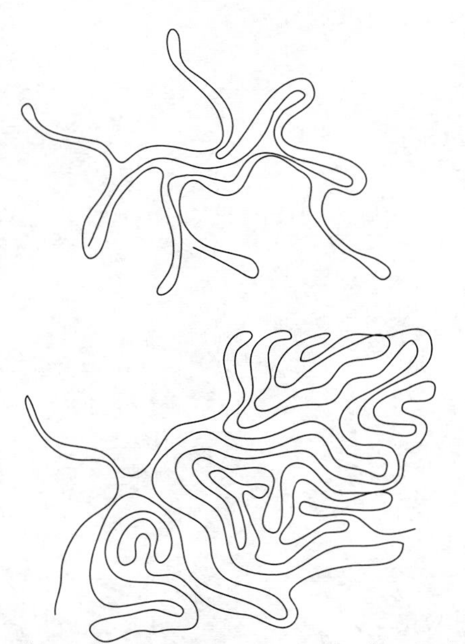

Worm-like shapes form basis of echo stippling.

Continue to echo and make new worm shapes.

It takes practice but I think you will like doing this type of meandering. It is particularly beautiful with variegated thread!

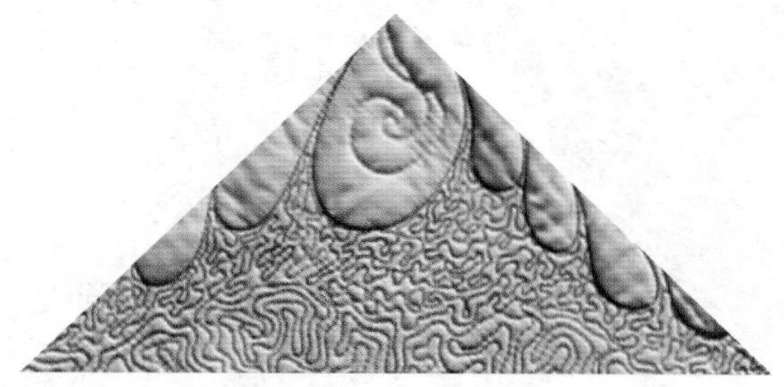

Echo stippling

Echoing

Echoing an appliquéd motif or a stitched design is not only popular, but also soothing and lovely. Freehand echoing does not have to be exactly ¼" apart. I am convinced that people hesitate to use echoing for that reason. If you want your echoing to be so exact, then mark it and follow your lines, or use the foot on your machine as a guide. I prefer to echo with more freedom, throwing in swirls or other designs within the echoes. Choose any shape to go into this area of the sampler and echo it.

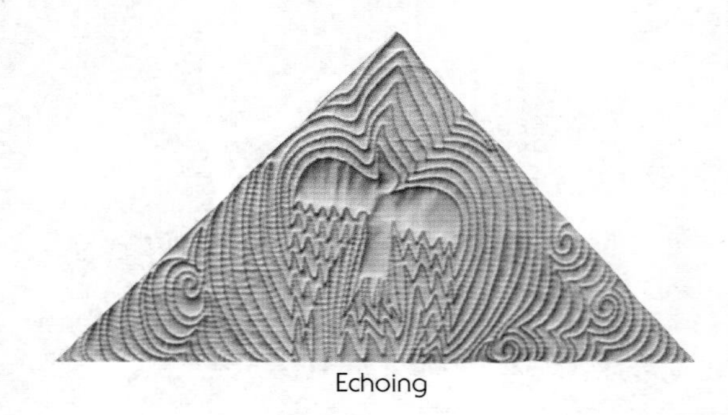

Echoing

Feather Meandering

Another interesting type of meandering that is popular and elegant is what I have named "feather meandering." It starts with simple crescent and swirl shapes (half-circles and pinwheels). Then, as you feel inspired, stitch in simple feather or flower shapes, continually echoing and swirling. I must say it is extremely fun to do on the longarm machine!

Feather meandering

Clamshells

Clamshells make a great background and are fun to do freehand. It is simply a half-circle shape. You can easily make them dimensional by gradually quilting them smaller and closer together on one end. Freehand clamshells are not meant to be exactly alike.

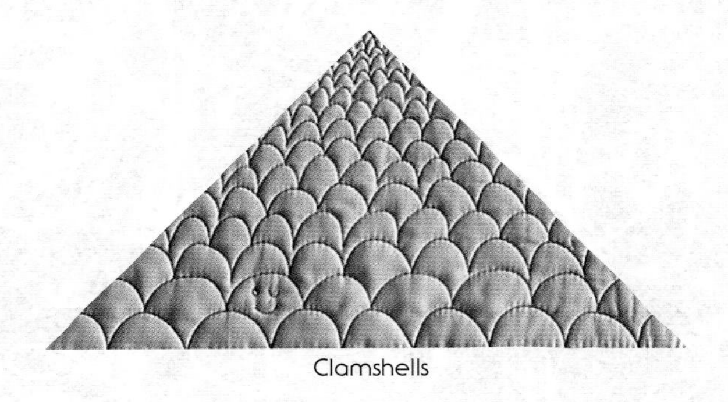

Clamshells

Lined Background

A straight-line background or channeled background can create an interesting texture around an appliqué or a quilted motif. This can be done using the channel lock, or holding the wheels of the machine on the vertical track if your machine does not have a channel lock.

First, quilt a motif in the middle area, then starting at the bottom (or nearest to you from the front of the machine), quilt back and forth every hopping foot width (¼"). Quilt up the sides of the block as you continue to quilt across. Be sure to secure the stitches on both sides of the motif with tiny stitches. Simply drag the thread across the motif as you are stitching—thread can be trimmed later.

Lined background

If you have the needle positioner on your machine, leave it in the "up" position to move quickly across the motif.

Angular or Geometric Meandering

This rather fun type of meandering is straight and pointed. There are no curves in it. It can be done large or small, combined with other types of meandering, crossed over or not crossed over.

It makes the quilt contemporary, fun, and playful. It breaks up smooth, round lines in a quilt and adds a lot of interest, especially with a contrasting thread. Use this for an entire border on a quilt. You will love it! As you are stitching it, think to yourself point. . . point. . . point. Do not stay too long in the points or you will get little balls of thread.

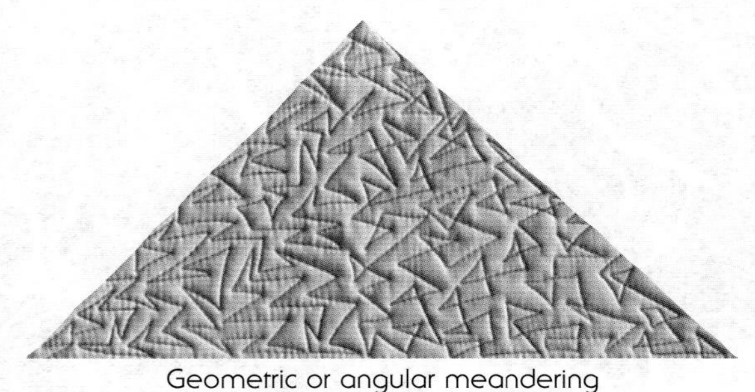

Geometric or angular meandering

Swirl Meandering

This swirl stippling or meandering is useful for water, angel hair, Santa's beard, trees, bushes, sky, etc. I try not to get into rows by varying the size of the circles. Think circular when doing this one! These are simply little pinwheels. Do not worry too much about getting into a corner because you can always echo your way out.

Swirl meandering

Start with a simple shape in the middle and stitch swirls around it. Remember to vary the size of the swirls.

Loop Meandering

This type of meandering is a series of little circles or loops. It does not matter if the loops change direction as you are quilting. Try to keep the loops all about the same size.

Loop meandering is a delicate looking fill-in background. It goes well around embroidery work. It is easy to make little stars or flowers or hearts as you are quilting the loops.

It is fun to write your name on the quilt. Write your name or your initials with the machine, then double back and echo what you have written. Then fill in with loop meandering.

Loop meandering

Thread Painting or Wood Meandering

To stitch this meandering, keep your speed up and pretend you are filling in a paper with your pencil. Stitch back and forth creating different lengths of lines. Try to keep your stitch length even.

To stitch a knothole, make an elliptical shape (a "UFO"), echo inside several times, then add a circle in the middle. Stitch your way out and fill in around it. This is a very dense quilting pattern. Make sure the rest of the quilt is balanced with heavy quilting or you will get puckers around the thread painting.

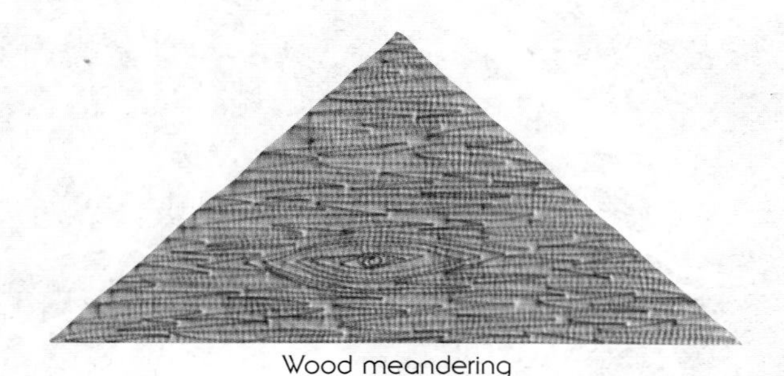

Wood meandering

Now you have finished the artistic freehand sampler. Take it off the machine, trim, and bind as desired. Congratulations!

GETTING STARTED—THE GROUNDWORK

During the past ten years, quilting (the process of stitching the quilt top, batting, and backing together) as a business has become very popular. I have observed that most quilters want to piece, appliqué, or otherwise complete the quilt tops, but do not have the skills or are not fond of the actual process of quilting. Many have tried quilting on their home domestic machines and have found it to be a tedious, slow job, even though it is faster than hand quilting. Others are simply not interested in this aspect of making quilts.

Longarm quilters have become popular simply by finishing other people's projects. Not many businesses have such a low capital investment with little or no advertising and are, for the most part, home-based. It seems to be an ideal job for a hard-working person who wants or needs to stay home for one reason or another. Notice I mentioned hard-working person? For good reason; this is not a business for the faint-hearted. It requires a lot of study, practice, and self-confidence.

One of the most important aspects of owning and running a home-based business or hiring a longarm quilter is professionalism. If you are going to have a business, you must treat it as a business. Be, or look, for a professional.

To Start Your Own Business

1 Make sure there are no laws or protective covenants in your neighborhood or area that would prohibit or restrict your business activity if you plan on doing business from your home.

2 Make up a simple financial business plan taking into consideration your start-up costs, how much money you have, how much you will need to borrow. Write down the pros and cons as far as the impact on your life and your family. Will you need help and support—whom, how, when, where?

3 Research quilting machines and choose the one that best suits your needs. Get the best machine you can afford. Anything else will be frustrating and costly in the long run. Talk to other longarm quilters, most of them have all the customers they can possibly service and are friendly and eager for you to join the longarm group. If possible, try out the machines at a show. Listen carefully to all the features included with the machine before you make your choice.

Some things to consider:

- What is the manufacturer's reputation?
- Do they show you how to take care of the machine?
- Do they train you to quilt with it?
- Do they show you how to use all the accessories that come with it?
- Do they deliver and set up the machine for you and make sure it is running properly?
- How do you get your questions answered regarding service?
- What is the warranty?
- How much room do you need?
- Is ongoing, advanced training available?
- Can your machine be upgraded if necessary?
- What is the resale on this brand of machine? (This will tell you a lot.)

4 Go to your financial institution and set up a separate checking account for your business after you have chosen and made arrangements to get your machine and training. Do not use your personal account. It gets really messy around tax time. Talk to an accountant if you feel inadequate in this area.

5 Check on the laws in your state regarding sales tax. Generally, you can contact the State Comptroller's Office or State Franchise Tax Board to get this information. If required, apply for and obtain your tax number and business license. Make sure everything you do is legal. Never apologize to a customer because you are required to charge sales tax. You did not make the law, but

you obey it. You need a resale number to buy supplies at wholesale prices. Some states have a tax exemption on the machine itself for manufacturing purposes; check on this in your state.

6 Keep good records and save your receipts. If possible, computerize your records to save yourself time and paperwork.

7 Check into credit cards if you feel it is necessary. Most home-based quilting businesses do not take credit cards. Make sure your customers understand this upfront and are prepared to pay with a check or cash when their quilts are finished.

8 Get business cards printed and carry them with you at all times. You will be surprised how many people will ask you for your card wherever you go.

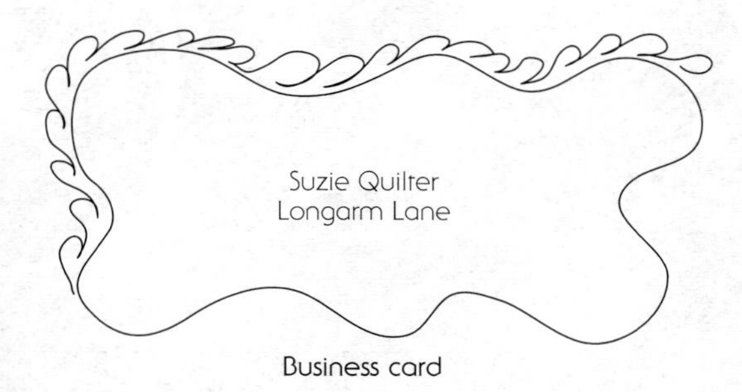

Business card

9 Design a price sheet or brochure including:

- Vital information on how to contact you (phone number, email, or website)
- Prices (page 88-92)
- Pattern choices (observe copyright laws, check with designers before printing in your brochure—many will give permission)
- How to prepare the quilt before bringing it to you (quilt top, pressed and threads clipped; quilt back seamed and 6"-8" longer and wider than quilt top)
- Batting choices you offer or should they supply their own?
- Explain the various types of quilting services you offer (pantograph, freehand, custom work, binding, etc.).
- Minimum amount—no matter the size of the project, you should have a set minimum dollar amount for your time and machinery.
- Deposit amount when you receive the quilt. This assures a speedier pick-up when the quilt is finished and it helps the customer budget the amount by spreading it out. This is generally 25-50% of the final payment.
- When are your appointment times to discuss the quilting? When can they bring or send the quilts to you? Remember that you are going to be working; you cannot be interrupted at your work, so set specific times to meet with your customers and stick to them. What is the turn-around time? When can they expect it to be finished? Some quilters allow customers to reserve dates for future quilts to be done—make sure to get a deposit for a reserve date.

I have seen some really wonderful brochures created by longarm quilters. Some of these brochures are tri-fold and in color. But do not let the lack of a fancy brochure stop you. My own brochure for the last nine years has been just a simple sheet of paper with my name, number, prices, and simple explanation of what to bring to me. A fancy fact-filled brochure gives a good first impression but your reputation will be based on your work, not your brochure.

10 Check with your insurance agent regarding insurance on the quilting machine and the customer quilt tops that will be in your possession. Be careful about accepting too many quilt tops at one time for insurance reasons and because storage can become a problem.

Notice I did not mention an assessment of talent? I believe any hard-working individual can have a successful longarm business. If you have a natural tendency to catch onto things quickly or some artistic ability, good for you; that is a plus, but not required.

You know yourself better than you think. You know if you have the desire to learn a new skill and are willing to work hard at it. You will be working for

4964 US Hwy 75 North Melissa TX. 75454
sales@lequilters.com Website www.lequilters.com
(972)562-6330 1-800-893-2748 Fax (972)562-3990

Quilting

Basting ....$0.005 \sq. inch (1/2 cent) (This service is for those who want to hand quilt)
Edge to edge (6" & up).$0.015 \sq. inch (1-1/2 cent) (Extra charge for smaller all over designs)
Custom Quilting..........................$0.03\sq. inch (3 cents) (Includes one border design)
Extra stippling or quilting.........$20 and up
Extra borders quilted.. ....$20 each
Trapunto Quilting ....$0.06\sq. inch (6 cents) (Prices vary)
Interpretive Quilting . ...$0.04\sq. inch (Prices may vary per quilt.)

Batting\Lining

Prices vary. Hobbs polys & cottons.

****Note** Tops should be pressed, threads cut, but not basted. Keep top, lining and batting separate.**

EXAMPLES OF APPROXIMATE PRICES FOR STANDARD SIZES (PRICES ROUNDED)

SIZE	SQUARE INCH	BASTE	EDGE TO EDGE	CUSTOM QUILTING
TWIN	68x90 = 6120	$31	$92	$184
DOUBLE	80x90 = 7200	$36	$108	$216
QUEEN	90x96 = 8640	$43	$130	$259
KING	96x108 = 10368	$51	$156	$311
XXL KING	120x120 = 14400	$72	$216	$432

Binding

Hand binding.... ....$.25 \inch
Machine binding..........................$.12 \inch
Curved edges-hand bind............$20.00 extra
Wall hanging Sleeve ....$0.30\inch

EXAMPLES OF PRICES FOR STANDARD SIZES (ROUNDED)

SIZE	PERAMITER INCH	HAND BINDING	MACHINE BINDING
TWIN	68x90 = 316	$70	$38
DOUBLE	80x90 = 340	$75	$41
QUEEN	90x96 = 372	$82	$45
KING	96x108 = 408	$90	$49
XXL KING	120x120 = 480	$106	$58

Prices subject to change without notice.

yourself and you may be the hardest taskmaster you have ever had. If you are still willing, go for it and never look back!

To Hire a Longarm Quilter

1 Check to see if credit cards are accepted if you choose this method of payment. Most home-based quilting businesses do not take credit cards.

2 Ask for a price sheet or brochure available that includes:

- Vital information on how to make contact (phone number, email or website)
- Prices (page 88-92)
- Pattern choices
- How to prepare the quilt before bringing it in (quilt top pressed and threads clipped; quilt back seamed and 6"–8" longer and wider than quilt top)
- Are batting choices available or should you bring your own?
- What are the various types of quilting services offered (pantograph, freehand, custom work, binding, etc.).
- Minimum amount (no matter the size of the project, the set minimum dollar amount for time and machinery)
- Deposit amount when dropping off the quilt. (This is generally 25-50% of the final payment.)
- When are appointment times to discuss the quilting? When can you bring or send the quilts?
- How soon is the turn-around time? When can you expect it to be finished? (Some longarm quilters allow customers to reserve dates for future quilts to be done—they usually require the deposit when the date is reserved.) Don't be deterred by a long waiting time, it generally means that the longarm quilter has a fine reputation.

3 Check to be sure that insurance is provided to cover your quilt top while in the possession of the longarm quilter.

4 Ask for references.

POSSIBLE SERVICES

There are many services possible in longarm quilting. Here are just a few that I have encountered.

Quilting Quilt Tops

As making quilts becomes more popular, the demand for quilters to complete the quilting process also increases. It seems to many of us who have been in this business for a few years that there will never be a way to catch up with the folks who enjoy making the quilt tops. Indeed, many of us have decided that instead of looking at it as if we are behind all the time; we view it as being booked ahead, a kind of job security.

I am often asked about the saturation of longarm quilters. I honestly believe that there will always be demand for good longarm quilters. There can be two longarm quilters right next door to each other and there is no competition. Each longarm quilter has an average of eighty customers who continue to give repeat business. Once a quilter starts piecing, do you think they will stop? My experience in a quilt shop tells me, "No."

Working With Decorators

Another wonderful service lies in the world of interior decorating—quilting custom comforters and bedspreads. I contacted the local decorators in my area when I first got my quilting machine and was instantly bombarded with comforters to quilt. Most of the decorators in my area were sending their work outside of the state to be quilted and were thrilled I was located so close to them.

The quilting on comforters and bedspreads is generally larger, more open designs that allow the fluffier polyester batting to puff up. These designs are faster and easier to quilt than anything else I have ever quilted.

There is a new product on the market for easily quilting comforters, bedspreads, or quilts. It is a good quality muslin fabric that has been printed with one of my pantograph patterns. The pattern printed on the fabric disappears with cold water. The project can be loaded "upside down" on the machine. From the front of the machine, the operator simply follows the printed design. Besides using the industrial quilting machines, this is an easy way for people with a regular domestic machine to quilt a pantograph on their quilt. The product is called Dreamline Fabrics and is manufactured by Benartex.

Pre-printed Dreamline fabric by Benartex

Sometimes the designers will ask for outline quilting. This kind of quilting is quickly and easily accomplished from the front of the machine. Rather than outline individual motifs, load the comforter on the machine sideways and make long runs on both sides of the motifs as in this illustration.

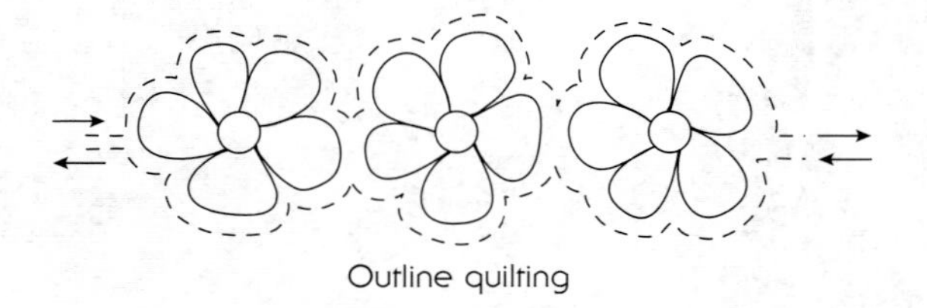

Outline quilting

Another product in the decorating world is quilted upholstery. Nearly every town has a business that specializes in upholstery or slipcovers for furniture. Oftentimes, the fabric used in the upholstery is greatly enhanced by quilting. The work is easily accomplished because there is no finish work involved for the quilter, just quilted fabric.

Occasionally, I have people call me and ask if I can quilt a duvet cover. They are tired of the filling (often feathers) flowing from one area to another. Indeed I can quilt it! I have also quilted feather mattress tops and even sleeping bags. The quilting machines are able to handle nearly any kind of fabric and stuffing. Your imagination is the limit.

T-Shirt Quilts

Quilts pieced using old T-shirts are becoming more popular around the country. It seems everyone has meaningful old T-shirts that they cannot throw away because of the memories involved, but they no longer wear them. When they discover they can have a whole quilt made of these old shirts, they are eager to have it done.

I know of several longarm quilters who have focused their entire business on completing this type of quilt. Once they have completed one for a student in a high school, sorority or fraternity, dance or sport club, it seems the entire school is calling them or dropping off bags full of T-shirts to be made into quilts.

This type of business can be as simple as performing the quilting only, or it can involve squaring and cutting the T-shirt logos, piecing them together (with or without sashing), quilting, and binding the quilt.

T-shirt quilt

Photo Quilts

As with the T-shirt quilts, another specialty business is quilting photo quilts. Lately, with the new printing technology, even novices are able to get their photos transferred to fabric and are looking for people to make their photo quilts.

The majority of people, however, want to be able to take their photos to a trusted professional and sometime later pick up a beautifully completed heirloom photo quilt. The entire scope of this business involves some equipment to transfer the photos onto the fabric, as well as completing the quilting. It is a lucrative, rewarding business, one that could keep an ambitious quilter wonderfully busy.

Photo quilt

Baby Nurseries

Baby nursery items and baby quilts will always be in high demand. With the help of the quilting machine, a baby bumper, quilt, wallhanging, dust ruffle, pillow, and other quilted items are easily coordinated to order. This can indeed be a "baby-booming" business.

Baby quilt

Antique Quilts

So far, my experience with quilting hundreds of antique quilts has been very gratifying. With some creative hard work and time on the quilting machine, I have been richly rewarded when my customers have literally cried as they see "grandma's quilt top" finally finished into the lovely heirloom quilt grandma hoped it would be.

The average longarm quilter will definitely encounter antique quilts. Most of these are brought, not by quilters, but by the general public. The longarm quilter is probably the last hope for getting this top completed. More than likely, it has been passed down for many years through the family and never quilted; therefore, sadly, never displayed or used.

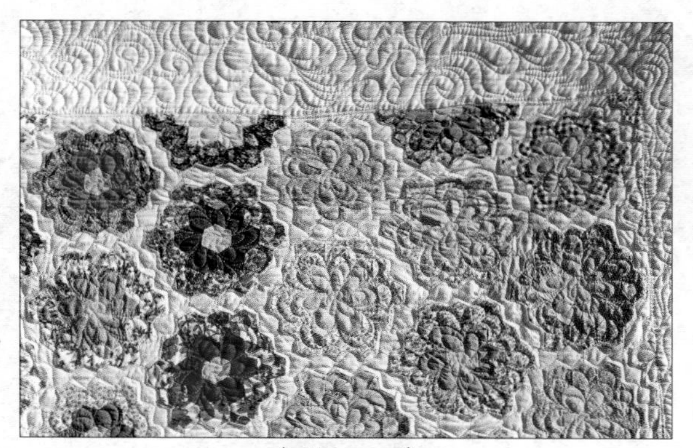

Antique quilt

There is definitely a market to specialize in quilting antique quilts, if that is your wish. It seems everyone has an old quilt top under the bed or in the attic or you can buy one at a quilt show. It is time to let people know these old tops can become beautiful antique quilts.

NOTE: This is a big responsibility. Be careful to examine the antique quilt top thoroughly before deciding to quilt it. Some of the older tops have deteriorated to the point that they no longer can be hand or machine quilted. Some of the tops have torn or disintegrated fabrics that must be fixed before any quilting can be done.

Luckily, I found a quilter in my area who specializes in the restoration of old quilt tops. She collects stashes of old fabrics and does extremely fine handwork for repairs. I refer my customers to her to repair the quilt tops, after which they bring them back to me to quilt and finish. If you are in business, look for someone with these skills that you can team up with to successfully complete antique quilts.

Wearables

Coats, vests, and a variety of other types of clothing are easily quilted on the longarm machines. For the most part, these items are marked or outlined on the fabric first, then quilted. After the quilting is complete, the piece can be preshrunk and made into the desired garment.

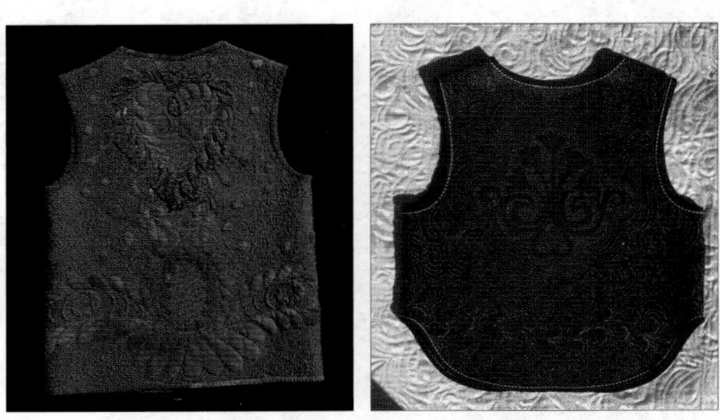

Vests using quilted fabric

Chenille Anything

It is so easy to make chenille on the quilting machines. Sew several layers of fabric together with lines approximately ½"–⅝" apart. The top layers of the fabric are then slashed; leaving the raw edges exposed creating a soft, kind of fuzzy, interesting effect. The quilting machines will quilt through several layers of fabric and batting at any angle.

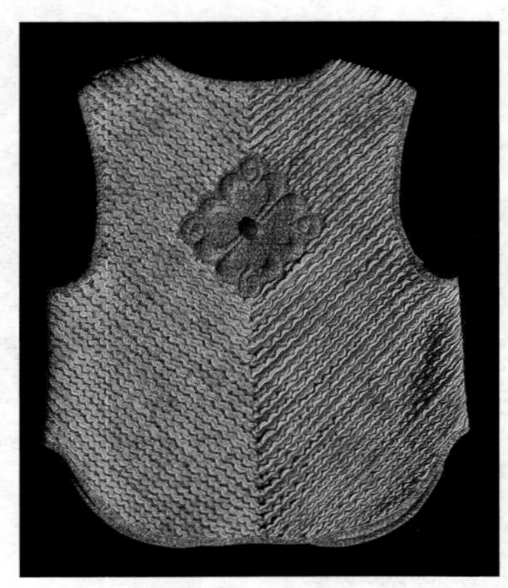

Chenille

Some of my students have completed their chenille vests in an afternoon class, although they still had to bind the edges! I have also seen chenille rugs that are absolutely breathtaking done on the quilting machines. Again, we are only limited by our imagination.

Fleece and Tricot Quilts

Fleece, fur, and tricot are a few of the fabrics that can be successfully quilted on the quilting machines. Depending on the regional location, some longarm quilters center their entire business around artfully quilting on these types of specialty fabrics.

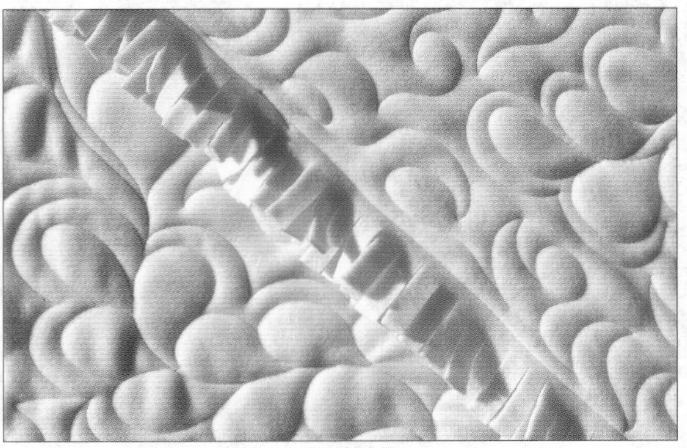

Fleece

The raw edges of fleece quilts can be fringed and will not unravel.

Renting Quilting Machines

The latest craze in this industry seems to be renting out the quilting machines to eager quilters. These are mostly people who do not or will not ever have the room or money for a quilting machine but want to quilt their own quilts.

I have had considerable experience with renting out quilting machines. I no longer do it, but applaud those who do.

You may want to think long and hard before renting out your quilting machines.

For Owners

1 There is a huge liability issue—the renters will be on your property, using your property. Make sure your commercial insurance company understands exactly the nature of what you will be doing with your business to ensure adequate coverage in case of an accident.

2 You need to train people to use the machines. This involves a great deal of your time. Deciding what compensation will be necessary for this aspect of the service.

3 You need to train people to supervise the renters using the machines or do it yourself.

4 People "tweak" everything on the machine, and I mean everything. If there is a knob, they will turn it. You will need an on-going maintenance person on the premises.

5 You will be held responsible if the machine is not sewing to their satisfaction.

6 How much do you charge for rental? When does time begin and end? Is the rate hourly or by the day?

7 When will you break even and actually start making money?

8 Will you supply the thread, batting, pins, scissors, and so on? Can they purchase these supplies from you?

For Renters

1 Make sure the business has adequate insurance coverage in case of an accident.

2 What kind of training is available? How much will it cost?

3 What kind of supervision is provided?

4 Is there an on-going maintenance person on the premises?

5 What is the help available if the machine is not sewing to your satisfaction?

6 What is the cost for rental? When does time begin and end?

7 Do I bring my own supplies, thread, batting, pins, scissors, or are they provided?

PROFESSIONALISM—WORK ORDER

Customer and Quilt Information

If you are in business, you must have some method of recording information on each quilt and a plan for filing and retrieving these records, especially since many customers become repeat customers. The information you need includes facts about the customer and details about the quilt and the work you will do on the quilt. Here is some of the vital information you want to include on your work order.

1 Work order number (start with four digits, e.g., 0001)

2 Customer name

3 Customer address (If this is a P.O. Box number you may want to get a street address in case you need to ship the quilt.)

4 Telephone (day, evening, and cell phone number)

5 Email (This could save on phone bills and is good way to send general announcements.)

6 Date quilt is due to be finished (Customer should understand this is an approximate time.)

7 Date quilt is finished (actual date finished)

8 Has customer been called that quilt is finished? (yes or no)

9 Date quilt is picked up (This way there will be no question the quilt has left your possession—you may even want a space for a signature of who picked up the quilt.)

10 Quilt description (It is important to mention the color(s), pattern of the piecing, and if the customer has a name for the quilt.)

11 Customer provides backing? (yes or no)

12 If quilter provides the backing: what type, color, width, and price?

13 Customer provides batting? (yes or no)

14 If the quilter provides batting; what type, width, and price?

15 Basting for hand quilting (Write in any specific requests.)

16 Regular pantograph (Which specific pattern?)

17 Petite pantograph (Smaller or more complicated—which specific pattern?)

18 Custom quilting (Includes one border design—which specific designs?)

19 Creative detail (Designed by you, heavier quilting, write what is discussed.)

20 Stippling charge (Show stippling strip to customer—what size stippling is chosen?)

21 Extra border designs (How many, which specific designs?)

22 Trapunto (What areas and what kind of batting for the trapunto?)

23 Seaming of backing (Yes or no; How many seams?)

24 Repair of seams or other repairs (Yes or no; You may want to have customer sign here.)

25 Thread (What kind, what color or colors?)

26 Prep work needed (trimming threads, pressing top)

27 Rush charge (if offered)

28 Binding (number of inches, machine or hand, curved edges, what fabric)

29 Wall-hanging sleeve (number of inches, what fabric)

30 Label (Is it provided? How and where should it be sewn on?)

31 Deposit amount (This should be at least 25% of the total ticket price paid to quilter when quilt is brought in to be quilted.)

32 Be sure any marks or torn areas in the quilt are noted on the work order.

A copy of the work order should be given to the customer before he/she leaves the quilt. The quilter may ask the customer to look it over and sign it before leaving.

If you do not have a computerized system, log the quilt in a notebook. If you do have a computerized system, it is already logged in the system. In either case, put a copy of the quilt order with the quilt and place the quilt on a shelf in numerical order. The quilt can be temporarily placed in a plastic bag and a numbered label placed on the bag. Some longarm quilters store the quilts on labeled hangers in a closet.

For insurance reasons and to ease storage/space problems, limit the number of quilt tops in your possession at any one time. This is why you will want to make reservation dates with your customers rather than try to store all the quilt tops at one time.

Computer Programs Make Record Keeping Easy

As your business develops, paper work can become a nightmare. For my own business, I use a program called Quilter's Business Suite. It was written specifically for longarm quilters, is user-friendly, and has all the information necessary for a longarm business. It is available through Linda's Electric Quilters, LLC (see page 133). Seriously consider computerizing all your customer quilt information for several reasons:

- Your records will include pertinent information on repeat customers such as name, address, phone, completed quilts, etc. When a customer brings another quilt you can bring up this information and will not have to re-enter it. It will save time for you and your customer.
- A mailing list can easily be generated to send information to your customers by regular or email.
- You can run a report by zip code to see where your target customers live.
- When quilt dimensions are entered into the program, the computer can automatically calculate square inches, etc. and the prices, according to the size of the quilt top.
- Prices can be programmed so the computer will automatically give totals, show deposits, add tax, and so on.
- Reports can be run to provide you with a list of when quilts are due to be finished.
- You can run reports on supplies needed to finish the quilts that are due, such as thread, batting, backing, etc.
- A computer program will help with the bookkeeping for your business; keeping track of taxable income, sales tax, supplies, etc.
- You can easily print a copy of the work order for your customer to take home. This gives them peace of mind, since they just left a precious piece of their life with you.
- Computerizing your business improves your professional image.

Work orders can be computerized or handwritten. Examples with the kind of information you want to gather from the customer are on pages 84 and 85.

OTHER PROFESSIONAL MATTERS

Check the Quilt

When measuring the quilt, lay out the entire quilt if possible. This way you can look over the quilt to note if there are any soiled spots, little cuts, or tears on the quilt. If the quilt is hand pieced, check to see if there are any seams that are not secure. If so, the customer needs to do the repairs, or you may include that as one of your services. In either case, be sure to note it on the information paper given to your customer.

Previously-Basted Quilts

If a customer brings a quilt that is already basted, make it clear that if the quilt is loaded "as is" it is impossible to control any tucks that could be quilted in the backing. You may want to offer the following options:

- You can quilt it basted, but there is a possibility of tucks in the backing (depends on their basting job).
- You must charge for your time to a take out the basting, and then it can be quilted.
- The customer can take out the basting and return it for quilting.

Another problem frequently encountered with previously-basted quilts is the likelihood of having the top, backing, and batting all trimmed to the same size. If this is the case, you will probably run out of the backing and batting at the end of the quilting process. If the top, batting, and backing are all the same size, the problem and possible solutions need to be discussed with the customer.

It is also important to note if the customer has a special quilt backing that needs to be matched to the quilt top. If so, it is easy to put in a little safety pin or a note to indicate which way you load it on the machine. It is next to impossible to guarantee that the backing can be perfectly centered in both directions. For example, if the customer has added borders all around her backing, it is easy to center

YOUR BUSINESS
ADDRESS
PHONE

ORDER DATE RECEIVED: ____________ DATE DUE: ____________

NAME: ____________ COMPLETE: ____________

ADDRESS: ____________ CALLED: ____________

STATE: ________ ZIP: ________ PICKED UP: ____________

PHONE: ________ WK PHONE: ________ EMAIL: ____________

QUILT DESCRIPTION: ____________

Top Size Top sq. in.

Customer provides own batting ❑ YES ❑ NO

BATTING LENGTH IN PRICE/IN $______

Customer provides own lining ❑ YES ❑ NO

LINING LENGTH	IN	PRICE	$______
Custom	$______	Basting	$______
Stippling charge	$______	Seaming	$______
Creative Detail	$______	Wallhanging Sleeve	$______
Edge to Edge	$______	Extras	$______
Petite Edge to Edge	$______	Extra Extras	$______
Trapunto	$______	Rush Charge	$______
Borders	$______		

Customer does own binding ❑ YES ❑ NO

BINDING DESCRIPTION: ____________

BINDING INCHES: ________ ❑ MACHINE ❑ HAND ❑ CURVED EDGE ❑ LABEL

THREAD COLOR: ________ THREAD CHARGE $______

MISC. CHARGES: ________ MISC. QTY. $______

PATTERNS NEEDED: ____________

ACTUAL SIZE: ____________

SUB TOTAL	$
TAX	$
TOTAL	$
DEPOSIT	$ ( )
BALANCE DUE	$
PAYMENT	$ ( )
BALANCE	$

---

123 Your Street
Your City, TX 75000
USA

123-123-1234
321-321-3210
name@yourdomain.com

INVOICE: ____________
QUILT: ____________

BILL TO
Quilting Store
Jane Doe
1234 Anywhere Drive
Anyplace, TX 75090
122-333-4444
contactme@internet.net

SHIP TO

INVOICE DATA
Quilted by: Johnathan D
Ordered: 12/15/2001
Reserved: 12/20/2001
Due: 1/4/2002
Completed: 1/3/2002
Picked up: 1/4/2002

MATERIALS	
Type: creative detail	($ 0.07)
Desc: Basic Example	
Size: 75 x 75	$393.75
Sq. inch: 5625	
Sq. feet: 39	
Linear inches: 300	
Batting: Hobbs 80/20	$ 3.75
Length: 75"	
Backing: Muslin	$ 0.00
Tread charge	$ 12.00
TOTAL	**$397.00**

OPTIONS"	
Wall hanging sleeve: 70"	$28.00
Number of extra borders: 1	20.00
Number of seams: 2	30.00
Binding: Machine bound	36.00
Stippling charge:	56.75
Rush charge:	50.00
Curved edge:	20.00
Piecework:	33.00
Research special thread	12.00
TOTAL	**$285.75**

COMMENTS
Add comments intended for your clients.

THREAD USED
Blue and yellow
Variegated
Orange cotton

PATTERNS USED
Flutterby
Customer (stars and swirls)

PAYMENT INFORMATION		
Subtotal:		$695.25
Discount: 10%		($69.52)
Taxable sub:		$625.73
Tax @ 8.25%	$51.62	677.35
Shipping:	$10.00	687.35
Paid:		($625.24)
Balance due		**$ 62.11**

Sample work orders

across the machine because you can start with the center point on both ends. However, you cannot guarantee that the top and bottom will be centered because you do not know how much the pieced quilt is going to stretch compared with the backing. You can measure as closely as possible, but because of the unknown factors involved, be careful about promising a perfect match, unless it is basted ahead of time. You can lose 2%–10% of the length in a quilt just by quilting it, depending on the amount of quilting and the kind of batting you are using. This is a significant factor when trying to center a backing or guess the finished size of a comforter. My suggestion is to let your customer know the difficulties you face with this situation and then, if they are willing, do your best.

Occasionally a customer will bring in a quilt that has been safety-pinned for basting. The safety pins must be removed before it can be loaded and quilted. In such cases I suggest the following options:

- The customer can take out the pins before leaving the quilt top.
- The customer can take it home and bring it back without pins.
- You can charge for the time it takes you to remove the pins.

While measuring the quilt, be sure to notice if the borders are flat. If the borders tend to be flared, then tactfully tell them, "As you can see, there is a little extra fullness in the borders."

There are a few options:

- Let the customer know that you can quilt it that way, but you cannot guarantee that the extra easing in the border will not mean a few tucks in the fabric. If so, you will try to hide the tucks in a seam if possible.
- Supply the customer with a sheet detailing how to sew borders on correctly so she can reapply the borders and fix it herself.
- Provide that service for a fee. (Do it yourself or pay a subcontractor.)

Note the option chosen by the customer on the work order before she leaves so the problem and solution is in black and white. As long as everything is candidly discussed with your customer everyone is satisfied. This also helps to educate the quilter; more than likely her next quilt will not have extra fullness in the borders.

Here is some information you can copy to give to your customers on adding borders to their quilts. Use your discretion.

ADDING BORDERS ON A QUILT

Measurements should be taken across the center of the quilt in two or three places for both the width and length.

To make a border with straight-cut corners:

1. Determine the length of the quilt border by averaging the two or three center measurements of the quilt body.
2. Cut two borders that length and pin them to opposite sides of the quilt. Match the ends and centers, then gently ease in any fullness.
3. Pin, sew, and press.
4. Repeat for the top and bottom borders measuring the width, averaging, etc.

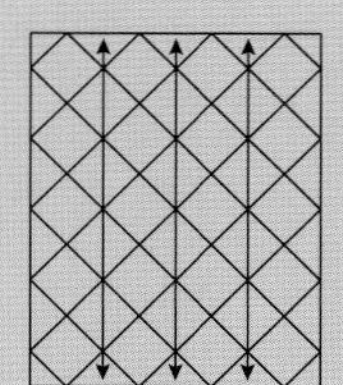

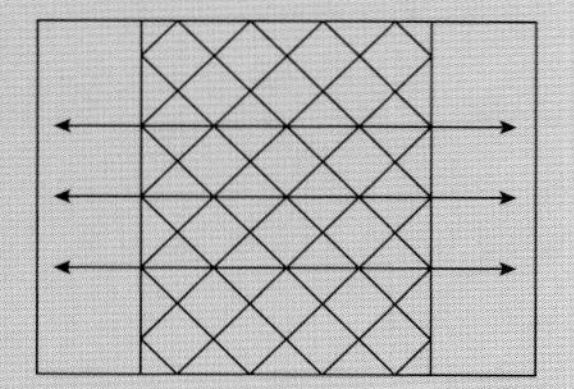

Measure in several places and average.

Do Not Set Yourself Up as a Quilt Judge

It is important not to give your customers the impression that you are judging their quilts. But there are issues that you must discuss and deal with as you are quilting their quilts in order to make them wonderful. You are their friend and you want their repeat business. You will watch them grow as "piecers" and yourself grow as a "quilter." They are, for the most part, very open and grateful for additional knowledge and information and love working with their quilter to make the quilt the masterpiece they envisioned.

Preparing Quilts

For the most part, customers prepare their own quilt tops and backings for quilting. Quilt tops should be pressed well and loose threads trimmed. Backings should be seamed with the selvages trimmed off. Quilts with selvages untrimmed create extra tension in the seams. Advise your customers to do this. If you do any of this extra preparation work, your customers should expect to pay you for it. You will have to determine how much to charge for these services. It might be an hourly rate. (You wouldn't want to know how much I would charge to iron.) You could also hire someone to prep quilts.

When seaming a backing, you can sew one seam right down the center of it. This generally saves fabric and is less expensive for the customer. Be sure to ask the customer how she wants it seamed.

When seaming a comforter or bedspread top or backing, there should be two seams. One of the panels should be centered. The other panel can be split, pattern matched, and then sewn on the sides of the center panel.

PATTERNS

Even at the beginning of a business, a longarm quilter needs a variety of patterns from which customers can choose. Usually a few basic pantograph patterns come with the machine. These are good to start and practice with, but they tend to be common and ordinary. In order to set yourself apart from other quilters, I suggest you find patterns that are more exceptional and distinctive. You may even design some of your own patterns as you develop your own style of quilting.

Copyright

In any case, please make sure you check the copyright statements on the patterns you use. Roll patterns made for longarm quilters generally allow you to use the pattern over and over for customer quilts. However, most of the roll patterns that I am familiar with do not allow "multiple commercial use." This means using the designer's pattern to manufacture quilts for a motel, condominium, or even a bed and breakfast. If you have any questions about what you can and cannot do with a pattern, contact the designer and ask permission. I know they appreciate the opportunity to clarify their intentions.

Copyrights mean you must obtain permission to copy or use the pattern for monetary gain unless stated otherwise. Some of the patterns will give permission to resize as needed.

Some patterns state "for home use." Generally this means if you want to use the pattern on a customer's quilt, the customer must own the pattern (or book) for his or her own use. For example, Hari Walner has a collection of lovely continuous-line pattern packets that are perfect for longarm sewing. If my customers choose one of her designs to be stitched on their quilt, I simply sell them the pattern packet. It is as simple as that. It is not a problem—have you ever known a quilter who did not love and have a collection of quilting patterns and books? The customer can use any of the patterns included in the packet for future quilts. Interestingly, I have observed that my customers have many books on piecing, but few on the actual quilting patterns.

Many articles and books have been written on copyright issues. Make sure you stay current on this issue and obey the law. When in doubt, "Do unto others as you would have them do unto you," or call, write, or email for permission or clarification.

Pattern Storage and Retrieval

I highly recommend that you create a good system for organizing and storing your patterns from the very beginning. Otherwise, locating patterns can quickly become a huge problem with time wasted. A well-rounded longarm quilter will use pantograph or "rolled" patterns as well as flat patterns, so provide storage for both.

Pantograph Patterns

Normally, the designer will number the pantograph patterns. A plastic bin or tub for each designer, labeled with the pattern numbers, is a good beginning to a storage system. Later, as more patterns are acquired, the numbered tubs can be divided. These tubs can be easily stacked and stored. This system works well for my business.

Other longarm quilters obtain or make tube containers to store the pantograph patterns. Find the system that works best for your space and use it. Putting the pattern away in the right place when you are finished with it is more than half the battle.

Flat Patterns (Custom Quilting Patterns)

Once a flat pattern is the right size for the quilt, it is a good idea to protect the pattern by laminating it or covering it with clear contact paper. The pattern may be used again and needs to be preserved in good condition.

Patterns for blocks, triangles, circles, etc., must be kept flat. Following a curly edge on a pattern with the laser light can produce a distorted pattern on the quilt. I organize small, flat patterns in plastic pages categorized in three-ring binders. The plastic pages are easily labeled with the pattern name or number. I have several three-ring binders divided according to the designers. Many of the pages have several sizes of each pattern that I have resized for quilts. I also keep a table of contents including the sizes available at the front of each binder. This helps me to know if I need to make a new pattern or size, or if I already have it in stock.

The larger flat patterns can be organized and stored in a file drawer of some sort. I buy large poster board, fold it in half, tape the sides together and label it. These poster board files store easily and keep even the largest patterns flat.

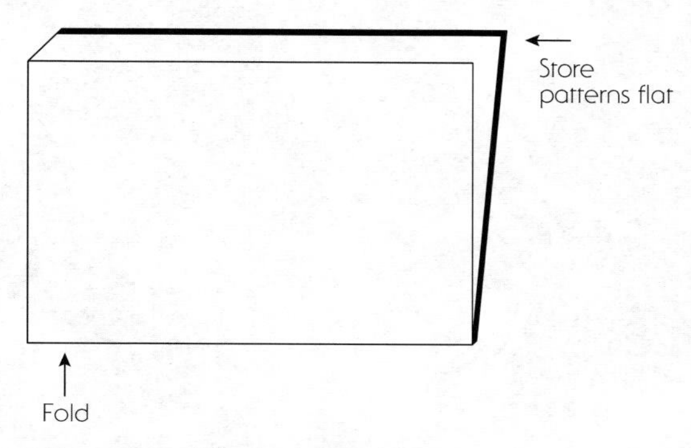

Poster board file for large patterns

A three-ring binder with an overview of the pattern selections in plastic pages makes a good reference book for your customers to browse through to choose the quilting patterns they want on their quilt. Make sure all patterns are labeled with a name or number for easy reference to put on the order sheet. Also be sure to include the copyright and designer's name for proper credit.

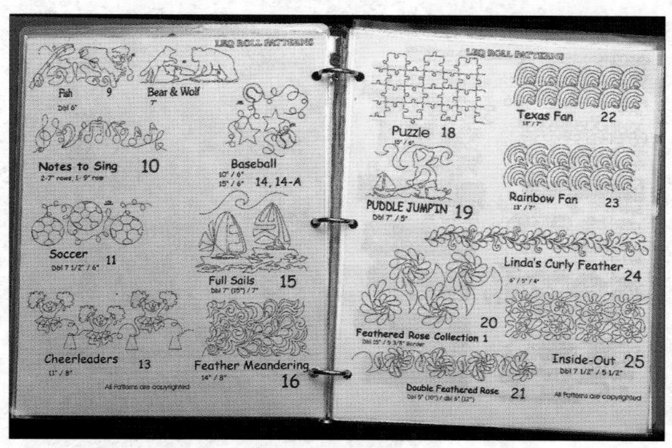

Pattern catalog

PRICING

Pricing Per Square Inch

There is no standard for pricing in the longarm quilting business; however, many longarm quilters charge by the square inch of the quilt top, with a minimum dollar amount for small projects. It stands to reason, of course, that there must be different "per-inch prices" for various kinds of quilting. The following chart defines some possible types of quilting:

Overall Quilting

- ***Basting for hand quilters*** - Three layers are basted together to be hand quilted, generally at 4" intervals.
- ***Pantograph Quilting*** - Pantographs with a fairly open design work
- ***Designer Pantograph Quilting*** - More complicated pantograph designs
- ***Petite Pantograph Quilting*** - Smaller pantograph designs (6" or less)
- ***Overall Meandering*** - Freehand large overall meandering (1-3" apart)
- ***Petite Overall Meandering*** - Freehand overall meandering (<1" apart)

Custom Quilting

- ***Custom (one border)*** - One border design, outlining blocks, simple block design
- ***Crosshatching*** - Entire quilt is crosshatch quilted.
- ***Creative Design*** - Longarm quilter decides quilting patterns, some freehand.
- ***Interpretive Design*** - Original designs by longarm quilter, heavily quilted
- ***Trapunto Quilting*** - Trapunto, heavily quilted, quilt show quality
- ***Stipple Charge*** - Using stipple strip (page 47), customer can choose size of stipple which can be added to any of the custom quilting categories.
- ***Extra Border Charge*** - Customer wants separate design in each border.

One of the advantages of charging by the inch is how easy it is to figure out how much it will cost to quilt the quilt. Length times the width of the quilt top equals the square inches. Most folks can easily multiply and thereby figure it out for themselves. They have a firm bid on the work when they leave the quilt with you. If the longarm quilter experiences difficulty, or it takes more time than expected for some unforeseen reason, it is the longarm quilter's problem, not the customer's. On the other hand, if the quilt takes less time than anticipated, the longarm quilter reaps the benefit and reward. Believe me, it evens out.

Various areas of the country charge different prices per square inch. Before you set up business it is important that you check around in your area and compare prices. When checking out prices, however, be sure to compare equal types of quilting. You can bet someone who charges the "same price for any size quilt" is not doing the kind of custom quilting you may be interested in doing.

As I have traveled and taught around the country from coast to coast, I have seen a disparity in prices. Generally, however, overall types of quilting vary from just under 1¢ ($.007) to 3¢ per square inch. The custom type of quilting varies even more, from 1½¢ up to 8¢ per square inch.

Pricing By Square Foot Or Yard

Longarm quilters who charge by the square foot or yard generally offer their customers a simple formula to figure out how much the quilting will cost. This could be incorporated into a brochure so prospective customers can predetermine approximately how much they will pay for the quilt.

- ***Square Foot Price*** - Length times width of quilt divided by 144 equals square feet.
  (L x W ÷ 144 = sq. ft.)
- ***Square Yard Price*** - Length times width of quilt divided by 1296 equals square yards.
  (L x W ÷ 1296 = sq. yd.)

The various types of quilting for square foot or yard are the same as for square inch.

When I have priced out the square foot and yard prices of some of my students and compared them with my square inch prices, I have found for the most part, they are nearly the same.

Pricing Per Hour

Another method of pricing the quilting service is by the hour. Most of the longarm quilters who use this pricing use a stopwatch while they are working on the quilt. Since I have never quilted by the hour, I interviewed a few of my students who successfully charge by the hour. When I inquired how they give the customer an estimate, they said they kept a log when they first started which gave them a good idea of how long each pattern (pantograph or overall meandering) took to quilt for a specific size quilt. After a few quilts they could give the customer a fairly close estimate of time for the work. They also stated that they look over the quilt carefully and take into account any problems they may encounter, such as ruffled borders, poorly pressed seams, etc., and add on extra time for anticipated problems.

You will need a very good reputation to charge by the hour for custom quilting. Many of those I interviewed say their customers are not concerned with how much it will cost; they simply want "their quilter" to do the job and they know it will be wonderful. It appears to me that trust is a big factor with this method of pricing. But, for that matter, any quilting on someone else's quilt top involves a lot of mutual trust. Quilters everywhere are known for their integrity and generosity.

Prices by the hour vary from coast to coast in the United States. I have heard everything from $15–$50 per hour. Indeed, knowing what you are making per hour can be comforting.

However, several issues are somewhat bothersome in my mind regarding this method of pricing. First, do you include the time when you have to pickout because you made a mistake? Second, as you gain more experience you become a much faster quilter. Does this mean you do more quilts for less money or do you continually raise the hourly rate? Third, do you charge the same rate for designing the quilting or thinking about how you are going to quilt it? And fourth, what if you forget to start or stop the clock—do you guess the time? I have never been good at punching a clock, so it is good that I am in business for myself.

Thread Charge

However you decide to charge for the quilting, I strongly suggest a separate thread charge. The prices for the quilting service are for the labor. Materials are extra. The thread charge is nominal (from $3–$5), but it allows the longarm quilter to buy more colors and have a larger variety for the customer. Any specialty thread is priced higher, of course (from $10–$25).

I do not charge for changing thread colors as long as it is the same kind of thread. It is very easy and fast to do on these machines. You tie the thread onto existing thread in the back of the machine and pull it through all the way to the needle.

My customers have never complained about the thread charge. I am prepared, however, to say "Bring your own thread, but make sure it is the good quality quilting thread that I use on quilts." They would have to pay much more for thread than my miniscule charge.

The thread charge money can be kept in a separate account to purchase thread. By charging for thread, you can legally buy thread wholesale since you will be reselling it to the customer.

My thread charge also includes a new needle for each quilt. I tell my customers this and I know my customers appreciate it.

Batting and Backing

Of course, if you are in business you will want to carry some batting choices for your customers. You will buy the batting at wholesale prices and sell it to your customers at retail. The batting is less expensive on the rolls and you sell it by the inch; therefore the customer is saving money by obtaining the batting from you.

The same applies to backing fabric. For the most part, this will be muslin. It is not necessary for you to carry muslin; most of the piecers will bring you their own fabric for the backing. However, a few will want muslin, either bleached or unbleached, on the back of their quilt. As your business grows, consider carrying some muslin choices, preferable at least 90" wide.

Extra-Border Design Prices

If the customer's quilt has more than one border on the quilt top and the customer desires a separate design stitched in each border, it is appropriate to charge for each additional border design. It takes time to set up the border and corner designs and skill to execute them properly. Around the country, longarm quilters charge anywhere from $20–$40 per extra border design in addition to their regular method of pricing per quilt top.

Repair Work

When the customer brings you the quilt top, lay it out with the customer present and look it over. You will be discussing not only how you will quilt the top, but any repair work that needs to be done before it can be quilted. Make notes on these; there may be seams that are coming apart or appliqué that is not stitched securely. It is important that you note this on your work order and decide with your customer if she is going to do the repairs, or if you will do them. If you are going to do the repairs, have a set per hour or per piece price in mind to quote. Most of this kind of work will range from $10-$20 per hour.

Preparing the Quilt for Quilting

The quilts are much easier to quilt if they are well pressed and loose threads are trimmed. This is a good suggestion to add to your brochure; however, if the quilt is not pressed, nor threads trimmed, it can still be quilted. If it does not matter to the customer, it should not be an issue for you.

Whether or not you want to do the prep work is up to you, but if you decide you are willing, you must charge for it. Again, I have heard of quilters who charge anywhere from $10–$20 an hour for prep work. If you start ironing and clipping threads for no extra charge, you will end up spending hours doing it. It is not just "part of the quilting process." It is part of the piecing process. If you are in business to make money you must make this very clear to your customers.

I believe it is a matter of educating your customers on how to prepare the quilt top for quilting. Carefully explain it to them and then leave it up to them. Of course, if you enjoy ironing . . .

Seaming the Backing Material

Oftentimes you may need to seam the backing material. Be sure this is noted on the work order and charge for each seam that you sew. Around the country, the prices range from $5–$15 per seam. This sounds like a good incentive for the customer to seam her own backing fabric.

NOTE: When seaming the backing fabric I use a very tiny zigzag stitch, which allows the seam to have a little give in it. After the seam is sewn, I remove the selvages. The price doubles if the fabric design needs to be matched.

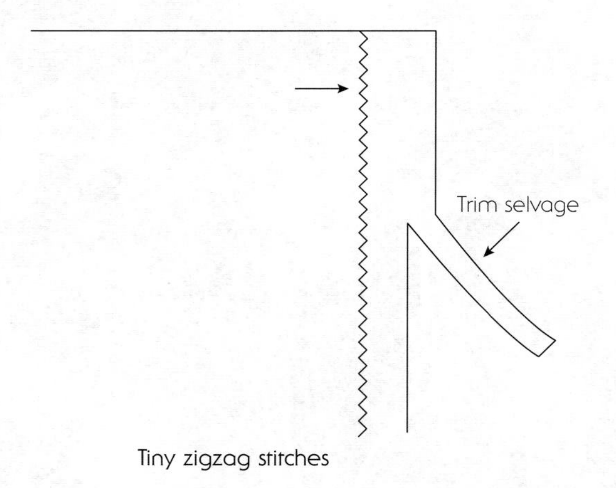

Rush Charge

A rush charge means that you will do overtime. Overtime pay is one and one-half to two times more than your regular charges. If you are willing to do a quilt when you would not normally be quilting, then perhaps you might consider a rush charge.

Some longarm quilters refuse to consider a rush charge. I believe it depends on how booked up you are with your quilting business. One thing for sure, it is not fair to push all your customers' quilt dates behind because someone else is willing to pay for their quilt to be completed sooner.

Binding

You do not have to bind quilts to be in this business. You simply say, "I don't bind." Most of the piecers want to bind their own quilts anyway.

On the other hand, binding quilts can be a part of your business. It is a nice service to offer, especially to beginning quilters and folks who do not sew but want their quilt completely finished.

You (the business owner) do not have to do the binding. I am not interested in doing the binding for customers. I only want to quilt for them. So, I found someone in my local guild who is very good at binding. She does the binding for my customers. It works for her, for me, and for my customers.

She does machine binding and hand binding. The prices range from 12¢–25¢ a running inch. The customer furnishes the fabric. My friend takes their fabric and cuts the binding, squares up the quilt, and applies the binding. Curved edges are $20 more per quilt. She also does wall-hanging sleeves for 35¢ a running inch. I have heard prices for binding that are much less, and some that are more. Check around for prices in your area before you decide what to charge.

You can make more money quilting than binding. If you decide to bind, make sure it is not taking away from your time quilting.

NOTE: Binding machines are available. They typically use a prepared binding fabric that comes on a large roll. It rarely matches what my customers want on their quilts. However, if you are manufacturing quilts to sell, the binding machine might be a good investment.

Labels

Some customers may bring you a label they have prepared and ask you to sew it on their quilt during the quilting process. This will take a little extra time but the charge should be nominal ($5–$10).

Miscellaneous Charges

Think about what you want to charge for other kinds of services that might be requested such as adding a fabric border around a quilt to make it larger. This can be priced out by a standard hourly rate or by the border (for instance $30–$40 per border).

If you have an embroidery machine, post your prices to create labels or other "per square" items.

Paying Employees and Subcontractors

My business was located inside a busy quilt shop for five years. I had several people who quilted full time for me in-store. At the same time several subcontractors quilted for me on machines in their homes. I am often asked how I paid my employees and subcontractors.

Paying Employees

At first, I paid my in-store employees by the hour. As time progressed and their skills improved, I not only raised the hourly rate but also added an incentive of a percentage per quilt.

Paying Subcontractors

There are some good longarm quilters who have a quilting machine in their home, but circumstances do not allow them to have a home-based business in their area. I was lucky enough to identify a few of these and have them work with me as subcontractors.

The subcontractors are always paid strictly on a percentage of the total bill. Those who do good custom work, earn a large percentage of the ticket. But I am still responsible for the quality and timeliness of all of the quilting. The customers are still my customers. It is a huge responsibility.

Check on the laws in your area regarding subcontractors if this sounds like something you may be interested in doing as a shop owner. These people have to be trustworthy to maintain your standards. You have much less control than you do with in-store employees. Although subcontractors are not employees, you do have to keep good records for tax purposes.

Prices Subject to Change

I believe it is important to mention that you can change your prices when you are more experienced and faster. People would not expect the prices of a beginning longarm quilter to be the same as an award-winning longarm professional. From experience, I can tell you that your customers will be loyal and their skills will grow with yours. They will sew better quilt tops and expect you to be the best quilter.

I worry when my students tell me they have very long waiting lists of customer quilts (more than one year). I interpret this to mean that they have not raised their prices according to their increased skill. They could be doing fewer and better quilts and making more money. Remember, when your waiting list starts getting long, by the time you raise your prices, you will not see the result of the raise until you have quilted your way through the list with previously negotiated prices.

WHERE TO ADVERTISE YOUR SERVICES OR FIND A LONGARM QUILTER

The places for professionals to advertise their services and quilters to find a longarm quilter are the same. Below are some suggestions.

Word of Mouth

There is absolutely no doubt that word of mouth is the number one source of advertising in this business. The professional's reputation as a good quilter is the best advertisement. Quilters have an underground communication system that spreads the word fast. If you are looking for a longarm quilter to hire, ask around.

Of course, this works in reverse as well. Unhappy customers tell all their quilter friends. That is why it is important to make each and every customer happy with her quilt. Being professional is a big part of this process.

Quilt Guild Membership

As a longarm quilter, join as many quilt guilds in your area as you can find. Many of the quilt guild meetings have a show-and-tell time where you can display your work. The members are the target audience for professionals and an ideal way to find longarm quilters. You will find many wonderful friends by being an active member of a guild. Get involved and contribute what you can.

Quilt Shops

Quilt shops can be a great asset for advertising quilting services and finding professional longarm quilters. Since completed projects make for happier quilters, most quilt shops should be happy to display a professional's business card. They also usually have a list of available quilters in the area. Professionals should ask to be added to the list, or, look at the list if you are seeking a longarm quilter. Check with all the quilt shops in your immediate vicinity. If you do not have many quilt shops close to you, check with shops that are further away. When piecers find good quilters to finish their quilts, they are not opposed to sending them via mail, UPS, etc. It may be worth the longarm professional's time to arrange a certain day per month when you could visit these shops and meet your customers there. If you are looking for a longarm quilter, keep in mind that you might be able to arrange to meet at your quilt shop. This is a win-win situation for the quilt shops as well, increasing foot traffic, customer loyalty, and thereby, profits.

NOTE: I am confused and disappointed when I hear that some quilt shops will not take a longarm quilter's business card or add their name to the list of quilters. The fact is, there are not enough quilters to quilt all the quilt tops that need to be finished. Quilt shops have more business when customers have choices of quilters to finish their work. The more quilt tops customers finish and have quilted, the sooner they buy more fabric for the next project. Healthy competition makes all of us better quilters.

Samples for Quilt Shops

Professionals can offer to quilt teacher samples for the quilt shop, possibly at a reduced rate. These samples generally hang in the shop for several months. Make sure that your name and vital information is attached to the sample for proper credit and advertising. (I would not quilt teacher samples for free. Do not give yourself away.) This would be another good way to find a longarm quilter and see examples of their work. Quilt shops greatly benefit from finished quilts hanging in their shop. They are more attractive and encourage prospective students to fill the classrooms.

Take Classes in Quilt Shops

Taking quilting classes in a quilt shop helps longarm professionals find prospective customers. Quilters love to see the work of their fellow-students in class. It might even catch of the eye of the teacher! This is also a good time for you to make more quilting friends and become part of this unique, friendly community.

Open House

Some of my students have held successful open houses when they were ready to start their businesses. Invite your friends, neighbors, and acquaintances over to see your new big toy. Let them see how it works and marvel at your courage to operate it.

One of my students sent quilting machine birth announcements to her friends. (Many longarm quilters actually name their machine.) It turned out to be a very successful advertisement for her business.

Charity Quilts

While you are getting started in your business, it is a good idea to volunteer to do a few charity quilts for local quilt guilds (they are non-profit and always have service projects), hospitals, nursing homes, etc. The contacts you make and the experience you gain while quilting will be invaluable, not to mention the service you are providing.

Local Paper

Putting an ad in the local paper will also attract attention; however, this is not your target audience of quilters. Since the general public reads the paper, you will attract the attention of many non-sewers. By that I mean, people who have a quilt top in their possession (probably passed down by grandma) but have no idea how to get it finished and certainly have no intention of quilting it themselves!

These people will most likely bring just the quilt top. You will need to furnish the backing and batting, as well as complete the quilting and binding. Since the majority of these passed-down tops are a double size, some customers may ask if it can be made into a queen or king size so they can use it on their bed. Consider ahead of time if this is one of the services you want to provide.

National Quilting Magazines

Most of the national quilting magazines have a classified section in the back of the magazine. Placing an ad in this section of the magazine will mean mail-order business for the professional. Be sure you are prepared with a comprehensive brochure to send out to people who request information. Also make sure you have a firm policy on your shipping arrangements and deposit agreement. Answering an ad will provide valuable information for quilters looking for a longarm quilter.

Note: Several students have told me they placed ads in these magazines and had to pull them out because they were swamped with quilt tops to quilt.

Decorator Shops

Look up decorator shops in your local yellow pages. Take samples of your work with you and visit these shops. Many of them are delighted to find someone in their area who can quilt comforters and bedspreads. I suggest offering a decorator's discount to these shops (10%–15%). They can keep you very busy.

Quilt Shows

Competition is healthy for all of us. Entering a quilt show will boost your confidence and attract the attention of other quilters. It also validates your work as a quilter. I cannot overstress this as a venue for advertising. It is a scary thing to do at first, but it is rewarding to see your quilt hanging in the show, with or without a ribbon. This is also a great place to find a longarm quilter. The longarm professional should be given credit on the quilt information sheet.

Like it or not, as a longarm quilter, you will probably see some of your work hanging in a quilt show. The customer owns the quilt and is free to enter it, but you should be given credit as the quilter. In fact, I encourage my customers to enter their quilts in the local shows. I know how much it bolsters their confidence and opens their eyes to excellence.

I suggest the first time one of your quilts is entered in a show you make a file on "show quilts entered." Write down the quilt, the piecer and quilter, the date completed, show entered, and if it won a ribbon. A picture of the quilt in the file would also be helpful. Watch this file grow over the years!

One-Time Special or Coupon

Another way to advertise services is to offer a one-time special. I say one-time because if it extends for a very long period of time you will not be making much money. Many quilters will use the coupon to test your work on their utility quilts before they give you their really good quilt tops. Always put an expiration date on the coupons.

Quilt Labels

Every quilt needs a label. Quilters intend to put a label on their quilt, but many do not get around to it. I offer my customers a free label when they pick up their quilt.

The label is inexpensively made with photocopy paper and transferred to white or ecru muslin. There are a variety of borders on the labels for special holidays and occasions. I have a place for the customer to write her name and the date. "Quilted by:" has my business name printed on the label in color. I have a fabric pen handy if they want to write the information on the label before they leave or if they want me to sign it. This is a nice convenience my repeat customers look forward to choosing. It is also a good advertisement as they show off the quilt to others.

Trading with Friends and Relatives

I want to say a word about quilting for free. Of course the decision is yours, but I would be careful about practicing for free on anyone's quilt. You have an investment in machinery and skill. Just a friendly suggestion, but when a friend or relative asks you to quilt something for them (practice for free, of course), kindly suggest trading time. While you are quilting for them perhaps they can clean, baby-sit, make dinner, or offer one of their skills in exchange. If you are looking for a longarm quilter, maybe this "trading services" arrangement will work for you.

Some people take advantage of longarm quilter friends who have purchased their machine to earn a living. The professional should decide the policy regarding these situations and stick to it. The friends and relatives should be considerate of this.

PROFESSIONAL ATTITUDE

Business at Home, Be Professional

Most longarm quilters are running their business from their homes. When someone works at home, often people do not take her work seriously. The prevailing attitude is that it is a hobby or something she does in her spare time. For this reason, it is extremely important to be completely professional when it comes to the business. This means setting a schedule and sticking to it. Otherwise, you will have people staying for tea and gossip when you should be working.

If you have a serious attitude, they will. This does not mean you are abrupt, rude, or otherwise unfriendly. It means you are a professional and can keep your personal life and your professional life separate. Here are a few suggestions that might work for you:

1. Schedule an appointment time for your customers to bring and pick up quilts and discuss the quilting. Do not say "ten-ish;" say "I have an opening between 10:00 to 10:30 a.m."

2. Always answer your phone with the name of your business, if your business number is the same as your home number.

3. Turn on your answering machine while you are quilting. You are not available at all hours of the day or night. State specific hours that you will be returning calls and make sure you do.

4. Set aside a specific area of your home to conduct your business affairs, if possible. You do not want people going on a "home tour" when they visit you on business.

5. If you are running behind on your quilt schedule, call your customers and let them know. Do not give personal excuses, e.g., children sick, house a mess, took dog to vet, etc. Just tell them when they can expect their quilt to be finished.

NOTE: If you are a stay-at-home mom running a quilting business, you will have emergencies and down days. Schedule your finished quilt dates later than when you actually think you can have them finished. An early quilt is a treat; a late quilt is stressful for you, your family, and the customer.

6. Consider designating one day a week for taking in and picking up quilts. Established customers will get used to this schedule and plan on it. Of course, there are always exceptions. Be nice but make the exceptions few and far between. Let these customers know you are making an exception, but that you rarely do it.

Shop Owners

The marriage between a quilt shop and a longarm business is mutually beneficial. Both businesses increase sales and support each other. There are several ways to incorporate a professional longarm machine quilter in a quilt shop.

- ***Referrals Only:*** As mentioned earlier, quilt shops can keep a referral list of longarm quilters or allow the quilters to display their cards on a bulletin board. The shop owner should be careful to remain neutral and make no recommendations, thereby not creating any liability for the quilt shop.
- ***Quilt Shop/Drop Off:*** Quilt shops can allow longarm professionals who work in their homes to make appointments with customers to drop off and pick up quilts at the quilt shop. This would be at a convenient time and place in the shop. It increases foot-traffic through the store and fosters loyalty in the longarm quilter and the customer. This probably happens with or without the quilt shop's blessing. The quilt shop may charge the longarm professional a small fee for the use of their shop.
- ***Preferred Longarm Quilter:*** Quilt shops might make arrangements with one or more longarm professionals that they deem to be worthy of

recommendation. The quilt shop may then accept quilt tops for the quilters or make the referral. Keep in mind that it takes a lot of time to measure and note the many details of the quilting process; therefore, the quilt shop would need to garner a percentage of the quilting ticket to cover the overhead expenses. An alternative would be for the professional to designate a specific day of the week to be in the quilt shop to accomplish this task. I have seen this work most successfully when the longarm professional is actually a relative or partner of the quilt shop owner.

- ***Divided Duties:*** Partners, relatives, or friends—all part owners of a quilt shop—may decide to divide the duties within the shop; one could be the in-house longarm professional. From what I have observed, this seems to work well as long as all the partners are working equally as hard.
- ***Sharing Space:*** One of the best arrangements I have observed is for a quilt shop to rent space within the shop to a longarm professional. Of course, this means the shop has to be large enough to make extra room for a quilting machine. I rented space inside a quilt shop for five years and I can tell you first-hand that their fabric sales increased, classes filled more readily, and more interest was generated in the quilt store in general. It helped off set some of their overhead as well. It took a while for me to get used to people watching me quilt, and many would come in just to see all the completed quilts ready for pick-up; however, my business soared. Having the machine somewhere other than in my house also made it easier to keep my business and personal life separate. My business dealings were always separate from the quilt shop's.
- ***In-house Quilting:*** Many quilt shop owners are now buying machines for their shops. This is another alternative in order to offer customers a complete quilting service.

Shop Owners' Dilemma—Becoming a Training Ground

With the addition of longarm quilting services, new problems tend to surface. I have talked to many shop owners who have trained several longarm quilters for their shop.

Employees who quilt everyday learn how to operate the quilting machines and become quite proficient and knowledgeable about quilting in general. Just when they really become "worth their salt" in speed and quality, many buy their own machine and start their own business. The shop owner starts over. It is called free enterprise and it happens everyday in America with lots of businesses.

There is always the risk of a well-trained employee leaving the company. My advice: as an employee, I would be careful of burning my bridges; friendships are very important. And as an employer, I would be mature and kind; you and your business will be just fine.

Still, the dilemma exists and so do the feelings. Perhaps a solution to avoid this problem would be a contract between the shop owner and the employee/trainee for a reasonable amount of time. If you are a shop owner or are thinking of hiring people to help with the quilting, be aware of these issues.

Professional Attitude Does Not Include Jealousy

On a more personal note, there is one more subject I feel needs to be addressed. It is a touchy subject because we all have felt a little jealous or resentful towards someone at sometime in our life. I see it a lot among quilters.

Here is the story: Once upon a time, when I was really young (about 28), I was very jealous of this woman who I thought could do, and did do, anything and everything. Actually, it was the everything I really resented. Well, one day I was confiding (okay, complaining) to another friend about the first woman, who was supposed to be my friend also. I was telling her about everything this woman did and why it grated on my nerves so badly. My friend looked me straight in the green eyes and said, "Linda, do you want her to be less than she is, just so you will be more comfortable around her?" That was not what I wanted to hear about myself. That was and is not the woman I thought I was or ever hoped to be. I resolved right there and then (and have been working on it ever since) to lift others, to elevate them, to hang on to their coattails, to beg for a ride, to learn from them, to listen, to lean, to be there for them, and most of all to rejoice with them in their victories and their talents, and spread the good news. How boring life would be if we all had the same talents. Celebrate diversity and stop whining. It has made all the difference in my life through hard times and good. Perhaps it will help you. We really are all on the same team you know.

I believe quilters become better quilters by sharing with one another. If the very best quilts in the world were not displayed in a quilt show, then where would I find my inspiration? Why should I resent the fact that someone won an award on his or her beautiful quilt? Our excellence is achieved through sharing; always has been, always will be. It is not hard for us to help each other through hard times. Why do we have difficulty celebrating each other's victories and achievements? That is what really separates a professional from an amateur. Decide which you want to be and do it today.

We all know our bodies get tired whether sitting or standing for long periods of time. Longarm quilting requires long hours of standing, reaching, and working with our arms and hands. The correct posture during the quilting process can relieve stress to the lower back. I have watched so many students lean, bend, and slouch during class when they could have easily avoided it by simply moving the quilt to a more accessible position on the quilting machine table. When your body gets tired, it is time to refresh with a rest or change. Proper exercise should be a part of our regular routine.

I asked chiropractor and personal trainer, Dr. Cari Hebert, if she would suggest some exercises to relieve the stress and strengthen the muscles I use in my work. Like you, I want to be able to continue quilting for a very long time.

After observing how I did my quilting, Cari offered these simple tips to stretch, relax, and strengthen the muscles we use everyday when using the quilting machines. These exercises can also help any quilter who loves to sew by hand or machine. Cari was kind enough to demonstrate the exercises. Thank you Dr. Hebert!

POSTURE

First, the proper height of the quilting machine table will do a lot to relieve stress on the back. To obtain the optimal height for most people, stand at the end of the table with your elbow bent at a 90° angle. The table end should be right at the bottom of your arm. This will work for the majority of people. Remember, everyone's body type is different, adjust the table so it feels right for you. You do not want to bend over in the front of the machine to see or sew.

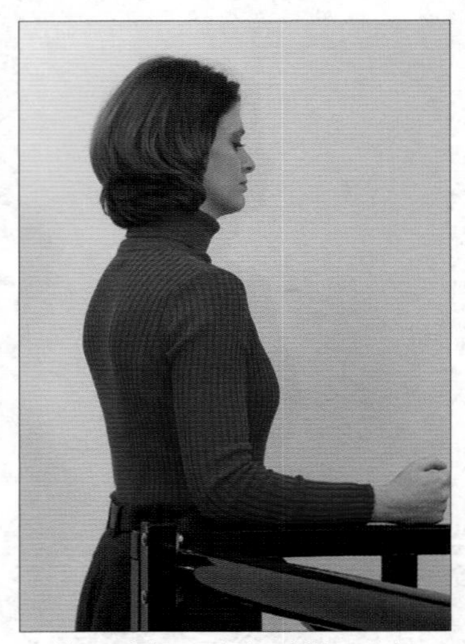

The table end should be right at the bottom of your arm.

When standing, your knees should be slightly bent, with feet pointed straight ahead. Keeping the knees slightly bent prevents the hips from rotating forward. Use the big muscles in the front of the upper legs (quadriceps) to control your posture when standing.

If you stand in one place for a period of time prop one foot up on a box or short stool. This will relieve some of the back tension that comes from prolonged standing.

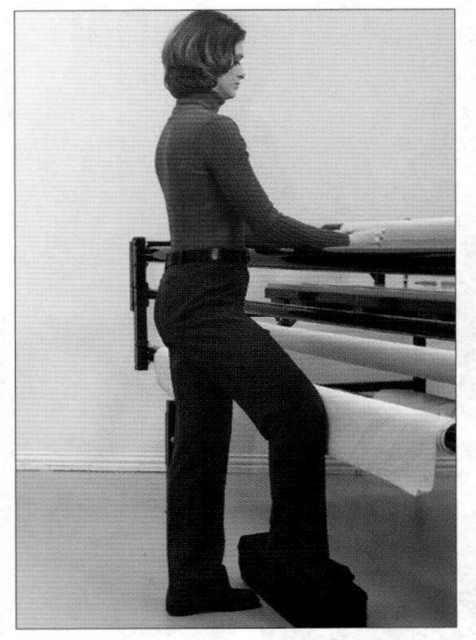

Prop one foot up on a box or short stool.

STRETCHING

Interlace your fingers with your arms stretched out in front of you at shoulder height. Turn your palms outward as you extend your arms forward to feel a stretch in your shoulders, middle of upper back, arms, hands, fingers, and wrists. Hold an easy stretch for 15 seconds, then relax and repeat.

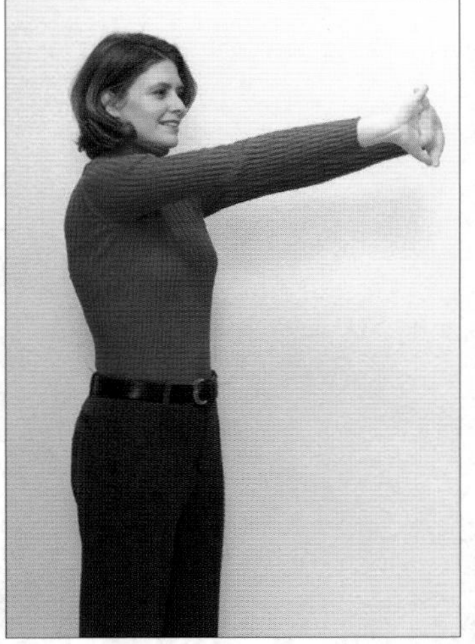

Upper body stretch

Interlace your fingers above your head. Now, with your palms facing upward, push your arms slightly back and up. Feel the stretch in your arms, shoulders, and upper back. Hold stretch for 15 seconds. Do not hold your breath.

Upper body stretch

To stretch the side of your neck and top of your shoulder, lean your head sideways toward your right shoulder as your right hand pulls your left arm down and across, behind your back. Hold an easy stretch for 10 seconds. Do both sides.

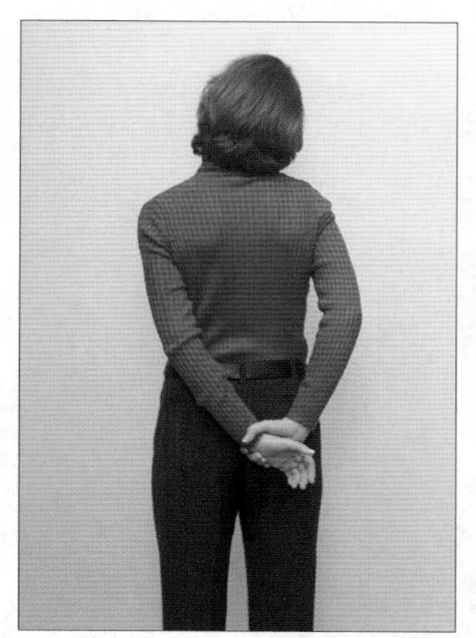

Neck stretch

Drop a towel behind your head. With your upper arm bent, reach up with your other arm to grasp the end of the towel. Gradually move your hand up on the towel, pulling your upper arm down until your hands are touching. Repeat with other arm.

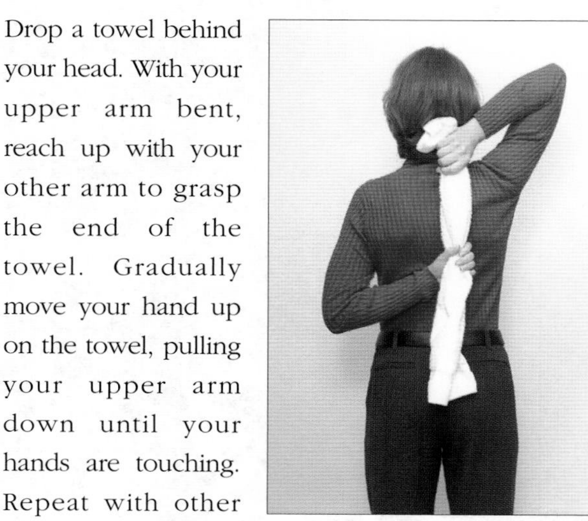

Arm stretch

Interlace your fingers behind your back. Slowly turn your elbows inward while you straighten your arms. If that is fairly easy, then lift your arms up behind you until you feel a stretch in your arms, shoulders or chest. Hold an easy stretch for 15 seconds. Keep your chest out and chin in.

Shoulders and chest stretch

STRENGTHENING

Wrist and Forearm Strengthening

Wrist flexion: Wrap soft rubber exercise tubing around your fist and secure the opposite end under your foot. Bend your wrist up (palm up) as far as possible. Lower your hand slowly, keeping your forearm on your thigh. Repeat with 12 repetitions and 3 sets. Do this every other day.

Wrist strengtheners

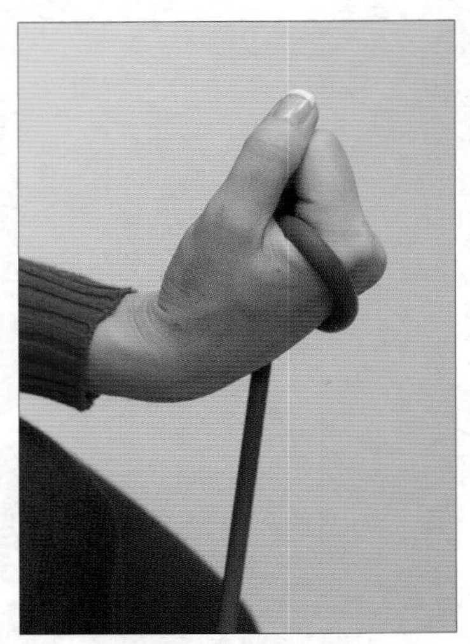
Wrist extension

Wrist Extension

With tubing wrapped around your fist and the opposite end secured under your foot, bend your wrist up (palm down) as far as possible. Lower your hand slowly, keeping your forearm on your thigh. Repeat with 12 repetitions and 3 sets. Do this every other day.

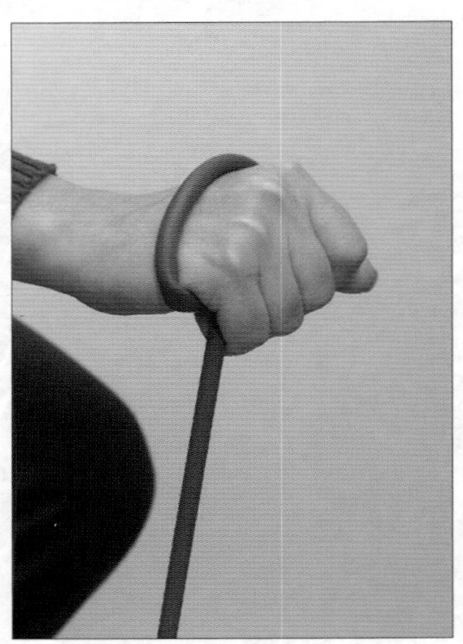
Wrist extension

Back Exercises

Sit on the floor. With tubing secured under the feet, slowly do a rowing motion squeezing shoulder blades together and release. Repeat with 12 repetitions and 3 sets. Do this every other day.

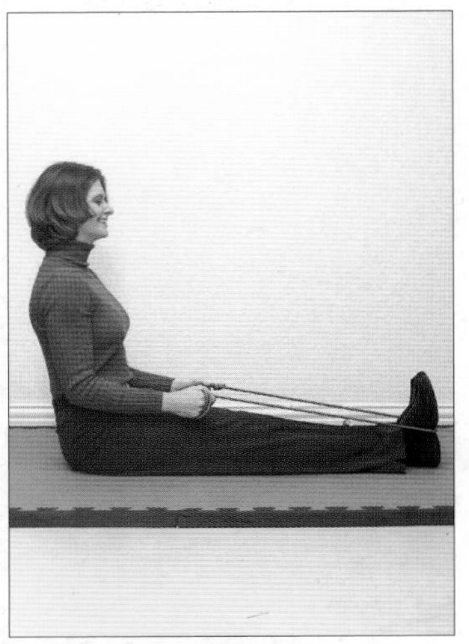
Back exercises

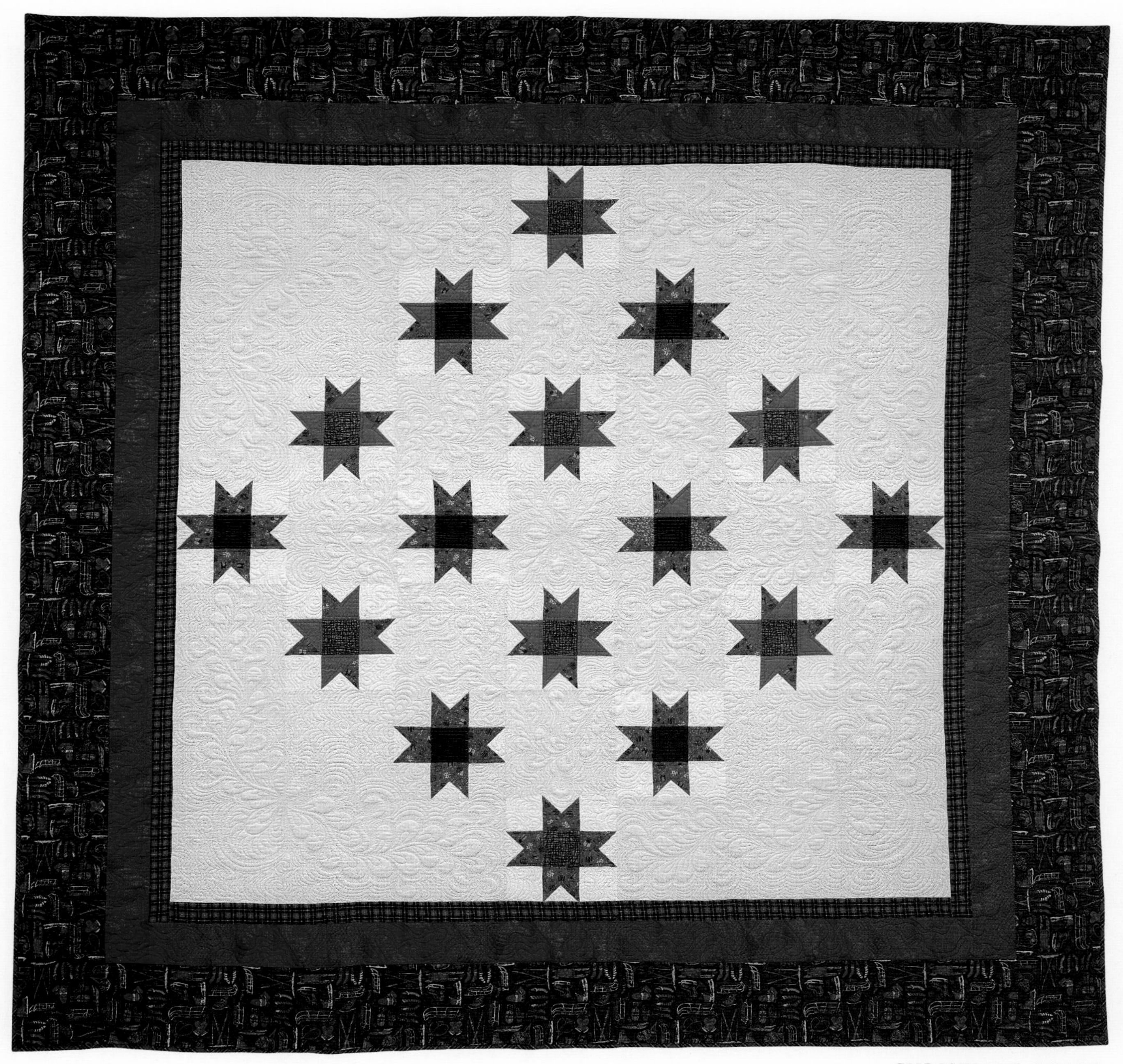

▲ **CHRISTMAS STARS**

96" x 100", 1998

Quilt top by: Frances Bagert, Princeton, TX

Quilted by: Linda V. Taylor, Melissa, TX

In the echoing process, I "lost" the freehand feather design; so I zigzagged between the feather and the first echo. I love what happened! This was the beginning of what I named "dimensional echoing." It raised and defined the feather without the usual tiny stipple all over the quilt. And it gives that tiny dotted effect which is exquisite. I used Quilter's Dream Cotton Supreme for good heavy cotton batting.

▲ TREE STAR

70" x 77", 1998
Quilt top by: Amy Stene, McKinney, TX
Quilted by: Linda V. Taylor, Melissa, TX

The pattern for this quilt top can be found in *At Home with Thimbleberries Quilts* by Lynette Jensen (Pine Ridge). I was very excited when Amy came into my shop and said she was selling this "tablecloth." It was the beginning of my love affair with trees. I also quilted bunnies, bears, squirrels, and birds around the trees (you must look closely to find them). The middle of the quilt was very plain so I wrote and trapuntoed from my favorite poem by Robert Frost, "The woods are lovely, dark and deep…." Also, in the outside corners I wrote another of his poems, "Two roads diverged in a wood and I—I took the one less traveled by. And that has made all the difference." This is also one of my favorite quilts, but I have never used it on my table!

▲ LOVE THAT BALTIMORE!

79" x 79", 1999
Quilt top by: Rosalyn Constant, McKinney, TX
Quilted by: Linda V. Taylor, Melissa, TX

This was Rosalyn's first Baltimore Album quilt. Linda did heavy quilting around all the trapunto designs.

▲ TREE OF HOPE
81" x 88", 1999
Linda V. Taylor, Melissa, TX

This was my first whole cloth quilt. I call it *Tree of Hope* because it was inspired by the 1890 *Tree of Life* quilt by Ann Robinson. As I studied her wonderful appliqué quilt, I realized nothing on her quilt was symmetrical. If she could do it, I could do it! I really love the folk-art look. I used RJR cotton sateen for the fabric.

◂ BRIGHT AND BOLD

72" x 72", 1994
Quilt top by: Alice Wilhoit, McKinney, TX
Quilted by: Linda V. Taylor, Melissa, TX

This quilt is a medley of traditional squares put together with a center medallion. Since Alice told Linda to "have fun with it," it is one of the first quilts she dared to use lots of different colors and kinds of thread for the quilting.

FIREWORKS ▸

74" x 84", 2001
Joan McGee, Richardson, TX

Joan started this quilt by taking a class from Alice Wilhoit on how to use a Creative Curves Ellipse Ruler. When she got back to finishing the center of the quilt two years later, she realized she did not have enough of the blue marble-like fabric to finish the quilt. Finally, she decided to be creative. I think her creativity made the quilt! It is quilted with mostly metallic decorative threads.

▲**ANGEL GATE**
59" x 76", 2000
Richard Larson, Plano, TX

First, Richard "thread painted" the original motifs with gold metallic thread and then quilted the whole cloth using freehand techniques. I particularly like the feathers around the outside edge of the quilt and I think the unusual shape of the quilt and tassel at the bottom add a wonderful artist's touch.

▲ AZTEC

75" x 75", 2000
Quilt top by: Cheri Meineke-Johnson, Corinth, TX
Quilted by: Linda V. Taylor, Melissa, TX

I envisioned heavy quilting for jungles and very angular geometric designs. I used bold bright YLI Jean Stitch thread to outline the prominent appliqué pieces and stayed with a matching soft cotton thread for quilting the ferns and Greek key designs. All quilting is completely freehand. Cheri cut all the pieces of this quilt from a single piece of fabric and then hand appliquéd them to the solid background fabric. The Swarovski crystals add highlights after the quilt is completed.

▲ **CITRUS WHIMSY**

54" x 79", 2002
Quilt top by: Cheri Meineke-Johnson, Corinth, TX
Quilted by: Linda V. Taylor, Melissa, TX

This quilt called for lots of colored threads and varied meandering techniques to complement the whimsical design elements. It has many playful areas on the quilt that needed special attention. As usual, Cheri designed and appliquéd the elements to a black cotton sateen fabric. The backing fabric is what she used for the inspiration.

▲ **LITTLE KATS**

47" x 47", 2001
Quilt top by: Cheri Meineke-Johnson, Corinth, TX
Quilted by: Linda V. Taylor, Melissa, TX

This is the little quilt Cheri made for me. I wanted to keep the quilting similar to what I had done on the larger *Kitty Kat Junction*.

▲ KITTY KAT JUNCTION

74" x 74", 2001
Quilt top by: Cheri Meineke-Johnson, Corinth, TX
Quilted by: Linda V. Taylor, Melissa, TX

Kitty Kat Junction is a playful, fun quilt. Cheri really made it simply because she fell in love with the little "Japanese kitties" in the fabric. The thread color changes "just happened" according to Linda, but the bright primary colors on the royal blue are dynamic.

▲ THE SUPPER

183" x 67", 1999
Quilt top by: Dr. Don Locke, Waxahachie, TX
Quilted by: Linda V. Taylor, Melissa, TX
Photographed by: Linda V. Taylor

Locke, a semi-retired dentist, combined more than 350 different fabrics to create a life-like scene. In only 2½ years, Locke took 51,816 pieces of fabric, some hand-dyed, others from as far as Scotland, and melded them into his modern-day masterpiece—*The Supper*.

He enlarged a photo of the DaVinci work several times on a computer until the blocks of colors (pixels) appeared. He used a wall in his studio to arrange the 1" squares (½" finished) into more manageable 8" blocks. The quilt has had a tremendous response from the quilting world and the general public.

Linda Taylor's story:
Don Locke first approached me about a quilt he was working on early in 1998. Every six months he brought the quilt into my shop to show me how it was progressing. Finally, one day while I was teaching a workshop, he brought in the finished quilt. It measured 15' wide by 6' high and was spectacular! It was breathtaking and caused more than a little stir in the entire quilt shop! Now the ball was really in my court and I had no idea of how I should quilt it.

I took several photos of the top and had them enlarged to 10" x 17". The quilt had to be loaded on the machine sideways because it was too wide to mount vertically. That meant I would be quilting it with all the figures facing sideways.

I stabilized the quilt by outlining most of the figures on the quilt and completing the outer walls. I proceeded to quilt the tablecloth and fill in between the figures. Then, the disciples had to be quilted. One by one the personages took on their own personality.

The lines in clothes, hands, and faces were a new experience for me since I have had absolutely no formal art training. I studied people's necks and the shadows on their faces. Any open hands on the quilt have my own lifeline since that was the only model available when I quilted the hands.

I took the quilt off the machine a couple of times and hung it up to study what I had done and what I felt needed to be done, because when I was working on the quilt close up it looked like a bunch of little squares. I had to stand back and squint to see the definition between the figures, as well as eyes, noses, hair, etc. When I remounted the quilt, I put it on going the opposite direction from the previous mounting. I was amazed that my perspective of the figures changed dramatically and I saw things I should quilt that I had not seen before.

I studied a picture of DaVinci's painting for long hours and compared it to the pictures I had taken before I started on the project. Many times I had to count squares to determine where I was on the quilt. I even drew lines on the photographs and used them like a map.

Mostly out of trepidation, I put off quilting the image of Christ until all the other figures were completed. This was the hardest of all because I know that everyone's perception of Him is different. I quilted my best for Him; and because of it—because of Him, I am a better person. For that, I thank you, Dr. Don Locke, for choosing me, for trusting me to quilt your precious quilt top. Quilted and finished at last, hopefully to be an inspiration to all who view it.

▲ **DEAR JANE & FRIENDS ALL GROWN UP**

72" x 90", 2001
Quilt top by: Linda Boeker Cordell, Arlington, TX
Quilted by: Sue Miklos-Champion, Gunter, TX

The design of this quilt was inspired by the Dear Jane book (Jane A. Stickle) by Brenda Manges Papadakis. The blocks were enlarged to 6" and completed in a friendship exchange with Linda's friends. Sue loves to do traditional quilting. She says the blocks on this quilt kept telling her to "stay with the traditional, please." She used several of Hari Walner's Continuous-Line patterns over some of the blocks. She used her acrylic circles for stained glass accuracy. The border triangles are freehanded.

▲ SUMMER STAR

60" x 60", 2000
Quilt top by: Alice Wilhoit, McKinney, TX
Quilted by: Linda V. Taylor, Melissa, TX

Alice expanded the center of the *Summer Star* quilt and added an appliqué design to bring her love for appliqué and piecing together. The light areas on the quilt were a perfect showcase for Linda's freehand feathers and echo designs.

◂ **TEXAS, OUR TEXAS**
68" x 78", 1998
Quilt top by: Alice Wilhoit, McKinney, TX
Quilted by: Linda V. Taylor, Melissa, TX

I trapuntoed all the design elements and many subtle Texas symbols in the borders—boots, cacti, horses, birds, and stars. The writing along the left border states: "The sun has riz, the sun has set, and here I am in Texas yet!"

FLAG DAY ▸
54" x 68", 2000
Quilt top by: Alice Wilhoit, McKinney, TX
Quilted by: Linda V. Taylor, Melissa, TX

This quilt name is very appropriate since Alice finished this quilt on Flag Day, 2000. The thirteen gold stars surrounding the Eagle medallion represent the first colonies. The white stars are appliquéd to the blue background. Linda softened the look of the flag by quilting red feathers swirling down through the blue and white stripes.

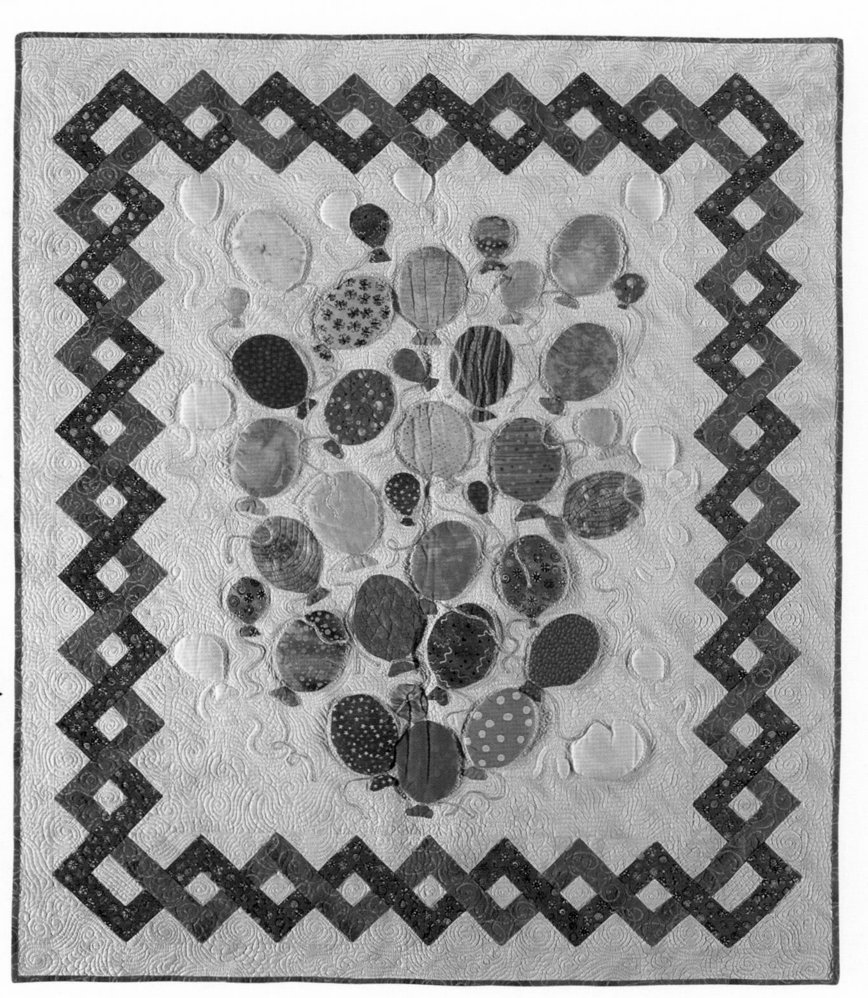

GRANDPA'S BALLOONS ▸

54" x 88", 2001
Merrily Parker, Springville, MO

Merrily made this colorful quilt to cheer up her grandpa. It is trapuntoed and heavily quilted.

◂ FIREWORKS

64" x 64", 1997
Quilt top by: Alice Wilhoit, McKinney, TX
Quilted by: Linda V. Taylor, Melissa, TX

Using the Ellipse Ruler by Virginia Walton, Alice created this quilt inspired by a fireworks show put on by her husband, Bill. This was the first time Linda even thought about quilting fireworks into a quilt.

◂ RUBY RED

40" x 48"
Beryl Cadman,
Castletownbere, Co. Cork, Ireland
Photographed by: Neil Porter

Beryl designed the red and white silk stripes with cotton, paper-pieced rubies in the center stripe. Red stripes were quilted with Linda Taylor's Feather Meandering design. White silk stripes were quilted with Keryn Emmerson's Feather and Cable design. Rubies were stitched in the ditch with meander quilting in the background.

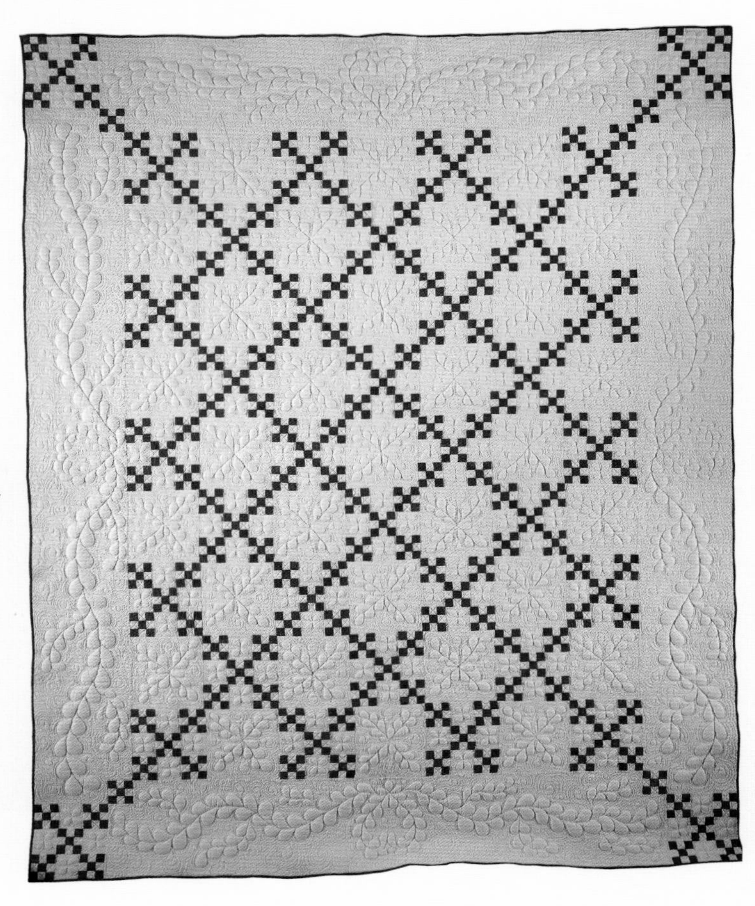

I LOVE FEATHERS ▸

78" x 99", 1999
Jana Menning, Highland Village, TX

No one gets as excited about feathers as Jana! When she felt fairly confident with her freehand feather medallion, she envisioned a whole quilt with feather medallions. She also wanted to try a whole quilt with trapunto. Now put red and white together—the combination is dynamite!

▲ WHACKY STARS

60" x 60"
Quilt top by: Katharine Guerrier, Worcester, UK
Quilted by: Beryl Cadman, Castletownbere, Co. Cork, Ireland
Photographed by: Neil Porter

The crazy Log Cabin and tilted Pinwheel blocks were devised by Katharine. The whacky stars are from Gwen Marston's book, *Liberated Quiltmaking*. Katharine gave Beryl a free hand to quilt. She used a variety of threads including variegated cotton, holographic, and metallic thread.

◂ TOUCH OF SPRING

55" x 59", 2000
Quilt top by: Alice Wilhoit, McKinney, TX
Quilted by: Linda V. Taylor, Melissa, TX

Alice used beautiful hand-dyed, soft pastel fabrics for the background and patchwork sashing of the center medallion. To complement the fabric, Linda used a beautiful variegated pastel thread for the freehand quilting all over quilt.

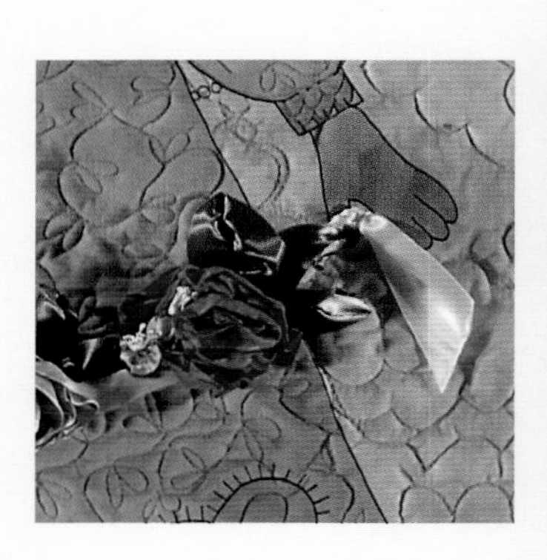

ANGEL ▸

48" x 72", 1999
Laurel Barrus, Centerville, UT

First, Laurel air-brushed the fabric using artwork created by artist Emily Dinsdale. Then she quilted it and embellished it with ribbons.

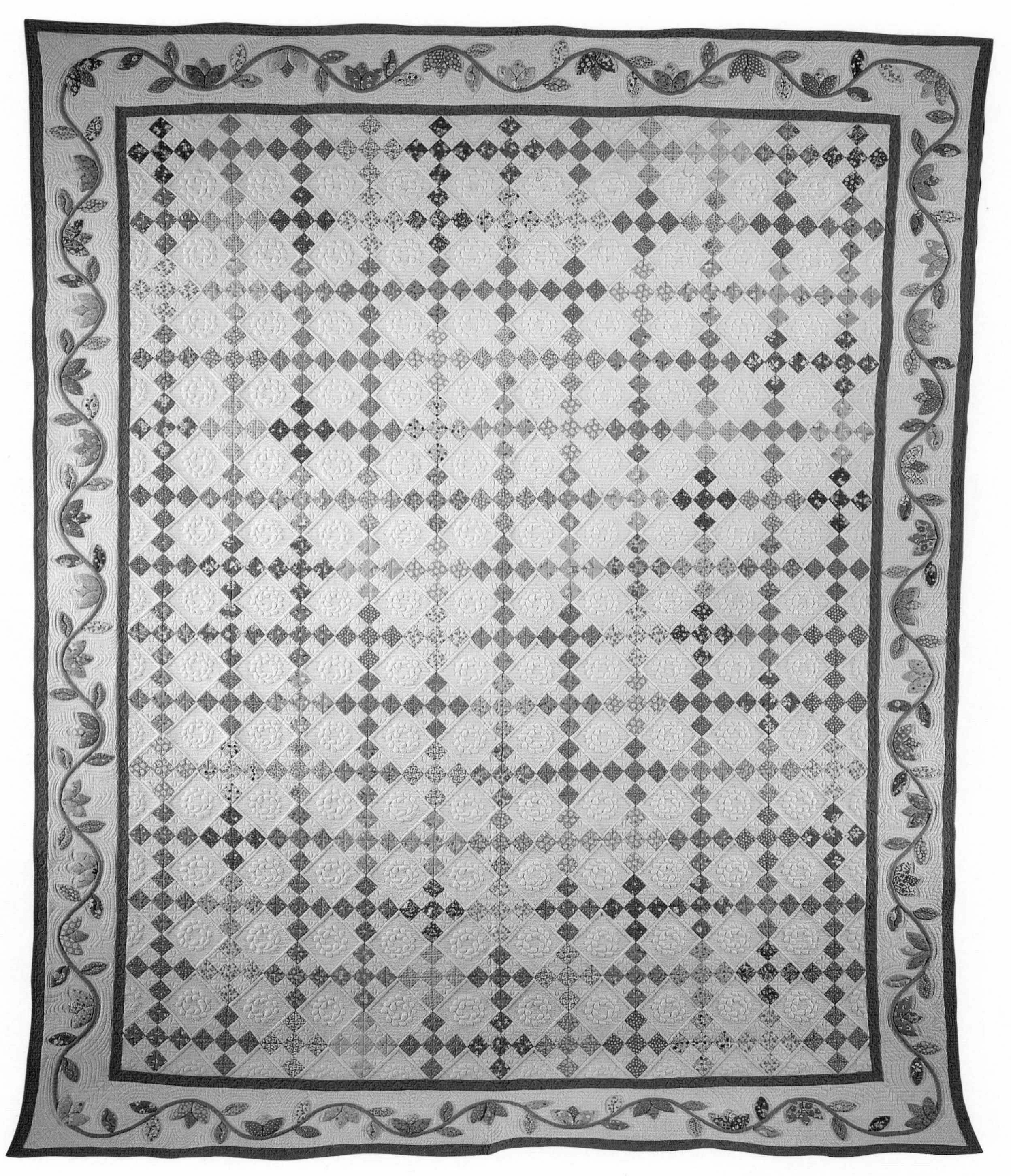

▲ **MY SHERBET GARDEN**

80" x 104", 2001

Jana Menning, Highland Village, TX

Although this is a simple Nine-Patch, she has elegantly quilted it. It has trapunto cording around each group of patches, which are cross-hatched. The border has a trapunto appliqué border with dimensional quilting using a stained glass design, then echoing to complete the dense quilted look. All the little feather wreaths are freehand and trapunto.

◀ **MOTHER NATURE'S REWARD—WILDFLOWERS**
56" x 68", 1998
Quilt top by: Alice Wilhoit, McKinney, TX
Quilted by: Linda V. Taylor, Melissa, TX

Traveling and playing in the Northwest inspired Alice to design this appliqué wildflower quilt. After Linda quilted the background with freehand feathers, leaves, and birds, Alice hand quilted around the appliqué and the leaf veins.

DETAILS OF SUMMER WEDDING ▶
90" x 108"
Beryl Cadman, Castletownbere, Co. Cork, Ireland
Photographed by: Neil Porter

Blue and white quilt based on a pattern in Lee Cleland's book, *It's Not a Quilt Until It's Quilted*, using Beryl's own freehand quilting designs. It was made for her brother as a wedding present and quilted with 100% cotton thread and monofilament thread.

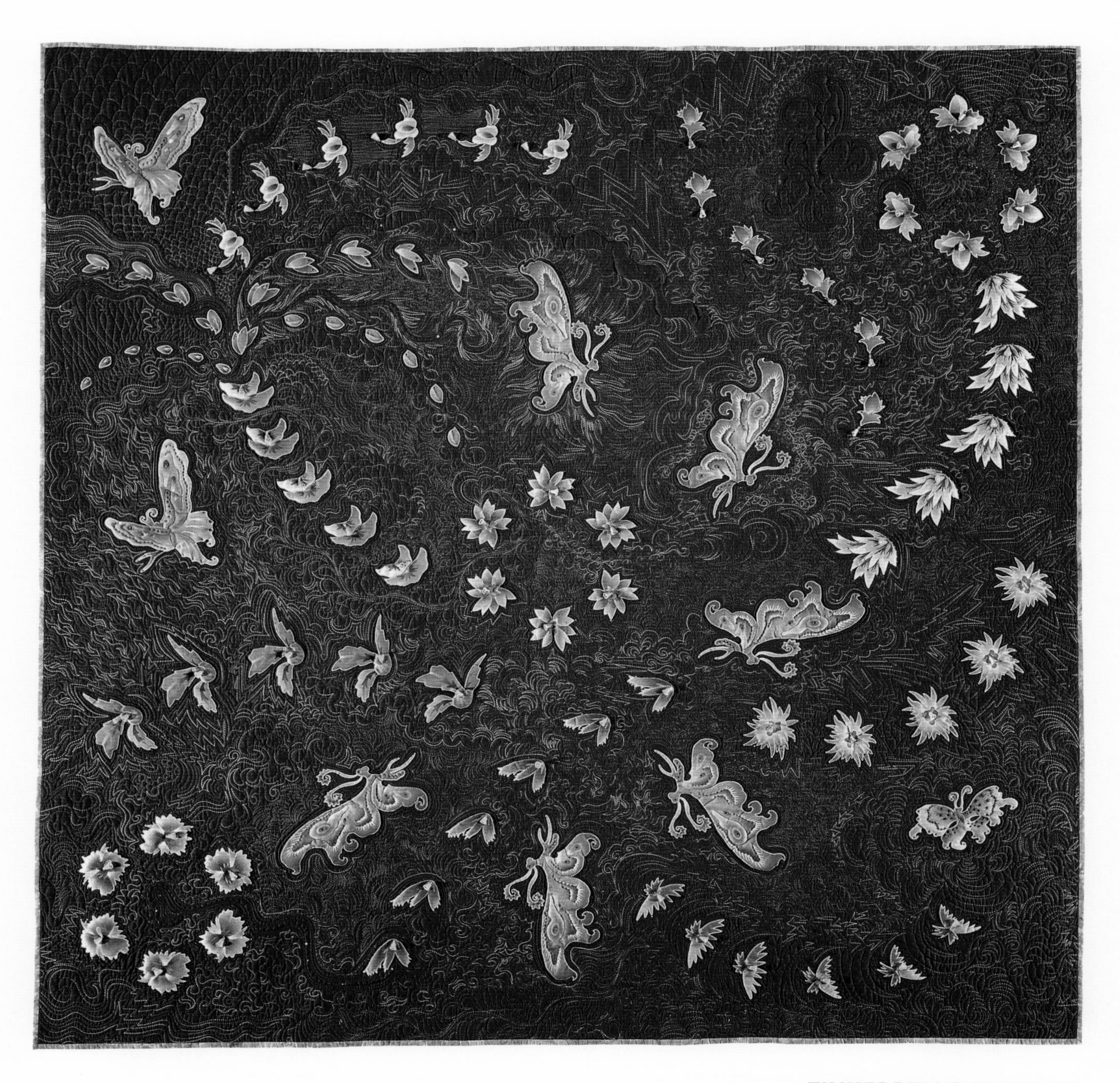

▲ **TINKERBELL'S FANTASY**

72" x 72", 2000
Quilt top by: Cheri Meineke-Johnson, Corinth, TX
Quilted by: Linda V. Taylor, Melissa, TX

Linda envisioned a kind of birth or transformation; each butterfly from the same source, each finding its own wings and way, and finally coming full circle in the cycle of life. The variety of colors and kinds of thread add depth and dimension to the quilting background. Freehand trapunto areas add interest and movement in the original interpretative quilting. Cheri cut all the pieces of this quilt from a single piece of beautiful Dutch fabric and then machine appliquéd them to the solid background fabric. The fiberglass bells and Swarovski crystals were added after quilting.

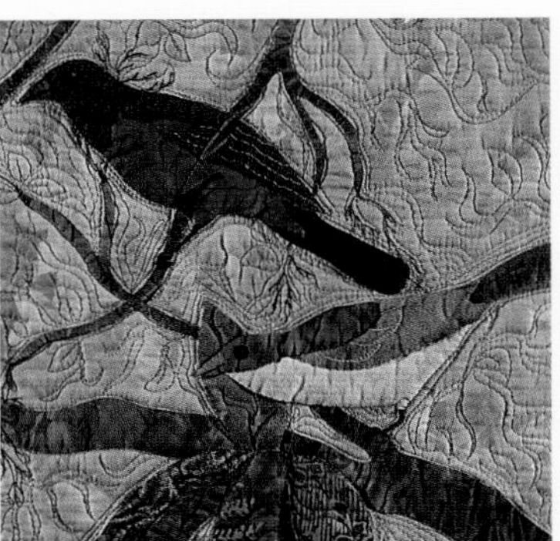

▲ **BIRDS IN FULL VIEW AND DETAIL**

72" x 90", 1999
Quilt top by: Alice Wilhoit, McKinney, TX
Quilted by: Linda V. Taylor, Melissa, TX

This quilt is Alice's interpretation of the window in her country home. The tree grows near the deck and there are many varieties of birds that come to visit. Linda continued the "window" theme by quilting the sashing to look like wood. The sashing, tree, and birds are all trapuntoed.

▲ONE DOZEN LONGARM ROSES
39" x 53", 2002
Hari Walner, Loveland, CO

Hari is having such a ball with her new longarm machine. She is quite used to quilting on her domestic machines, but using a new tool can be exciting. She put on this piece of muslin just to "practice," and look what happened! Hari says using the machine as a pencil is the most fun you can have. She stenciled the shading on the muslin after she was finished quilting.

▲ **MILLENNIUM M & M**

75" x 78", 2000
Quilt top by: Cheri Meineke-Johnson, Corinth, TX
Quilted by: Linda V. Taylor, Melissa, TX

Cheri's design elements are amazing. The blue, freehand feather-fern laps around each of the design elements pulling the eye back to the "mother ship" which has little "M & M" springs as a crown. Each of the outer design elements has different colored thread and freehand designs to set them apart and yet tie them together.

▲ MAGIC CARPET

78" x 83", 2001
Quilt top by: Cheri Meineke-Johnson, Corinth, TX
Quilted by: Linda V. Taylor, Melissa, TX

Cheri saw much more in the fabric than I could have imagined. *Magic Carpet* turned out to be a very elegant quilt garnished with more than 9300 Swarovski crystals. I could not believe the gorgeous "button" design work created by Cheri. This was one of the first quilts I envisioned with freehand trapunto. All the motifs are original designs. Other trapuntoed areas on the quilt are freehand. The motifs are stitched with metallic thread. The rest of the quilt is quilted with Mettler poly embroidery thread.

KRISTEN'S DRESDAN PLATE

68" x 89", 2001
Quilt top by: Jo Cechan, Greenville, TX
Quilted by: Bettilu "Pug" Wichern, Greenville, TX

Pug started to work for me in my shop when she was seventy years old. She worked for two years and then bought her own machine and started her own quilting business at home. Her work is phenomenal. I call her my "clone" because she can copy anything I quilt. She says you are never too old to learn something new.

RHYME AND REASON

77" x 78", 1999
Merrily Parker, Springville, MO

Merrily made this quilt based on a class she took at a quilt store. Everyone else was using plaids; she chose Bali prints. Instead of appliqué in the border, she chose to trapunto the design work.

▲ JOY

59" x 74", 2002
Quilt top by: Betsy Wilhoit-Perkins, Flower Mound, TX
Quilted by: Linda V. Taylor, Melissa, TX

Betsy based this quilt on the design of the quilt *Coriolis* by Judy B. Dales. Betsy's sense of color, precise piecing, and design work is developing quickly. Her creativity follows closely in her mother's (Alice Wilhoit) footsteps. Linda free-hand quilted all the design work.

◀ **PATRIOTIC HOPSCOTCH**

90" x 94", 1999
Quilt top by: Amy Stene, McKinney, TX
Quilted by: Linda V. Taylor, Melissa, TX

H.M. Wyant called this quilt *Yankee Doodle Diagonal* in her 1990 book, *Yeah, Yeah, USA*. Amy pieced this quilt top and sold it to me. I knew the beige triangles on the sides were perfect for a trapunto eagle. It is one of my favorite quilts.

BIG BLOCK QUILT ▶

98" x 98"
Quilt top by: Louise Riley, Blythe, UK
Quilted by: Beryl Cadman, Castletownbere, Co. Cork, Ireland

Louise did not want the thread to interfere with the strong design so Beryl used monofilament on the top and cotton thread in the bobbin. Louise now has a reversible quilt, pieced on one side and whole-cloth muslin on the other side.

Quilting was done with Linda Taylor's Feathered Mum edge-to-edge design.

THE ELEGANCE OF RED ▸

63" x 74", 2001
Allison Bayer, Plano, TX

Allison was inspired by the quilters of Welsh heritage. For the beautiful freehand middle medallion, Allison used metallic thread to quilt two layers of bronze tulle over a cotton burgundy fabric. A pre-printed tree skirt was cut into fourths for the corners of the quilt. Then she trimmed the quilt with gorgeous gold bias tape and braided trim. Truly ingenious, Allison!

◂ APRIL IN PARIS

28" x 28", 2002
Hari Walner, Loveland, CO

This lovely little quilt is a gem. Hari used her original pattern "April" from her book *Trapunto by Machine* for the center medallion. The solid fabric is cotton sateen quilted with a slightly darker thread for effect.

▲ **FLYFISHING I & II**
100" x 130", 1999
Quilt top by: Cheri Meineke-Johnson, Corinth, TX
Quilted by: Linda V. Taylor, Melissa, TX

Cheri decided to make two of every quilt, one for herself, and one for me. *Flyfishing I and II* were the beginning and end of this idea. They are really two different quilts; however, Cheri's appliqué flows from one into the other, and I mounted and quilted them at the same time. After they were completed, it just seemed that they belonged together so Cheri whipped them together at the side binding. One of the best features of the quilting is the many thread color changes and the way the quilting tends to lap around the fabric circles.

▲ MONKEY SHINE

68" x 69", 2000
Quilt top by: Cheri Meineke-Johnson, Corinth, TX
Quilted by: Linda V. Taylor, Melissa, TX

Inspired by her love for monkeys, Cheri appliquéd this playful quilt. The design work is strong. I used lots of variegated YLI Jean Stitch thread for accent.

▲ **SCREAMING PEACOCKS**

80" x 80", 2002
Quilt top by: Cheri Meineke-Johnson, Corinth, TX
Quilted by: Linda V. Taylor, Melissa, TX

Cheri cut all the motif design work from a very colorful fabric, pieced, and then appliquéd it to purple cotton sateen. With the exception of *The Supper* quilt (page 110), I have never spent so much time quilting on a quilt—eighty hours. Every square inch is very heavily quilted with intricate freehand designs. The larger designs are also freehand and trapunto.

Alice Wilhoit Designs
publisher of patterns, designer, teacher
P.O. Box 785
McKinney, TX 75070
972-540-5803
FAX: 972-540-2479
email: awilhoit@earthlink.net
website: www.AliceWilhoit.com

American & Efird (A & E) Inc.
distributors of threads
400 East Central Ave.
Mount Holly, NC 28120
800-438-0545
website: www.amefird.com

Beautiful Publications, LLC,
publishers of continuous-line quilting patterns by Hari Walner
7508 Paul Place
Loveland, CO 80537-8732
970-662-9950
email: quilting@earthlink.net

Benartex
manufacturers of fabric
1460 Broadway, 8th floor
New York City, NY 10036
212-840-3250

Cheri's Crystals
Cheri Meineke-Johnson
distributor of Swarovski Crystals
3955 Summit Ridge Drive
Corinth, TX 76210
940-498-9517

Creative Designer Lines, LLC
Linda V. Taylor
author, designer, teacher longarm workshops, Quilt 'N Sleepover Retreat Center, videos and books
4964 US Hwy. 75 North
Melissa, TX 75454
800-893-2748
FAX: 972-562-6330
email: Linda@lequilters.com
website: www.lequilters.com

Custom Quilting, LTD
Beryl Cadman
distributor of longarm supplies, patterns, Gammill Quilting Systems Dealer
Beal Na Tra/Derrymihan West
Castletownbere, Co. Cork
Ireland
email: patches@iol.com

Hobbs Bonded Fibers
manufacturers of Heirloom Cotton batting and polyester batting
P.O. Box 2521
Waco, TX 76702
254-741-0040 (wholesale only)
FAX: 817-772-7238

International Machine Quilter's Association, Inc. (IMQA)
For membership information send to:
P.O. Box 86
Seaton, IL 61476
website: www.IMQA.org

Linda's Electric Quilters, LLC,
distributors of longarm supplies, thread, publisher of patterns, longarm videos, Quilter's Business Suite
Dealer for Gammill Quilting Machines
4964 US Hwy. 75 North
Melissa, TX 75454
800-893-2748
FAX: 972-562-3990
email: contact@lequilters.com
website: www.lequilters.com

RJR Fashion Fabrics
manufacturers of fabric, finishers of Quilter's Sateen
13748 S. Gramercy Pl.
Gardena, CA 90249
800-422-5426 (wholesale only)
website: www.rjrfabrics.com

Unlimited Possibilities
newsletter for longarm quilters, editor Marcia Stevens, co-owner of Machine Quilters Showcase
Little Pine Studio
218 N. 10th Street
Brainerd, MN 56401-3420
218-828-9116
email: mstevens@brainerd.net

YLI Corporation
distributors of thread for longarm quilting, cotton, poly, metallics
161 W. Main Street
Rock Hill, SC 29730
803-985-3100
website: www.ylicorp.com

Longarm Quilting Machine Manufacturers

A-1 Quilting Machines, Inc.
3232 E. Evans Road
Springfield, MO 65804
800-LONG ARM, 800-566-4276, 417-883-6883
FAX: 417-883-2883
email: a1qm@aol.com
website: www.long-arm.com

American Professional Quilting Systems
8033 University Blvd., Suite F
Des Moines, IA 50325
800-426-7233, 515-267-1113
FAX: 515-267-8414
email: apqs@netins.com
website: www.apqs.com

Design-A-Quilt
305 Jefferson Street
Paducah, KY 42001
800-346-8227, 270-442-0105
FAX: 270-442-6495
email: designaq@vci.net
website: www.designaquilt.com

Gammill Quilting Machine Company
P.O. Box 230; 1452 West Gibson
West Plains, MO 65775
800-659-8224, 800-748-8105, 417-256-5919
FAX: 417-256-5757
email: gammill@townsqr.com
website: www.gammill.net

KenQuilt Manufacturing Company
121 Pattie Street
Wichita, KS 67211
866-784-5872, 316-303-0880
FAX: 316-303-0882
email: sales@kenquilt.com
website: www.kenquilt.com

Legacy Quilting Machines
600 North 500 West, Suite #C
Bountiful, UT 84010
801-294-4800
FAX: 801-294-5466
email: nitinc@legacyquilt.com
website: www.legacyquilt.com

Nolting Mfg., Inc.
Nolting Longarm Quilting Machines
1265 Hawkeye Drive
Hiawatha, IA 52233
319-378-0999
FAX: 319-378-1026
email: nolting@nolting.com
website: www.nolting.com

Nustyle Quilting Machines and Supplies
Hwy. 52, P.O. Box 61
Stover, MO 65078
800-821-7490, 573-377-2244
FAX: 573-377-2833

Proto Inc.
2608 Lowell Road
Gastonia, NC 28054
704-824-3131
FAX: 704-824-8587
email: proto@loclnet.com

Statler Stitcher
manufacturers of Computerized Longarm Quilting Machine Add-on
700 W. Rt. K
Columbia, MO 65203
573-449-1068
FAX: 573-815-0406
email: paul@statlerstitcher.com,
website: www.statlerstitcher.com

Bibliography

Hari Walner. *Exploring Machine Trapunto,* Martinez CA: C&T Publishing, Inc., 1999.

Harriet Hargrave. *Heirloom Machine Quilting,* Martinez, CA: C&T Publishing, Inc., 1995.

Marcia Stevens, "Unlimited Possibilities Newsletter", Brainerd, MN: Little Pine Studio, 2001.

INDEX

PATTERN INDEX

ABOUT THE AUTHOR

In the early 70s, Linda pieced and quilted several full-size quilts, but found quilting on her domestic machine was like wrestling a bear.

In 1993, she heard someone mention a "quilting machine." That is all she had to hear; she wanted one. Off she went to the Texas State Fair to see her first quilting machine. She was too embarrassed to try it but wrote a check for the down payment. Then she went home to figure out how to pay for it and where to put it. Meanwhile, her husband was off fly-fishing in Wyoming.

"I had quilting lined up to do before the machine was delivered, and I still have quilts in line." Her quilting machine was in her living room until she moved her business (Linda's Electric Quilters, LLC) to a quilt shop in downtown McKinney, Texas. Five years later, Linda's husband and partner, Rick, built a spacious studio for her and her eight machines. Here she teaches students from all over the world how to use the longarm quilting machines. Her new studio also includes wonderful retreat facilities for her students. Linda says, "It's like having a sleepover with my best friends every weekend."

Linda's work has been displayed in many venues and published in several quilting magazines and books. She has won numerous quilting awards in the IQA, AQS, and NQS quilting shows. She has appeared on several television shows with various quilting experts.

She has her own pattern line and has produced five "how-to" videos for longarm quilters, as well as four longarm quilting idea books.

"I never had a business plan. All I know is that something magical happens when I start sewing on that machine. Being able to share how I feel and what I have learned on the quilting machine with enthusiastic students brings great joy and satisfaction to my life."

As one of the innovators of the art of longarm machine quilting, many of Linda's ingenious inventions have been incorporated as custom features on the quilting machines today.

Linda is also quick to tell you that she is, first and foremost, the proud mother of three lovely daughters and four incredibly gifted grandchildren who are the light of her life.

Top of pattern

Top of next row offset

* SEE PAGE 50 FOR DUPLICATION INFORMATION.

* SEE PAGE 50 FOR DUPLICATION INFORMATION.

* SEE PAGE 50 FOR DUPLICATION INFORMATION.

* SEE PAGE 50 FOR DUPLICATION INFORMATION.

* SEE PAGE 50 FOR DUPLICATION INFORMATION.

* SEE PAGE 50 FOR DUPLICATION INFORMATION.

* SEE PAGE 50 FOR DUPLICATION INFORMATION.

* SEE PAGE 50 FOR DUPLICATION INFORMATION.

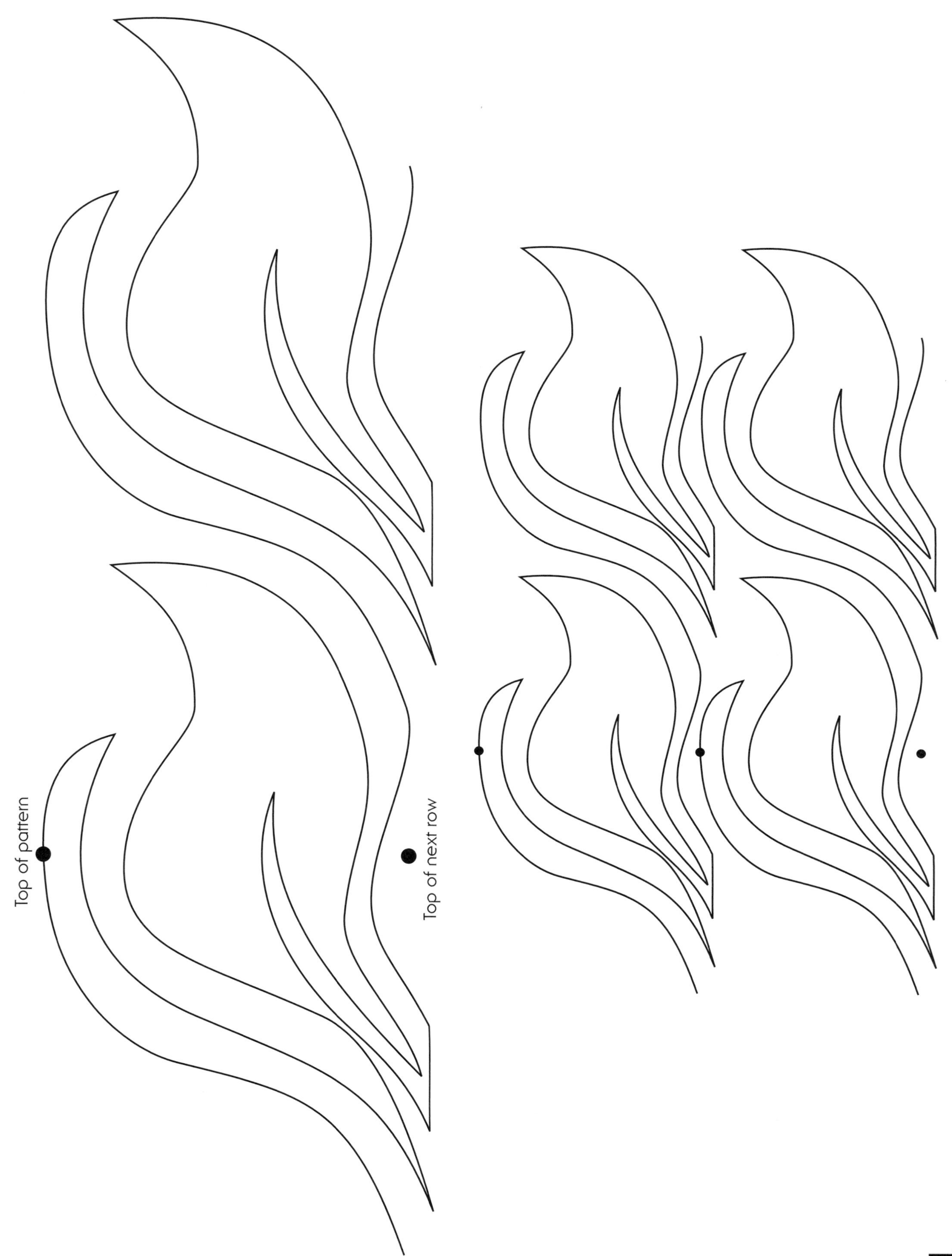
Top of pattern
Top of next row

* SEE PAGE 50 FOR DUPLICATION INFORMATION.

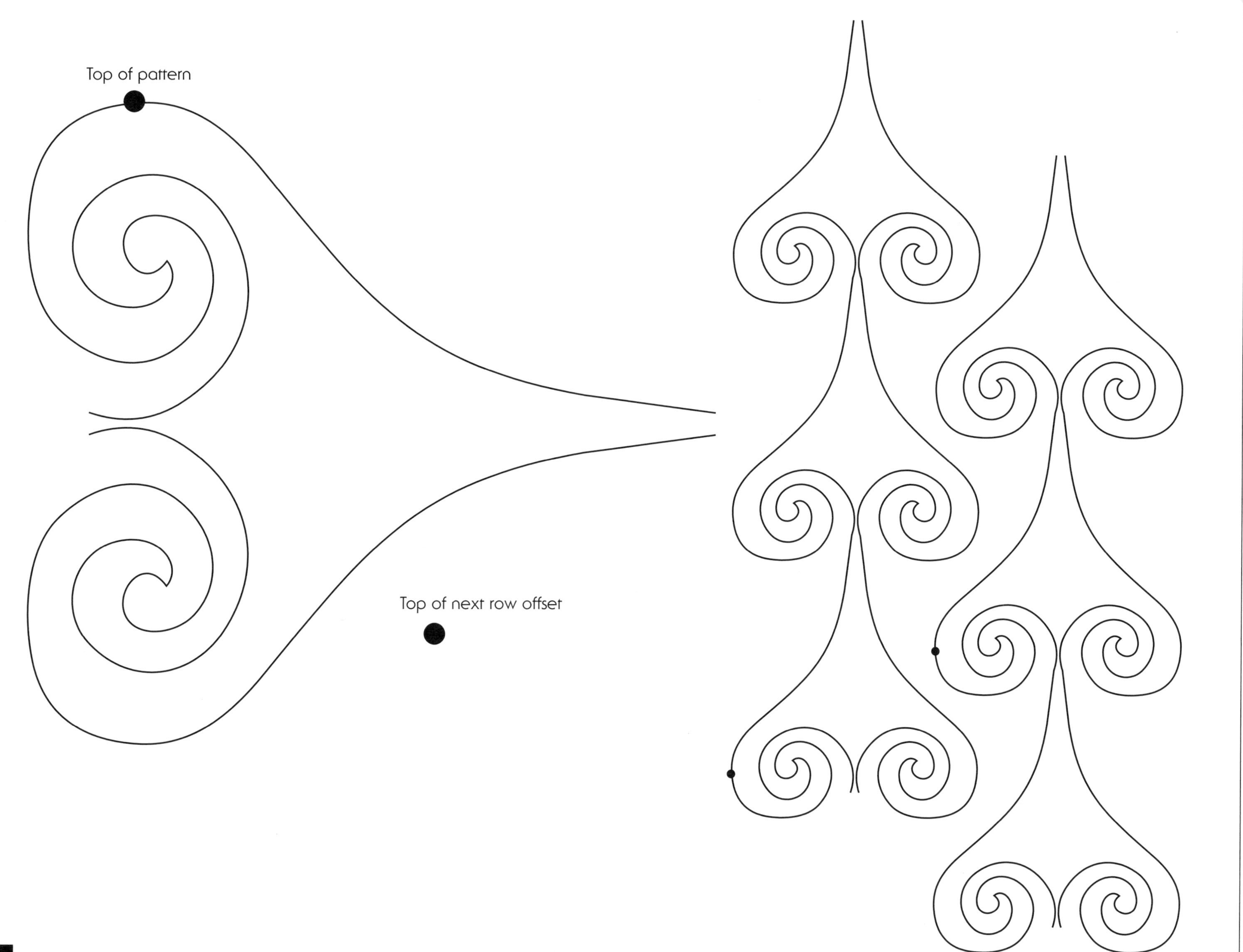

* SEE PAGE 50 FOR DUPLICATION INFORMATION.

* SEE PAGE 50 FOR DUPLICATION INFORMATION.

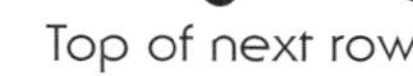

* SEE PAGE 50 FOR DUPLICATION INFORMATION.

* SEE PAGE 50 FOR DUPLICATION INFORMATION.

* SEE PAGE 50 FOR DUPLICATION INFORMATION.

* SEE PAGE 50 FOR DUPLICATION INFORMATION.

* SEE PAGE 50 FOR DUPLICATION INFORMATION.

* SEE PAGE 50 FOR DUPLICATION INFORMATION.

* SEE PAGE 50 FOR DUPLICATION INFORMATION.

* SEE PAGE 50 FOR DUPLICATION INFORMATION.

* SEE PAGE 50 FOR DUPLICATION INFORMATION.

* SEE PAGE 50 FOR DUPLICATION INFORMATION.

* SEE PAGE 50 FOR DUPLICATION INFORMATION.

* SEE PAGE 50 FOR DUPLICATION INFORMATION.

* SEE PAGE 50 FOR DUPLICATION INFORMATION.

* SEE PAGE 50 FOR DUPLICATION INFORMATION.

* SEE PAGE 50 FOR DUPLICATION INFORMATION.

* SEE PAGE 50 FOR DUPLICATION INFORMATION.

* SEE PAGE 50 FOR DUPLICATION INFORMATION.

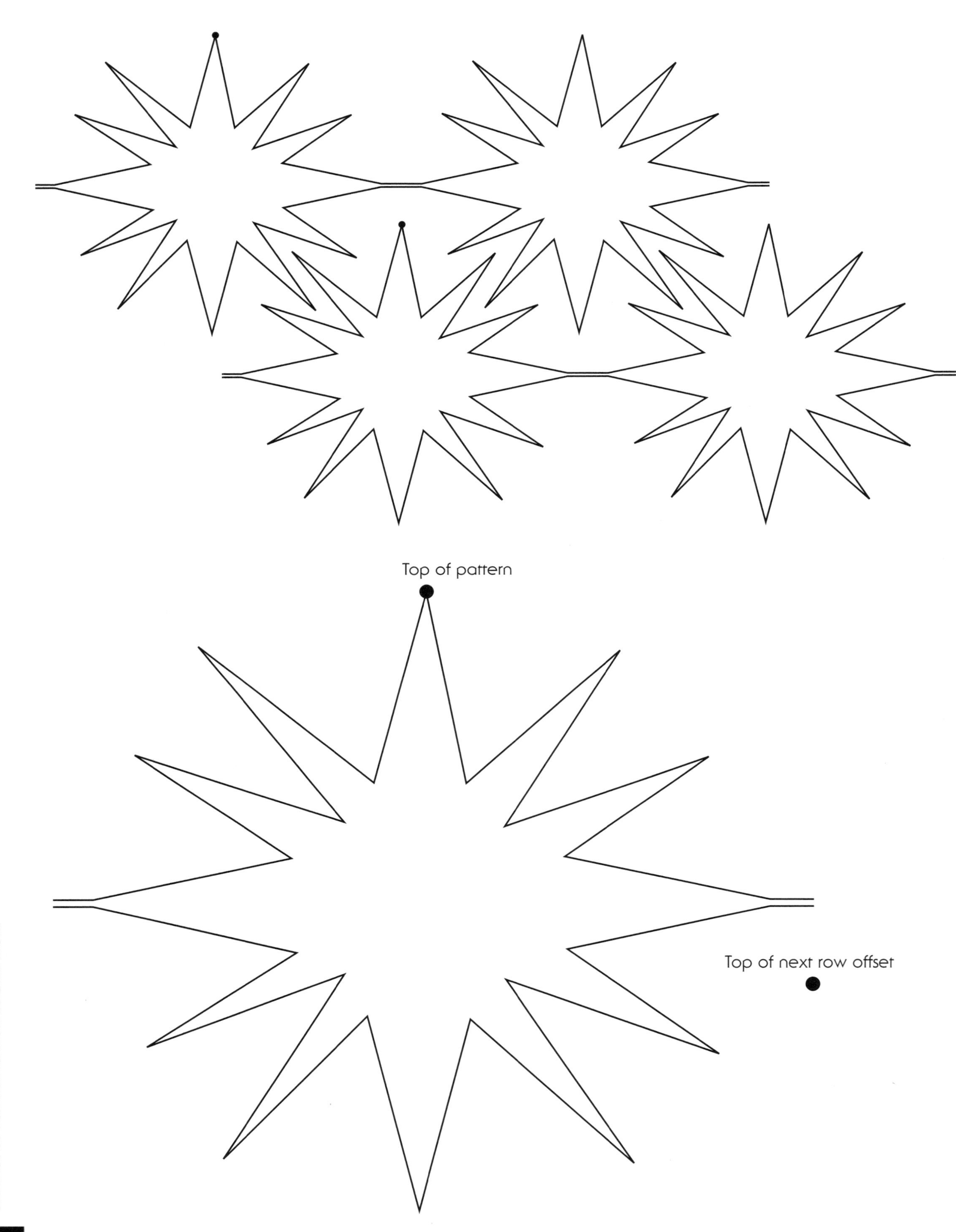

* SEE PAGE 50 FOR DUPLICATION INFORMATION.

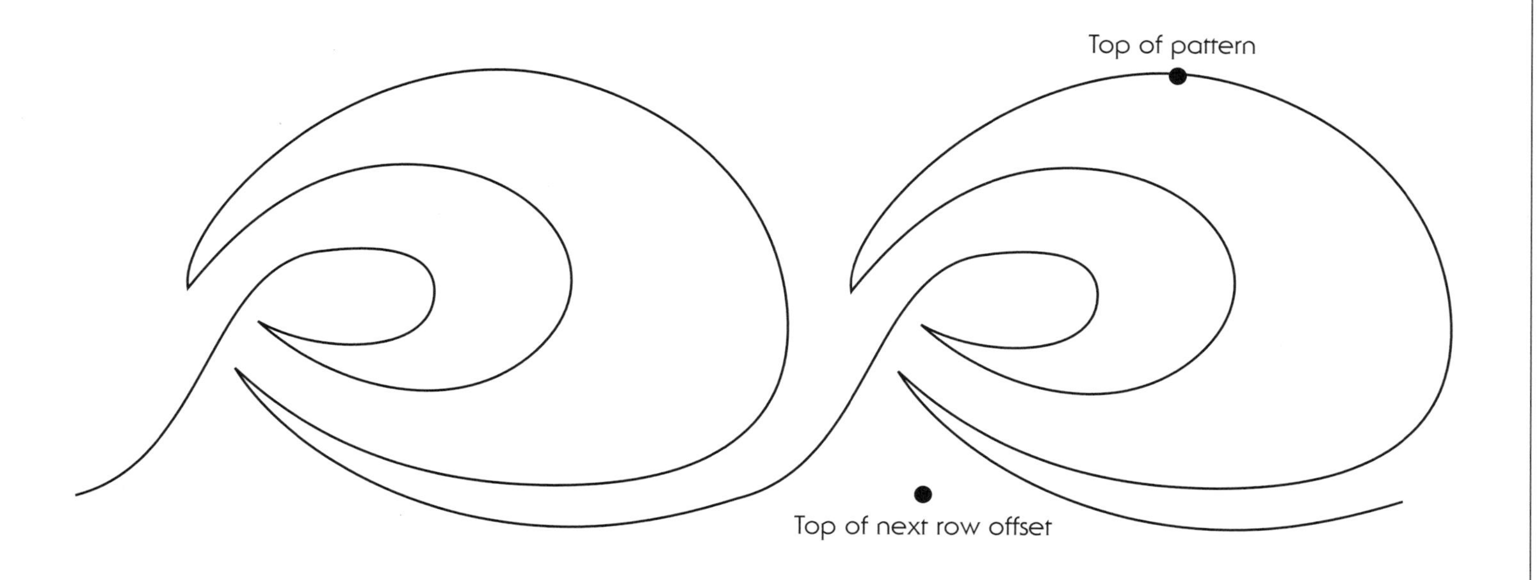

* SEE PAGE 50 FOR DUPLICATION INFORMATION.

* SEE PAGE 50 FOR DUPLICATION INFORMATION.

* SEE PAGE 50 FOR DUPLICATION INFORMATION.

* SEE PAGE 50 FOR DUPLICATION INFORMATION.

* SEE PAGE 50 FOR DUPLICATION INFORMATION.

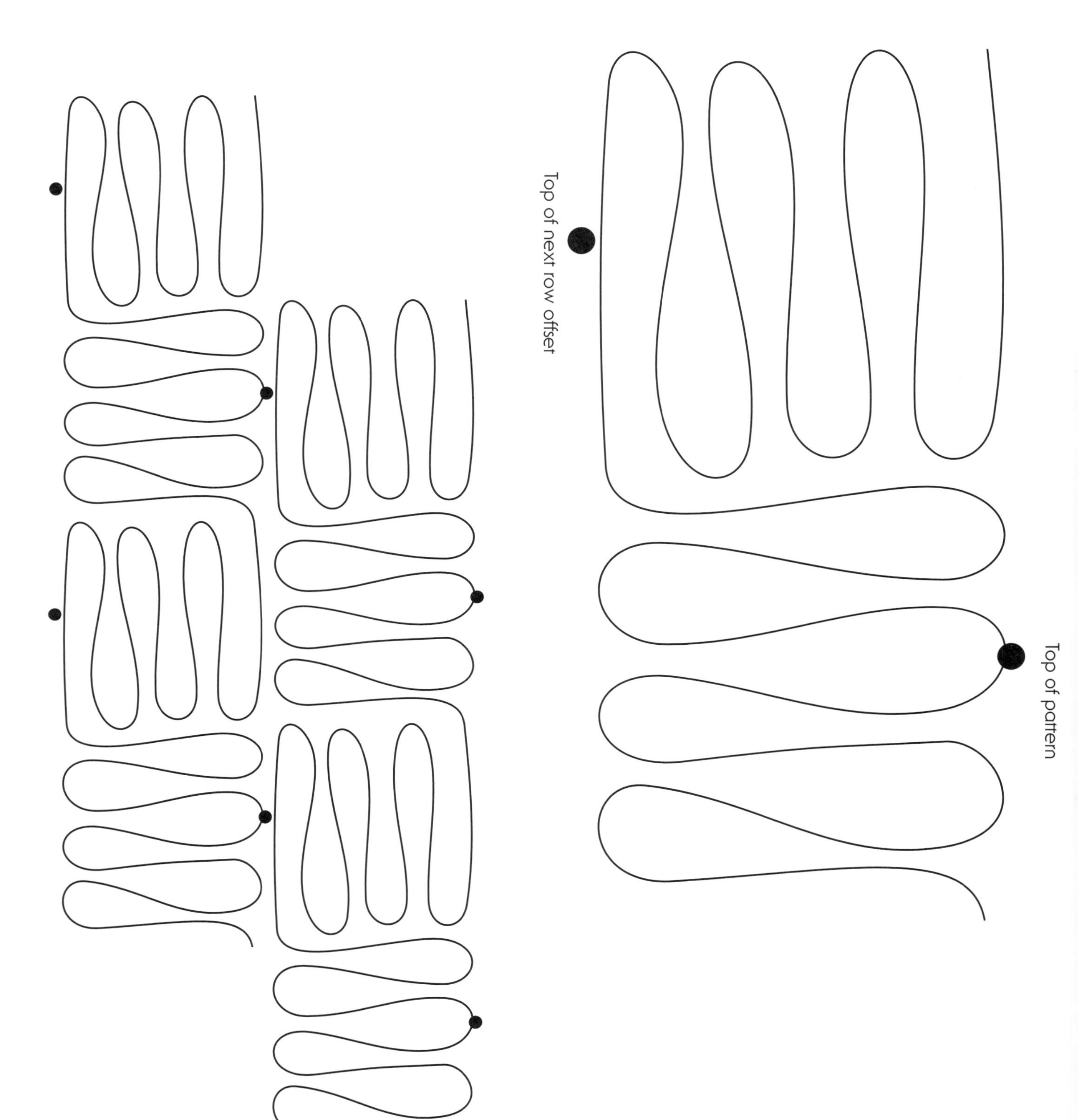

* SEE PAGE 50 FOR DUPLICATION INFORMATION.

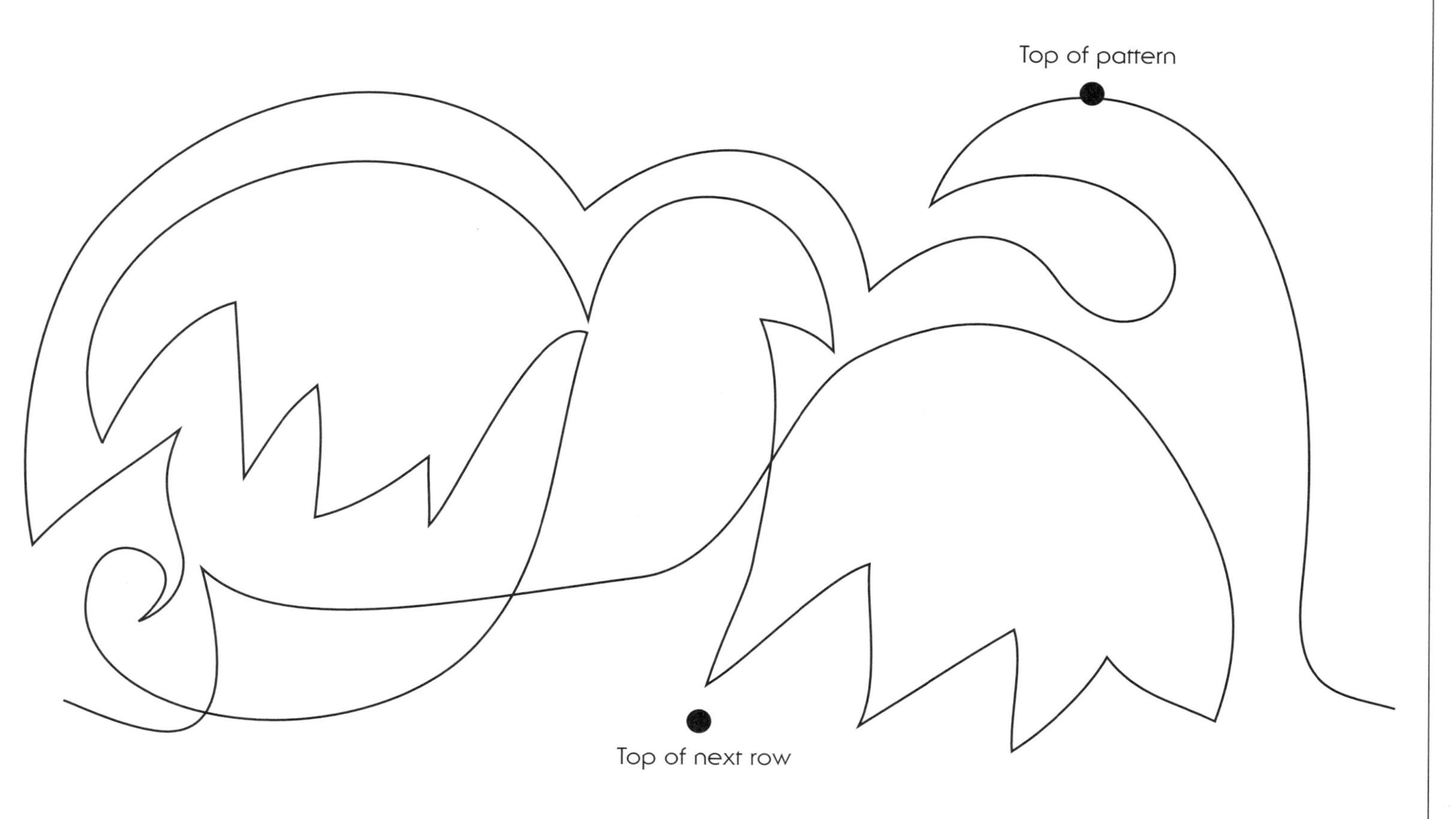

* SEE PAGE 50 FOR DUPLICATION INFORMATION.

* SEE PAGE 50 FOR DUPLICATION INFORMATION.